Michael Bloomfield

If you love these blues

Michael

Bloomfield

If you love these blues

by Jan Mark Wolkin & Bill Keenom

Miller
Freeman
Books
San Francisco

Published by Miller Freeman Books
600 Harrison Street, San Francisco, CA 94107

An imprint of Music Player Network
    www.MusicPlayer.com.
    Publishers of *Guitar Player, Bass Player, Keyboard, Gig, MC2,*
    and *EQ* magazines.
    A division of United Entertainment Media, Inc.

Distributed to the book trade in the U.S and Canada by
Publisher's Group West, 1700 Fourth Street, Berkeley, CA 94710

Distributed to the music trade in the U.S. and Canada by
Hal Leonard Publishing, P.O. Box 13819, Milwaukee, WI 53213

Cover Design: Rich Leeds
Cover Photo: Peter Amft
Text Design and Composition: Leigh McLellan
Editor: Jim Roberts

Library of Congress Cataloging-in-Publication Data

Wolkin, Jan Mark.
    Michael Bloomfield : if you love these blues / by Jan Mark
Wolkin and Bill Keenom
            p.   cm.
    Discography: p.
    Includes bibliographical references and index.
    ISBN 0-87930-617-3 (alk. paper)
    1. Bloomfield, Michael—Interviews. 2. Blues musicians—
United States—Interviews. I. Keenom, Bill. II. Title

    ML419.B58 W65 2000
    787.87'1643'092—dc21
    [B]

                                                00-057319

Printed in the United States of America

00 01 02 03 04 05   5 4 3 2 1

Contents
....

by Carlos Santana

Foreword

The first time I saw Michael Bloomfield play guitar was when the Butterfield Blues Band came to San Francisco. I was still in Mission High School. And it literally changed my life enough for me to say, "This is what I want to do and want to be for the rest of my life."

I zeroed in like a laser beam on Michael's way of phrasing on the first two Butterfield albums. For a while my band was playing a lot of their music. We would play "Born in Chicago"—that was part of our repertoire. One time we opened up for them, and we played those songs before they played them, which was kind of funny.

That band really captured us. All the material we had before, we just put it aside and started working around their songs. "Born in Chicago," that was the anthem. People used to sing "do-do-do-do, *do*; do-do-do-do, *do*." That's it. "Born in Chicago." People were singing that in school. So, needless to say, that band was very, very important.

* * *

The first time I played with Michael was at a jam session at the Fillmore West. I was just a cat who came from Tijuana, and I played guitar. It was a Sunday afternoon jam. Jerry Garcia was there. Jack Casady on bass. And Michael Bloomfield on keyboards.

I saw Mike's guitar. A friend of mine said to Bill Graham, "Listen, Bill, this Mexican kid from Tijuana loves B.B. King and loves Michael Bloomfield. Do you think you'd let him play?" Bill said, "I'm not in charge. Go ask Michael Bloomfield." And my friend asked him. Michael looked at me, and he looked at his guitar and said, "Go ahead, man. There's my guitar."

And it was like—I felt like somebody had just given me a key and opened a huge door for me. I picked up his guitar, put it to my ear to make sure that it was tuned, and when everybody said what they had to say, they let me play. Bill Graham liked it and he asked me, "Would you like to open up for Howlin' Wolf and Steve Miller?"

So Michael opened the door for me to be in the field that I'm in today. That was my first connection with Michael Bloomfield. I have that guitar—it's a Les Paul. I've seen a lot of pictures of him in the early days with it.

I was able to really breathe, playing that day in front of Michael and the rest of them. For some reason, when you're young you have this attitude that you can do anything you want to do. And it wasn't about a competition.

● ● ●

One time we were at the Fillmore, and I could tell he was embarrassed because he had a whole bunch of people around him. He was being adored like he was the center of the galaxy. And he was kind of looking at me like, "God, I wish we could just get out of here and do something else."

I remember saying something really nasty, something really bad. I don't know why I said it, to this day. I asked him to forgive me. We worked it out before he left. But I said, "Man, one of these days, I'm going to cut you." And I was like a player, like a gunslinger. As soon as it came out, I just felt so terrible. I felt awful saying that to this beautiful, kind man. And he just looked at me and said, "Oh, that's okay, I want you to, man. You will. One of these days you'll be better than me. It's okay, man. I want you to."

He had the wisdom to say, "I want you to and I know you will. I encourage you to do it." That hurt even more. Everybody was looking at me like, "Man, why would you say something like that to Michael?" And I'm going, "I know."

I saw him four or five years later; he came to the Fillmore when they were closing. The day that they closed we were in there. I kept apologizing the whole night for saying that. "Oh, God, remember that? I don't know why I said that. Oh, man, I'm sorry." And he said, "Man, don't worry about it. We all do that, man. I know where it came from. Don't worry about it."

So he gave me a strong inner lesson. He put it right to me. He gave me inner confidence, and another kind of wisdom—so that now I don't have to do that to anybody. I don't have to compete. I think that consciously and unconsciously he instilled those values in me, not just playing blues guitar.

● ● ●

We had a bond, Michael and I. He passed something to me and I have to guard it very, very carefully because what he passed down to me is that the art of music is about making a bridge between the flesh and the spirit. He did that very well. Regardless of what he took or what he didn't take. All of that was irrelevant.

I'm very blessed that I have had tremendous teachers and guides. And Michael Bloomfield was one of them.

I

························

1943 to 1965

Born in Chicago

Michael Bloomfield I was born in Chicago, and raised up to the sixth grade in Chicago, in a hillbilly-Jewish neighborhood. Chicago has these border-line neighborhoods, and the street bordering the lake, Lake Shore Drive, is sort of a wealthy Jewish neighborhood known as the Gold Coast, and then just one block going west it's a hillbilly-Puerto Rican mix neighborhood, and that's where I did all my hanging out and where I went to school.

When I was a little kid, driving around with my folks, we'd go through certain parts of town, and go to the black parts of town, and I'd hear music coming out of record stores and juke boxes. I never knew what it was but I knew it just knocked me out.

I moved to the suburb of Glencoe when I was in the sixth grade, 12 years old. I have one brother, Allen, who's 18 months younger than me. My brother, my cousin, and most of the people in my peer group, my friends, were pretty socially into it, man—they were either jocks or good students. I wasn't into the scene—I was just a fat kid. God almighty, it was a bad adolescent puberty thing. I just never got it together. Bad at school, bad at sports, bad at all kinds of crap.

Allen Bloomfield When we were growing up, Michael and I lived at 424 Melrose, in an area that abutted a fairly affluent street called Lake Shore Drive. When we walked out of 424 Melrose, at the corner was ABC Toyland. ABC Toyland was the place where Whitey, the hood of the neighborhood, used to smoke cigarettes. ABC Toyland was where you used to get an Oscar Mayer hot dog with relish and mustard on it. You looked at the gifts that you might get.

We had these really heavyweight Schwinn bikes with fat tires. They were indestructible. Now, I was very meticulous. I polished my bell and had my head lamp working. My bike was in good order. I used my kickstand. Michael, on the contrary, would ride his bike and drop it when he was off it. That was how he parked it—he just let it crash to the ground.

It was a neighborhood. It was our place, and there was always activity. You walked down the block, you saw your friends, and you hung out.

Finally, in their wisdom—and I use that word with a tremendous question mark—our parents decided that we should go to a suburb. So we moved to a place called Glencoe, an elite suburb with prestigious public schools. We lived in a formidable stone-and-Ludowici-tile house. It had six bedrooms and was quite opulent. We lost the Schwinns along the way and ended up with English bikes, Raleighs. We got these two fine English bikes, which we immediately ruined.

Once we moved to Glencoe, we had a real deterioration of the type of synchronicity that we developed when we were in the city. All of a sudden, we were the outsiders. We didn't have any friends. We didn't have the appropriate clothing. We were, in a sense, strangers in a strange land. And this was tough.

You walked down the block and saw nothing but old people. And if you weren't into a sport, you weren't into anything. If you weren't into an academic thing, you weren't into anything. It was just the beginning of getting into puberty, so that was a tough time for us. I think it was an especially difficult time for Michael to assimilate.

Dorothy Shinderman We moved to Glencoe because I thought that the schooling would be better there. That was the biggest mistake of my life. He should have been in a highly progressive school. We put him in the wrong schools. Glencoe was a very wealthy area, and their standard was: you had to conform. God forbid you should be a nonconformist. And Mike was a nonconformist.

Fred Glaser Mike was originally a year ahead of me in grade school in Glencoe, a rich, upper-middle-class Jewish suburb. He was a real obnoxious kid in a certain kind of way. If you didn't like him he was a little, fat, obnoxious, wise-guy kid.

We were lawbreakers from the very first. We just had it in us. We weren't authoritarian people or establishment people. I think we were born that way—I really do. Because I was a troublemaker all my life, and so was he. There were four of us, and we did everything wrong. We were famous as the bad kids in town. You know, that Bloomfield boy, that Glaser boy, that Greenspan boy, that Ruby boy—they were all bad seeds.

The Glencoe House.

Mike was into throwing eggs at people, and he dragged me into that. We used to go around town, hiding in the bushes and waiting for convertibles to drive by, throwing raw eggs into cars on the highway. And then they would stop and come running after us. We would laugh and run away through the woods.

He was fearless and would do anything. One time we were standing in his garage at night, and he decided he was going to egg his neighbor's house. He didn't like his neighbor. So we loaded up with eggs and ran down the driveway and across the street to his neighbor's house, and we threw, like, five eggs each on the neighbor's windows. Then we ran back to his garage. But the light was on, and we were perfectly silhouetted on the driveway. So this guy's watching us running back into the house and closing the door and hiding. He called the cops on us, and we got arrested.

This was in a town where nobody did anything wrong. You have to get that clear. This was a town of perfectly behaved little kids, where all the parents were lawyers or doctors or psychiatrists, perfectly proper people. And nobody did anything wrong.

Bob Greenspan I knew Mike from the time we were 13 years old. Everybody laughed at him, and he was an outsider in the school. He was the type of guy that athletes would laugh at. He had a very strange, peculiar way of walking, and he was known to be a very uncoordinated kid.

He was the type of guy they'd stick out in right field in a baseball game. One time a ball was hit to him, and he tried to catch it and fell down. He tripped on himself and fell flat, and everybody laughed at him.

Allen Bloomfield Michael went away to a camp called Ojibwa, which is a jock camp. Most of the kids that go there are going to be precocious in sports, which is the last thing Michael is. Well, unexpectedly, our father drives up and there's a baseball game going on. There's nobody to greet him at the main lodge, so he meanders around until he hears the sound of the ballgame.

He's an avid jock; he's been an athlete all of his life. He was a professional boxer before he did a lot of other things. He's a tough guy, okay? He looks out, and there in far, far right field—there's Michael. He's not even facing the infield. He's got a stem of dandelions and he's blowing on it, watching the little parachutes come down. The batter hits a ball out Mike's way, and they yell, "Hey, Michael! Hey, Fatso!"

The ball comes by, and Mike's watching the laces revolve, man—he doesn't even make an attempt to get it. Instantly, Harold connects to the whole thing and grabs the owner of the camp and lays into him for allowing his son to be neglected.

Two weeks after that happens, it's time for him to come back. I go out with my mother to pick up Michael, and I end up with an earache and have to sleep over. Michael and I are in the cabin, and he's got this enormous trophy—a really big trophy, like one of those professional bowling trophies. And I said, "What did you do for this?" And he sheepishly said to me, "I told the best ghost stories. Camper of the Year."

If there ever was an Achilles heel for him, man, it was in the area of sports. Or learning how to ride a bicycle. Anything like that. It just wasn't his forte. And he always took a lot of shit because of it.

Fred Glaser I remember being at the ice skating rink the first time I met him. People were pushing him, and he kept falling down. There was a goofy little kid I knew named Ricky Freedman, and he knew Mike from class. Ricky and I just happened to be near him that day, sitting on the bench, when he came crawling over after falling down for the hundredth time. And he got to telling me about his record collection.

Then Mike invited me to come down to the Covenant Club, where his dad was a member. He said we could go down and take a steam bath, lift some weights, play ping-pong, and go swimming. I didn't know what that was or what that meant. It just sounded like fun to me.

He wanted friends, and nobody would be his friend. So if you were friendly to him, he was instantly friendly. I mean, in five minutes he said, "Come over to my house on Saturday, and I'll take you down to my dad's club. We can go swimming and take a steam bath. We'll get some lunch down there, and I'll take you around, man. I'll show you everything. It will be my treat."

Allen Bloomfield In Chicago, there were city clubs, and we belonged to the Covenant Club. There was a lot of anti-Semitism, and to get into the Chicago Athletic Club or the Harvard Club you had to be non-Jewish. But places like the Covenant Club and the Standard Club were Jewish clubs, so we could belong to those.

Fred Glaser The Covenant Club was one of those old Jewish athletic clubs where the main athletic event was sitting around smoking cigars and playing poker. Nobody did anything more athletic than play poker. Lifting your arms up to deal the cards was as athletic as anybody got.

Allen Bloomfield We used to go to the club and go swimming. They had a punching bag and weights, and there was a running track on the second floor that you ran around on an angle.

Then you'd go into another part, and there was a Turkish bath. They had these black guys that worked there, and they'd wrap a towel around themselves, which gave them some authority because we were all naked. There were old Jewish guys, sitting on these marble slabs, and they would get wet messages. These black guys would soap and lather them up and move them around on these marble slabs, and they'd be ahh-ing and saying, "Oh, that's so good, Sammy." We'd watch that, you know, and that would be a chuckle. Then we'd go into the Russian room, which was very steamy.

In there, they had these felt hats, and you put them in ice water. As you went higher and higher on the tiers of what's called the Russian *shvitsbod*, it got hotter and hotter. And so what you would do is: you'd invert your hat over your face and breathe through it, because it was so hot, man, it hurt your lungs. You couldn't do that too long, because you became claustrophobic. The steam would come, and you'd say, "What if we could never get out of here? We'll be stuck in here!" So we'd freak ourselves out and go charging out of there. Then we'd go and shower. And then we'd run to the dining room.

Fred Glaser The old guys, the *alta kockers*, the old Jews, sat around in the steam room for an hour or two with a towel wrapped around them, and they'd lose a few pounds. And then they would eat a nice lunch—a big, heavy lunch of pot roast or veal chops or T-bone steak.

After the steam room, we'd shower and go to the dining room. You couldn't come into the dining room without a sport coat. We'd show up in jeans and T-shirts and old shoes, and they'd make us wear these big, baggy sport coats that were 10 sizes too big, and a tie that didn't match, so it looked terrible.

These old guys would look at us like we were some kind of animals. Michael's father would be embarrassed to introduce him. "Sit over there, Michael, and don't tell anybody you're my son. I'll take care of your check later. Just sign your check. Go sit over there and don't bother me."

It hurt, but we would go and sit where he told us. The black guys would be nice to us—they'd wait on us and give us extra chocolate in our phosphates and all the good stuff. So we learned how to get around people by doing that. It was just another example of the way we would go around white people and be treated well by black people. It was another way of connecting with blacks and breaking away from the whites.

Michael Bloomfield My dad was a kitchen-appliance manufacturer: pots, pans, salt shakers, ketchup squeezers, mustard squeezers. That's what he wanted me to do, but that's not where I was at, exactly.

Dorothy Shinderman Harold, his brother, and his father were in business together. They did hotel, restaurant, and hospital supplies. They manufactured all those sugar dispensers, the ones with a chrome top and the little flap over the hole. They did stainless ware. Not for the fine restaurants where they had elegant equipment, but the roadside places. They made a fortune on it.

Allen Bloomfield Sam Bloomfield, our grandfather on my father's side, came over from Russia and was a self-made man. He came over at nine years of age, and he made several significant fortunes in his lifetime. He also had several significant financial disruptions.

He was the vulcanized-tire king at one time. After he was the vulcanized-tire king, he put all his money into real estate in Florida. The stock market crashed, and he lost it all. Then he got it back together, got some money, and opened up sporting-goods shops in Los Angeles. He owned 40 sporting-goods shops in Los Angeles. And then the earthquake came and wiped him out completely.

Sam Bloomfield came back to Chicago and saw a way to merchandise pies with this pie case that's connected to a counter. It makes them visible, so they buy the pie when they're drinking coffee. He saw the money in that, so he got the guy who made the case to sell him the patent. He got one of his sons to manufacture it and the other son to sell it.

They were constantly involved in business. It was the language they spoke all the time. Everything was addressed to the buck, everything was addressed to productivity, everything was addressed to the ability to make money. Based on that, Sam Bloomfield ended up fine-tuning his sons to be successful in a very legitimate way—not to say that he was illegitimate—but in a legitimate way to grow a company and go through the metamorphosis of an American success story.

The work ethic was something that was a given from a really early age. My dad, when he was 14, had a gas station. I mean, you were expected to make money. If you didn't have the ability to add and calculate quickly and find the leverage point, that was regrettable.

Michael Bloomfield The first person in my family who played music, that I knew of, was my cousin. He started playing guitar, and I wanted a guitar 'cause he had one—just sort of a relative rivalry. I demanded to get a guitar and got one, and then my brother wanted one. So I picked up the guitar because my cousin had one and my brother had one, and we were all playing. My cousin sort of put it down, my brother put it down, but I didn't. I had a real cheap little 3/4-size Harmony guitar.

Allen Bloomfield Simultaneous to moving to Glencoe, our cousin Chuckie got a guitar. Michael wanted one, and I got one, too. The guitarist who taught Chuckie was my mother's hairdresser, Tony Carmen. We were playing together for a little while, and then I put it aside. But Michael stayed with it.

At 13 years of age Michael has his *bar mitzvah*, and it's like his first performance, if you will. He goes beyond the call of duty of just reciting the *Haftorah*, which is the part you have to memorize. You have to verify that you can read Hebrew. In a sense, it's a rite of passage into manhood, and it's also the beginning of taking on full responsibility for your actions. All of those things are implicit in the tradition.

Michael added certain dramatics to it for—I don't know, we'll just call it "theatrical effect." He would look up at the ceiling, raise his eyes, and sort of have a dialogue with, if you will, or speak directly to, The Absolute, with what he was saying. It was beyond what would be considered the normal *bar mitzvah* thing.

And he looked quite funny, because he had on this sharkskin or silk suit, which was really fancy for a kid of 13, and a tie with a big Windsor knot and everything. He got a lot of gifts, and a lot of people came. You have to understand that the *bar mitzvah* was a big event. Hundreds of people would attend, and there was social status in having a big *bar mitzvah*.

I was getting more and more envious by the moment, as he was getting more and more gifts and more and more attention, and he saw that. He was the type of guy who would say to me, "Take. Take whatever you want, man. Go on, take something. You want something, you like something, take it." He was always like that.

One of the things he got was one of the first portable transistor radios. It was an ivory-colored job with a telescopic antenna and a waffle front.

Dorothy Shinderman He had a wonderful *bar mitzvah*. It was just projecting what he learned, and he did it beautifully. He didn't balk at studying for *bar mitzvah*. He knew he would be onstage.

He got a transistor radio. It was a little radio you could listen to under the sheets at night in bed, and he would listen to that every night. He would hear these blues stations. A lot of music came out of Chicago—black, country western—and he listened to everything. He became very interested in it through the radio.

Michael Bloomfield The AM radio was a freaky thing with me. Just to hear the music that I loved—to hear Sun Records, Elvis Presley records—to turn on a radio, and maybe get John R. from Nashville or something, playing this music that I just loved. It was like a whole world opened to me.

My first rock & roll influence was Scotty Moore, Elvis's guitar player. Also Cliff Gallup, who played with Gene Vincent's Blue Caps. Man, I had every Elvis Presley magazine—this little fat Jew with his hair combed like Elvis Presley, waddling around. It was very serious to me. It knocked me out—not just the music but the social-aesthetic thing at that time. I saw myself, in my mind, as this lanky hillbilly, and the radio was a reinforcement of that whole lifestyle.

Fred Glaser The maids always had the radio on, and they listened to black music with people like Muddy Waters and B.B. King and Ben E. King and Bo Diddley and Jimmy Reed—those were the day-to-day people that black people were listening to, when we were listening to Elvis and Buddy Holly

Michael's bar mitzvah,
1956.

and some of those early guys. So we heard this music around the house. And we liked it. We didn't know what the hell it was, but it was cool music.

All of these people—Roy and me and Michael and Greenspan and every person you knew—had a black maid. And those maids listened to WVON on the radio all day while they were cleaning the house. That was the black music station in Chicago; the letters stood for the Voice Of the Negro, VON.

The key to what it was really all about was breaking away from these rigid, conservative white people and being attracted to these liberal, non-judgmental, kindly black people. That's what the music is. The music is the outpouring of that feeling; it's a visceral creation—you know, a creation of that feeling. We just wanted to be among these nice people and have some fun and not be screamed at, because we liked music and art, and we liked to sit around.

It was interesting music. And the more we would listen to it, the more we would like it. I would go up to my room every night when I was supposed to go to bed, at 10 o'clock, and I'd turn on Sid McCoy, who had the 10 to 11 o'clock jazz show, and then Norm Spaulding, who was on from 11 to midnight. If I could stay up, I'd listen to Pervis Spann—he was on from midnight to 6 a.m. And he played the real blues. He played Muddy and Wolf, Little Walter, and all those people.

Pervis Spann, the Blues Man. He'd talk to the women: "I want you women to call me and tell me how bad your men have been treating you. I'll tell you, I'll treat you right. I'll show you some real loving. I'll be good to you. I don't want no men to call me." And he'd talk about made-up political campaigns, like running Muddy Waters for President.

All of us had bad parents and bad parenting, but we loved the maids. Our parents were mean, unpleasant, middle-class people who didn't understand us. The maids were cool, hip, sophisticated people who did understand us and liked us. So naturally we were attracted to them, and we were attracted to black culture.

Bloomfield had a whole black family living in his house—the same family for years and years. Bernice was the maid. Her husband, Freddy, was the gardener and the fix-it guy. We weren't that rich, but we were comfortable. And we had a maid who came in a couple of times a week to clean the house.

People like Roy Ruby had live-in maids. Roy didn't have a whole family, but they had a live-in maid at his house. She spent her whole life with him, protecting and guarding him. It was like *Gone with the Wind*. When his parents wouldn't talk to him and wouldn't give him any money, she'd give him money. When he was in California, strung out on dope, and he'd run out of money at the end of the month, before his trust check came, the woman who had been his maid when he was a boy would give him $30. And he would go and score some dope.

Roy's father was a professor at Roosevelt University, and his mother had been a concert pianist. They were real intellectual, rich people. His family owned a store in Chicago. It was a famous, high-priced, super-exclusive grocery store that had only the finest foods imported from all around the world. It was the finest grocery store in Chicago. His mother came from that family. She had a lot of money, and she married Lionel Ruby, who was a college professor.

Joe Greenspan—Bob's father—was one of the major political pollsters in Chicago. He was a behind-the-scenes political figure, one of those smoke-filled-back-room guys that you read about in the papers. A Damon Runyon character. They lived out in Glencoe because they wanted the status. Even though Joe wasn't one of those kind of people, he wanted to raise his kids out there, in a nice place.

Bloomfield was very rich. Ruby was very rich. Greenspan was upper middle class. We were sort of like over-reachers. My mother was an over-reacher, and she wanted to live where all her friends and relatives lived, so she dragged my father out there. And we just managed to hold on.

In the '40s and '50s, my father had been a studio musician who played with the big bands when they came through Chicago. They would travel with a core group and add studio guys for the local gig—pickup musicians. My father was one of those.

My mother talked him into stopping playing music and taking a job with her father's company. That's how we got money and got to Glencoe. Mike liked my father because my father had been a musician all his life. He told my father that he wanted to be a disc jockey, and my father said, "That's crazy. Get a real job. You don't want to be a musician. You don't want to be a disc jockey. That's no kind of a job."

When I would tell Michael's father that I wanted to be a writer or a college professor, he'd get mad at me. He'd say, "Your parents spent good money. They raised you in Glencoe and got you a good education. You want to be a goddamned college professor? You know how much money they make? They don't make shit. Get a real job. Go into business. Make something of yourself. Be a businessman, make some money, make your parents proud." And I'd be shocked. What could be more noble than being a college professor? What could be more meaningful than that? He would just make fun of me.

We all had run-ins with each other's parents, but my father was a cool, easy-going guy. He didn't bother anybody. He would play the violin around the house, and Michael would sit and listen to him and try to accompany him. He could play a little piano, and they would play duets. Michael liked him, and he liked me for that reason, because this was the first real musician he'd ever met—a guy who had actually played music for a living. That fascinated him, so he used to come to my house all the time.

He would walk into these beautiful houses—I mean, Glencoe, man, I want you to understand this town. Everybody was a millionaire in this town. Oriental rugs and big huge windows, white couches covered in plastic, white rugs and everything. Beautiful stuff. And Michael would come in and immediately knock over a $500 lamp. He'd bang his fingers on the piano, right after my mother had just had the maid rub it down and clean it up real nice. He'd come in with his dirty hands and start playing the piano. And he had a funny style of playing—he played real loud and heavy.

My mother was used to playing classical music, really dainty and light and everything. So he'd start banging away, playing rock & roll music. She said, "Stop that noise, stop that noise! What's that racket? Michael, stop that. I bet your mother doesn't let you do that in your house." And he said, "No, that's why I come over here. You're such a wonderful woman, Mrs. Glaser. You're so charming. You have this piano here, this beautiful piano.

I want to play music for you on your piano." She said, "Well, play it some-where else. Wait 'til you learn how to play, and then you can come back."

He would knock over food in the kitchen. He couldn't eat at home when his father was there, because his father just hated him, so he'd eat at our house a lot of the time. When his father was gone, then the maids would make dinner and he would eat there. I would eat there too.

Michael came to my house a lot as a kid, because my parents were pretty easy-going and didn't lay into him too heavily. They would bother me, but they weren't as heavy as his parents. They'd let us have a little more room and a little more space. My father liked talking to him, because it made him feel good that here was a young kid who looked up to him for doing what he had done all his life, for doing the work that he was most proud of. He kind of liked Michael, even though he would tell him he was nuts.

I didn't like his father much. And his father didn't like me—each of our parents thought the other one was the bad influence. My parents said, "Stay away from that Michael, he's a bad guy." And his parents said, "Stay away from that Freddy, he's a bad guy." And Roy was supposed to stay away from everybody. All of our parents thought the other kids were a bad in-fluence, but we were all bad. We'd go to each other's houses and hide out.

There was a place called Harry's Delicatessen where we used to hang out. Harry was this old Jew with a mustache, a stooped-over guy who had escaped from Germany and come to Glencoe to open a delicatessen, some-how. We would go there for lunch and skip school for the rest of the day. He would never report us, never turn us in. He would let us drink choco-late phosphates for free and let us charge corned-beef sandwiches to our parents' bills because we didn't have any money to pay for them.

We would hang out there—just sit around in the booths and talk to each other, and talk with him. He would tell us about Germany, and about the Nazis and the concentration camps, and about art and life and how to be hip. He would say that our parents were nice people but they were square. He would say, "You shouldn't be so bad. You're embarrassing your parents." He was like an old philosopher type of guy, one of those older people that kids gravitate to. We spent a lot of time at his shop. We would never go home. We didn't like our parents. We didn't do homework. We didn't do schoolwork.

We went to real conservative schools, the best schools. New Trier High School, where we all went, is, like, the best public high school in the coun-try. But we didn't like it. Bloomfield got thrown out.

Allen Bloomfield New Trier High School had a thing called "Lagniappe" that was like amateur night. The kids put on a program. Michael had a rock

& roll band, and the show's director told him, "You can play whatever the tune is, but you can't do any type of encore." Michael and his band brought the house down—and, of course, they played an encore. And then they kicked him out of school.

Fred Glaser He got thrown out of New Trier, which was very hard to do in the first place, because they had a lot of weird kids there and they could usually accommodate them, but they just couldn't accommodate him. So he went to a school in Massachusetts for a while.

Dorothy Shinderman He was sent to Cornwall Academy in Massachusetts. It was terrible on him. That was the worst thing my husband could have done, because Michael was a free soul. Michael had a lot of talent inside and it had to come out. I don't think he was there for even a year. He wanted to come home. We were thinking he needed strict training, but that's just what he didn't need. He needed freedom to advance his own talents.

Fred Glaser They shipped him out there. And all that did was introduce him to drugs faster than it would have happened in Chicago. At the same time, Roy went to a prep school called Windsor Mountain. Both of them came back the first Christmas after our sophomore year with pot in their pockets. That was the first time I smoked pot, when I was about 14. They

Courtesy Allen Bloomfield

Dorothy, Michael, Allen (standing), and Harold Bloomfield, 1956.

had both started smoking pot in prep school. All the things that our parents thought they were doing to get us on the straight and narrow wound up making us wilder and crazier.

That experience introduced him to drugs and East Coast intellectuals and kids who were more sophisticated than we were—who were like us but were even more sophisticated than we were about books and literature and stuff like that. Power and prestige. We were like hillbillies, in that sense. We were from Chicago. We didn't know as much as, say, a kid from New York and Long Island and the Hamptons. Those people knew about books and records and being college professors and being sophisticated people. So we picked up a lot of that from them.

We were rough around the edges, but we knew about blacks and they didn't know about blacks. They knew about drugs and girls and power and politics. They introduced us to books like *Catcher in the Rye* by J. D. Salinger. Michael got it from kids at his school, and Roy got it from kids at his school. That got us into the left-wing intellectual bent. From J. D. Salinger into Norman Mailer and Saul Bellow, and then into the whole radical literary movement, Allen Ginsberg and Kerouac and that group.

They sent him off to what they thought was a nice, middle-class, intellectual prep school, where he'd get a good education and settle down, but he got introduced to more radical stuff, to intellectual radicalism. That, combined with the street radicalism of the South Side, made him, like, a whole radical. Now he had an intellectual background, and he was learning about the people who had gone to the South and made field recordings of blacks for the Library of Congress.

We didn't realize that the black people we were hanging out with were something that serious intellectuals would think about or care about or put in the Library of Congress. For all we knew they were just a bunch of niggers having a good time. That was fine with us. But then we found out that people like John Hammond Sr. and Alan Lomax and Charles Seeger had recorded people like that and considered them great poets and artists. Tremendous people, historical people. So that proved to us even more that these white people we knew were really stupid. They didn't know anything about what was going on. They knew nothing about life at all.

Michael Bloomfield The guitar was the only damn thing I had. That and the AM radio. Just being a social misfit was a help, because I took the guitar to be my own. I took it to be a thing I could do. I wasn't even aware that I was any good for a long time. I was left-handed, and it was real hard for me to learn 'cause I learned right-handed. It was the only thing that I focused on, because it was the only thing I could do with some success.

Dorothy Shinderman When he started his music, I didn't fight it. And I never told Michael to take lessons. It was all his own—he wanted it. I had a hairdresser who was a guitar teacher, and he gave him a few lessons, not for very long, just to get the basic chords. And the rest Mike did all on his own.

It's the genes. He got the talented genes from my family's side. My mother's parents were born in Czechoslovakia, and her whole family was interested in music. Most were violinists. They played Hungarian music, and they were all very talented. My mother was an actress, and my aunt was a very fine pianist. I graduated from the Goodman Theater. We were all in the arts, to some extent. There was that tendency for everybody to be talented.

If anything, he should have gone to a school of performing arts. But he learned in spite of not doing that. He learned from every black man he ever met that could play an instrument. And that's why he was such a good blues guitarist.

Harold's idea was that Michael would eventually be in the family business, be a businessman. My husband did not appreciate Michael's love for music. Whether it was blues or jazz, it wouldn't make any difference. He was against it. He didn't want his son to be a musician. That's not a business. He didn't understand it, and that's the sum and substance of it.

I wanted Michael to do whatever made him happy, and I knew he was good at it.

Michael Bloomfield My father used to break the guitars. He called them "fruit boxes," and he'd just take 'em and break 'em up. He wanted me to be everything that I wasn't. He wanted me to be a jock, he wanted me to be a good student, he wanted me to be this and that. He just didn't understand.

Allen Bloomfield There was a story Michael told about our dad smashing the guitars and calling them "fruit boxes." I think that was just a fabrication. I never heard him call them "fruit boxes." Our father was not the type of guy who would smash a guitar. It was never, ever going to be something on that level. He'd hit you in the face. He'd correct you instantly. There was no lag time in that. He'd never take it out on a guitar. He would go right to you.

I felt the pressure of those expectations while I was growing up, too. I mean, it was measurable in grades in school, in athletic performance, anything like that—it was highly competitive. It was competitive inside the family, and it was competitive outside the family.

It was very difficult. On the other side, my mother was an actress and came from a theatrical background. It was really an amalgamation of the precision of my father and the theatrical creativeness of my mom that kind of fused together to give Michael some of his skills. Because as Michael's skills were applied to music, he really had a discipline that he brought to learning a number of different styles. He had the desire to separate himself from whatever his pleasure was for the purpose of becoming a better player, and that in turn became his ultimate pleasure. And he noodled all the time. He'd be in his room and he'd be playing, running his fingers up and down constantly. He'd be watching Lawrence Welk on TV, and he'd be playing. Michael and his guitar were inseparable.

I think it took about a year for him to figure out where it was at, and then Tony Carmen couldn't really expand upon what he had learned. He got this chart book, and he would play anything and everything that was in it. It was show tunes, all types of music that was popular from the '40s up to the late '50s.

The only moment I can recall where my father and my brother shared anything in common was when Michael would play show tunes for him. Dad liked a lot of show tunes, and Michael would bring his guitar and amplifier into Dad's bedroom and play every one of them for him. Every one of them. Now, I don't think he did that for anybody else in his life. But for that type of appreciation, for a sense that he could get his father's love, he was banging out those show tunes.

Michael Bloomfield I took lessons for about a year or so. I learned dance-band guitar, straight rhythm chops. I was the only person who knew I was getting anywhere at it, until I got to be around 15 years old. When I was about 15, I was a monster rock guitar player.

The first blues I remember was a T-Bone Walker song called "Glamour Girl." That was just a whole other thing. I was playing the same notes that they were playing, but when I would take my solos they weren't the same. What I was playing was like fast bullshit—it wasn't right at all. Those cats were using the same notes, and it was all right. I just couldn't figure out the difference.

Ya Got It?

Dorothy Shinderman Fred Glaser, Roy Ruby, and Michael would go to blues clubs and try to hear the great blues artists. Fred and Roy were very, very close to Mike. When you live in a suburb like that, there aren't many way-out kids. They come from proper families, and they do the proper thing—they graduate and become doctors or lawyers. There aren't that many musicians and artists, especially in the northern suburbs.

Roy and Mike would take a train into the city. That's when they started going down to the black neighborhoods. They would sneak away and go to Maxwell Street and hear the music. I didn't even know at the time that they were doing it. I would go crazy—I wouldn't know where he was.

● ● ●

Roy Ruby Before we went to the South Side, Mike and I were "folkniks." I mean, we were white kids that had heard about this other kind of music. Before I went away to school, Michael and I would go down to Maxwell Street, or we would go to the Gate of Horn to see Josh White and Odetta. These were the first two black artists that we were super-excited about. Both of them were very nice and talked to us.

Michael Bloomfield There were black artists that we liked, like Chuck Berry and stuff. But that was just what we considered rock & roll.

Roy Ruby That was rock & roll, yeah. The first blues, where we really knew it was blues, was Josh White, I'll bet. And we got a record by T-Bone Walker called *T-Bone Blues*, on Atlantic.

Michael Bloomfield Best album he ever made in his life.

Roy Ruby "Stormy Monday." That's when we heard "Stormy Monday."

Michael Bloomfield And "Mean Old World," and this incredibly good song with a harp called "Play On, Little Girl." We talked to Josh White a couple of times. My family's maid knew him personally—Mary Williams.

Roy Ruby That's right. That's how we met him. We went down there and we said, "We know Mary." She had called up and everything. We were real young. Later on, I realized where he was at. At that time, he was pretty nice to us.

Michael Bloomfield She had known him, and he got us into the club. We went to the back room. Yeah—the very first trip, man, when we went down to the Gate of Horn. God, going in the back room there. The first thing is: they wouldn't have even let us in there. But Josh White got them to give us special seats up in the balcony. They didn't serve black and white together.

Roy Ruby Let's see—the first time we went to the South Side, we saw Guitar Junior, and a fat lady in a red dress who played the saxophone. We were at the front table, and we were underage. Mike sat in on guitar. The club was called the Place.

Michael Bloomfield And what did the lady with the saxophone say to you?

Roy Ruby She said, "Ya got it?" I said, "Got what? What do you mean?" She said, "Ya got it?" I said, "I don't know. What? Got what?" She said, "Ya got it, don't ya?"

And by now everybody's laughing. The whole place is breaking up, people are falling all over. Here are these two 14-year-old white kids in the middle of this place. This is before the blues movement started. These people were friendly. They didn't know about white people. Everyone's cracking up, and she's saying, "Ya got it, don't ya?" And I'm saying, "What do you mean? Wh-wh-what do I have?"

This goes on for about 25 minutes. I'm completely embarrassed, crawling under the table, don't know what is going on. It's like being in Africa, and they're like, "What's the password?" When I finally give up, and I'm about to slink out the door, she finally blasts out the answer. She turns around, takes the saxophone from her mouth, spreads her arms wide, spreads her legs, leans back, looks at the ceiling, and screams, "Ya got yo' ass, don't ya!"

The people are rolling around on the floor. And I'm slinking out the door. That was my first experience with Chicago blues.

Michael Bloomfield Don't you remember the show at the Regal, man?

Roy Ruby Oh my God, that's right. My mother's maid took us to the Regal Theater.

Michael Bloomfield That was incredibly nice. Wow—I don't know why she did that. Just because she's a sweet lady. And we saw Art Blakey & the Jazz Messengers, Sonny Stitt, Sonny Rollins, Miles Davis. Don't you remember that guy saying, "Play 'Moanin',' Blake-ley [*sic*]?" Remember that guy saying that?

Roy Ruby Miles was there. "Bye, Bye, Blackbird." That was his hit then.

Michael Bloomfield And remember those kids sitting behind us calling me "Fatboy"?

● ● ●

Fred Glaser There was this black world that doesn't exist anymore. It was part of the old jazz world—"black-and-tan" clubs. Those were the mixed jazz clubs in the '40s and '50s. There were clubs where whites could go in black neighborhoods, and it was okay because they were there to hear the music. In the late '50s, there were blues clubs that were like black-and-tan clubs, where white people could go to hear the blues. But hardly anybody went.

And so, when we got to be about 15 years old, these maids—Michael's maid, primarily—would take us to these clubs. The maids would invite us down to their apartments on the South Side on a Sunday afternoon and make dinner for us. And they'd have relatives over. A big Sunday dinner with fried chicken and okra and squash and sweet potatoes. And they'd play the records of these people, of Wolf and Muddy and Chuck Berry before he was a crossover artist.

We would take the El downtown on Sunday afternoon, and they would take us out to these clubs, to Pepper's Show Lounge on 43rd Street or Theresa's on Indiana Avenue—these famous blues clubs. Here was this other world that was totally unimaginable to us. And we were just overwhelmed by this music.

And then, as we got a little older, we would go on our own. There was this older guy named Al Scher—a big fat guy with long, black, greasy hair.

He was a couple of years older than we were, and he had a car. He would drive us down to the South Side and take us to these clubs.

To get out at night, I'd tell my parents I was going to sleep at Mike's, and Mike would tell his parents he was going to sleep at my house. We'd meet by the movie theater downtown—there was one little movie theater in this town. Al would pick us up, and we would drive down to Pepper's or Theresa's and hang out there.

The black people would be so amazed to see these little, white Jewish kids down there listening to music that they wouldn't bother us. They were amazed. And they would talk to us. When they discovered that we knew about Muddy Waters and Howlin' Wolf and Little Walter, they were amazed. They couldn't believe it. They would sit at the table and talk to us and buy us beer and keep us company. And they'd take us out in the alley to smoke joints. They liked us, because no other white people were coming down there at that time.

It was fun. It was nice, and if you wanted a beer, they wouldn't say, "Hey, you can't touch a drink. Wait 'til you're 18. You can't drink." They said, "Hey, man, have some beer. You want a cigarette, pal? Sure, fine."

Michael Bloomfield In the blues clubs, first of all it was noisy. There was a band, and the band was pretty loud, 'cause most of the time it was electric. The harp was through an amp, and there was a couple of guitars through an amp, an electric bass, and drums. Spann played an electric piano in Muddy's band. That band was loud, and they played from 10 to 4 in the morning, seven sets.

And it'd be crowded. If it was a Saturday night, everybody was determined to get it on. They'd be jukin'—they'd be jukin', Jack! Just into getting it on, man. And they'd be partying. The women'd be dressed up as fine as they could be, with red hats on their heads, and wig hats on their heads, and the cats'd be pressed out slick. I remember—back then, there wasn't no naturals. Everybody had conks, man. Some dudes, some young badges, would have them rags on their head in the afternoon but come night, they'd be polished, gleamin'—everybody'd be gleamin'. Determined to party.

They had their wages in their pocket, and they wasn't gonna blow the whole wages or nothing like that, but by God they was gonna take their wife and have a good time. And dig that music. They wanted to dig that music. They wanted that singer to talk to their ear, man.

Cats'd be up in front of the bandstand screaming at you, man, telling you to "Play that music!" Lord, they would want to hear that music. And when you played that music, oh man, you'd be talking right to these people, and they'd be screaming back at you and dancing and everything. Lots of times there were incredible good feelings, just the best feelings of all. Because there was so much correspondence between the musicians and the people. Sometimes a cat would be up there, and the groove'd be so strong, the joint would be jumping, people'd just be rocking and screaming and shouting.

Come late at night, come the midnight hour and after, come into the morning hours—cats'd be playing slow and laid-back and bluesy. They'd be playing nothing but the blues, there wouldn't be no fast songs. All the rock & roll would be out of the way; all the jump blues would be out of the way. Cats'd be laid back, tired, their hands'd just be crawling over the strings, bending a note, and people'd be slow-dragging across the floor. It was just the blues.

There'd be a blue light, maybe, and the club'd be all smoky, and there wouldn't be any fancy step-dancing anymore. It was sort of like slow dancing at a high school sock hop. Your arms'd be around a chick, and you'd just be rocking back and forth, and the blues would be slow and easy and mellow.

All the cutting contests, the hot licks and show stuff, was over. Y'know, cats'd always be bringing up guest stars, 'cause they'd wanna get off the stage and get a drink and set with their woman for a while. But late in the evening, all the guest stars'd been up and down, and the cats'd be playing the blues, and it was just beautiful.

Many's the time, come four o'clock in the morning, people'd go home and all the musicians'd go out and get some chicken or ribs someplace, and be so relaxed and mellow. It'd just be great.

● ● ●

Fred Glaser There was Pepper's Show Lounge. There was Theresa's on 47th and Indiana. There was McKie's Disc Jockey Show Lounge on 63rd and Cottage Grove. There was the Purple Door—that was more like a folk place; that was over by the University of Chicago on 57th Street. And Silvio's Lounge, where Wolf played, on Lake Street on the West Side.

Roy Ruby Silvio's, Lake and Kedzie, under the green El tracks. Now, you see, this is on the West Side, which is worse than the South Side. And Howlin' Wolf is performing.

Fred Glaser He'd be crawling around on the stage. He used to do his act— he'd crawl around and do "Howling for My Baby."

Roy Ruby And he'd say, "I want to do this one for my white friends. I've got some white friends here tonight. Put the spotlight on them."

Fred Glaser He'd say, "Stand up, white people. Here they are—give them a big hand. They're right at this table, right here. Now, I want all you people to be nice to these white people out here in the audience."

Roy Ruby Silvio's is in a black neighborhood surrounded by whites on the West Side. I can't describe to you what it's like to be a black person living in that area of the West Side. It would be like living in Khe Sahn as a Marine in Vietnam, you know—being surrounded by the enemy. And this was a rough fucking place, man. Because, you see, the black people that lived in this area had constant warfare with the whites that lived in the area. And so when young, white, blues aficionados would show up, I mean, who knows? You were a white dot walking down the street, like the reverse of a black man walking in Glencoe.

Fred Glaser People would look at you, man, remember that? So we'd just drive up, park right in front, and run in to safety.

Michael Bloomfield The violence was part of the thing. I grew to accept it after a while, and just watched out that I wouldn't get caught in a heavy scene. The only thing that would scare me would be groups of kids—10 kids from, like, 10 to 14 years old, walking in packs with big sticks. They were called Paddywackers. They'd catch a little paddy, a little white cat, and wack him. That scared me—no way you could get away from that. I got beat up a couple of times from that kind of jive.

See, if they went across this freeway, into the mayor's neighborhood—this sort of white, middle-class, Polish neighborhood—the same thing would happen to them, man. There dasn't be a black cat walk that neighborhood, 'cause he's gonna get his.

Chicago's a borderline city—one street can make the difference between whole neighborhoods. Like it's all black for miles for one direction, then one street, one expressway, and it's all white. And those lines never cross. In the hillbilly ghetto of Chicago, there's one little black area, a few blocks, and those cats never stray from that area. They never even walk out of it, except to go to the subway to go to work, because the rest of it's just stone cracker country.

Roy Ruby We'd go to Pepper's, and we'd go to the front door—the gate—and we'd say to the guy, "Well, we're friends of Muddy, and he said we could come in," and they'd hassle us for a while.

Michael Bloomfield Muddy Waters, he was like a god to me. Well, if he was a god, B.B. King was a deity where I couldn't even imagine ever knowing someone of his magnitude and greatness. But Muddy was in Chicago. I would go down the street, and from two blocks away I'd hear that harmonica come out of the club. I'd hear that harp, and I'd hear Muddy's slide. I'd be tremblin'. I'd be like a dog in heat. I didn't know what to do. I'd get into that place, and I'd be all a-quiver.

Do you remember when they wouldn't let us in? We stood out in front, me and Roy Ruby, and just peered in the window. We were too young to get inside. We had phony IDs, but they just laughed at us. I would stand all night in the window, in the worst section of town. Muddy came out and shook our hands, all for naught. We still couldn't get in. A big brown hand that was bigger than both my hands, engulfing one hand.

Roy Ruby At Pepper's there were different cliques. There was one group that would stand along the bar along the back wall. And then there was the audience who'd sit in the chairs that were arranged out in the auditorium. And then there was the front bar, where you first walked in.

Michael Bloomfield Do you remember the dirty dancing at that place? All the women who would lift their dresses over their heads and shake it right in your face. Oh, man, it's so embarrassing.

Muddy played at Pepper's Show Lounge. Theresa's had people like Little Walter and Jimmy Reed and other people—not quite such big names. They would let us in there. They wouldn't serve us drinks, but they'd let us sit in the back and drink Cokes and stuff like that.

The musicians, like Muddy, would get up on the stage and tell everybody to let us alone, that we were some of his white friends from the North Side coming down there to hear the music, and nobody better mess with us or they'd have to mess with him. He'd take care of it. We were his friends. Nobody'd better fuck with these white boys out here, or they'd have to deal with him. So people wouldn't bother us.

Roy Ruby You didn't sit in at Pepper's until some time after that. It was a year or two after you first sat in at the Place before you were allowed to sit in at Pepper's.

Michael Bloomfield It was weird. I got to play Muddy's guitar with that raised action, so he could play slide on it real easy—the red Telecaster. I went down there, thinking that I was really some hot stuff, 'cause I had some fast fingers, and I had plenty of licks.

I was, like, 15. And the minute I got in, man, I said, "Let me play. Let me up on the stand and play." But I didn't have no soul or nothing. All I had was that speed and some brash Jewboy confidence. I would go down there, and I wouldn't know what the hell made my music different—why I couldn't really sound like them other cats.

I could already play rock & roll. When I around was 15, I started working with rock & roll bands in this real funky town called Highwood, Illinois, where the Fort Sheridan army base is, way up in the north suburbs. I worked with a Jerry Lee Lewis imitator, a hillbilly about 32 years old named Hayden Thompson.

Fred Glaser Hayden Thompson made a couple of small-selling records. He was a little bit older, and he fronted kind of a bluesy rock & roll band in this white Italian town. It was the only town where you could drink anywhere along the North Shore. It was an anomaly from all these rich towns. It was a town where the army base was, so you could drink there. And it's where all these Italian gangsters lived, so there were bars where heavyweight street Italians hung out. Hayden had a rock & roll band there, and Michael was his rhythm guitar player.

Michael Bloomfield And then I started working with my own little band, in this bar called PG's Club 7. We had a harp player—Jim Schwall, from Seigel-Schwall. He played harp with us then. I was working, and I worked every kind of gig—fraternity parties, Jewish Centers. But all my hanging out, when I wanted to sit in and learn, was down on the South Side. I'd be hanging out down there to learn. I'd be sitting in constantly.

Bob Greenspan We got together with Vince Vidi, a guy who was about 10 years older than us. I was singing and playing the guitar. It was Mike, myself, and a guy named Jerry Pasternak, who was a drummer. Vince lived in Highwood, which is north of Glencoe by about six or seven miles. And they had all kinds of bars back then.

Vince was a piano player, and the group was called Vince Vidi & Them. I don't remember how Vince found us or we found him, but we played our first professional job in a little crummy bar called the Club 7 in Highwood. We were 15 years old, so we had to stay in the back room until it was time to start. We couldn't play for shit back then. But that was the first professional gig that Mike Bloomfield ever played.

Fred Glaser By the time Mike was 17, he was as good as any of the professional musicians. He would get up onstage with Muddy's band, and he'd play as good as Muddy's guitar player would play—as good as Muddy, in his own way. And the people would flip out. They couldn't believe it.

He was a little, fat, Jewish kid then. He looked real Jewish and funny-looking. He had curly hair, and his name was Michael Bloomfield. Muddy would say, "My friend Michael Bloomfield from Glencoe is going to come up here and play the guitar with us for a couple of numbers now. Want you all to listen to him real good, and want you to give him a nice, big round of applause when he finishes. He's a great musician and a good friend of ours." And everybody would laugh and say, "Come on, man, get that fucking kid off."

They laughed at him. And then he started to play, and they'd shut up. He started jamming with the band, and he was good. He was real good. Three or four minutes into a song he started taking off, and people would sit back and listen and start dancing. And they realized he was great. And they started applauding him.

Later on, we got to be friendly with Muddy and his wife and Otis Spann. They all lived in the same building. We would spend a day there. We'd start out at Muddy's house for dinner, and his wife would make, like, gumbo or bouillabaisse or some real hot New Orleans kind of dinner. And then we'd go downstairs to where Spann lived, in the basement, and jam. Michael would play and Muddy would play and Spann would play the piano. They would all jam down there.

Michael Bloomfield A lot of these cats was old enough to be my father. And I had that sort of feeling—they were like dads, y'know. Like a father relationship. And I had to be polite. They were the older masters of this thing. It was like being with old classical musicians. They were the classics of the blues. I was very, very polite.

When I was 17, I thought I was good enough to gig in black places and hold my own. You had to hold your own. If you shucked, then you had no business being there. You'd not only be a white kid, you'd be a fool. You'd be a punk and a fool. You couldn't shuck. Just to be in that environment, and to be accepted in that environment as a man when in my own mind I felt like a little kid, was a very flattering thing.

I can't say I wasn't scared, 'cause I was scared, lots of times, because it was a rough thing, man. I saw knifings and shootings—it was a man's world. There was no jive. The kids were scary, man, the youngbloods, the low-riders in the street. They were scary. It was a very violent scene, man. Cats that didn't get a lot of bread.

It's a sociological thing about ghetto society. When a man can't get a job and maybe his wife works for some white man's family, and it makes him feel bad because he can't be supporting her and she has to work for some damn fool white people, he goes out and gets drunk, and he has to assert his masculinity in some sort of way. It's a wretched, undignified, terrible scene for a man to be in, and some terrific violence went down—terrific in the sense of terrifying.

And there was an amazing amount of fantastic passion and getting it on, too, man—an incredible love for the music. It was just an amazing thing for my eyes to behold. To see that lifestyle, and to be swept into it.

One time I was standing in a bar, and a guy walked in, and he took a woman's head and slammed it on the bar and said, "Bartender, give this bitch a beer." Her severed head was on the bar. This guy had cut off his old lady's head in some horrible fight, and he slammed it down on top of the bar and said, "Bartender, give this bitch a beer." That freaked everybody out.

The cops were paid to let that stuff go. The white cops were glad when black cats shot each other. They'd be delighted. In their eyes, man, it was just two dead niggers. They'd be happy about it. And black cops were paid off to let that stuff go down.

Chicago was graft city. Cats busting hookers and getting free lays. Busting a hooker and getting paid off at the same time. It was just graft city. Everybody robbed from everybody else. Everybody was guilty, and everybody was innocent. They were the poor, innocent, guilty children of a messed-up ghetto society.

Several guys took me to be almost like I was their son—Big Joe Williams, Sunnyland Slim, and Otis Spann. They took me to be like their kid, man; they just showed me from the heart. They took me aside and said, "You can play, man. Don't be shy. Get up there and play." What I learned from them was invaluable. A way of life, a way of thinking, a whole kind of thing—invaluable things to learn.

I used to hear Elmore James, Sonny Boy, Little Walter, Howlin' Wolf, Muddy Waters, Freddie King, Albert King—way before they were known anywhere but the ghetto. Lowell Fulson. Otis Spann. And many of the smaller, more obscure cats—J.B. Hutto, Jimmy Rogers, Eddie Taylor, this guy named Little Mac.

By the time I was around 17, I was interested in it from a musicological standpoint. I was trying to discover where the old blues singers lived. I met cats like Washboard Sam and Jazz Gillum and Tommy McClennan and Kokomo Arnold. I used to have a band with Big Joe Williams, Yank Rachell, John Estes, and play with guys like Little Brother Montgomery. By then it was a scholarly thing. Like Paul Oliver and Sam Charters, I wanted to know the story of the blues, and the best way for me to learn was to actually meet the guys.

Hyde Park
White Blues Kids

Michael Bloomfield I had played a lot of folk music—stuff like Gary Davis and Doc Watson and Travis picking. I was doing this when I was 17 or 18. I was playing acoustic guitar, really a stone folkie. I played with a lot of bluegrass bands and did a lot of country blues. Tons of country blues styles.

There's a lot of music in Chicago: blues, of course, and bluegrass and country music, all over the place. Great Puerto Rican music over on Clark Street, over on West Division Street, and there was Greek music—really good, the real stuff, man, the real nitty-gritty music, all this ghetto music. There were sections where there were old Jewish people, Talmudic Jews, Hasidic Jews. They'd be chanting in these old synagogues, and you'd think you were in Israel 2000 years ago. The music sounded like blues, the wailing of it.

The Puerto Rican music, when they were singing these really romantic songs about death and pathos, it was like flamenco singing. The ghetto musics of the world are related to each other, musically—even the scales are the same. The sob, the cry—it's all there. Grief don't know no color, no nationality.

The hillbilly area was another music scene. You'd hear mountain songs, right out of the Kentucky mountains, cats singing 'em, women singing 'em while they was working. It looked like *Let Us Now Praise Famous Men* or right out of the dust bowl. Okie stuff. It was just amazing.

I wanted to make sure I could play like Robert Johnson, play like Furry Lewis, and play all this stuff, too. And I still didn't know how it all fit in. But all of it came together—it sort of melded together and coalesced and came out in my playing. Still, in my heart of hearts, I would strive to sing like Ray Charles if I could, and play exactly like B.B. King. If I could play exactly like B.B., be B.B. Junior, I'd be content. But I had to accept myself for what I was.

Norman Dayron The first time I met Michael, I was a student at the University of Chicago. I was in my junior year—the fall of 1960. Michael wasn't attending school regularly. I was about to be 20, and he had just become 17, I think. He was kind of a truant.

I met him in a music store called the Fret Shop, on the South Side of Chicago on 57th Street. There were old wood-frame stores that looked like a Western movie set, left over from the Columbian Exposition. Little bohemian stores had opened up in these old buildings—a guitar store, a music store, a place that sold health food, I think, well before its time.

The Fret Shop was run by this guy named Peter Leibundguth. He repaired instruments and ran this little shop as a labor of love—he never made much money, I don't imagine. The Fret Shop was where I used to go to get strings and so on, because I played a little guitar and a little banjo and was into folk music. At the university, we had this thing called the Folklore Society. It was a group of people who liked authentic music—who liked mostly rural, Southern music, both black and white.

There were some people who liked blues, and there were some people who liked Clarence Ashley and Southern Appalachian mountain music and that kind of thing. Everybody played a little bit. Nobody was real good, but everybody could sort of play a little bit and sing. And I was one of those people who played a little bit and sang and wasn't very good.

I went into the Fret Shop one day to get some banjo strings and to hang out, because people just hung out there. I'm standing in the shop, and I hear this fantastic three-finger guitar playing—very fast, very clean, three-finger playing. I thought it was a record or something. I thought Pete was playing this very hip thing, so I turned around to see where this music was coming from, and I see this guy sitting on a metal chair, bent over one of the guitars that was in the store. So I walk over and just watch him for a while.

He's playing at a whole different level than any of my friends are, or anything I'd ever seen in person. And yet it was very different from anything I'd heard on record. It was just—the music was just dancing out of him. I mean, it was just so alive. It was almost like he had this perfect tension between his fingers and the strings, and it was just tremendously alive music. Most of that stuff, even the traditional stuff, was always performed very routinely. The point I'm trying to make is that this was real different sounding to me. It was alive in a way I'd never heard before, and I was fascinated.

I kept watching the guy, and then I struck up a conversation with him and found out who he was. It was Michael. I asked him some questions about where he came from, was he a student and so on. And he said, no, he had been kicked out of high school.

I asked him about the music. I said, "Where'd you hear that?" He told me he'd heard it on the radio. Because of the atmospheric conditions around Chicago, he could pick up bluegrass stations like WWVA from Wheeling, West Virginia, where you could hear the Stanley Brothers or the Blue Sky Boys or the Delmore Brothers, as well as some of the more commercial things. But I think you heard more of the pure stuff than the commercial stuff. You could hear Bill Monroe. You could hear Ralph and Carter Stanley.

I think he also heard WDIA in Memphis, which is where he may have heard B.B. King for the first time. He could hear stations in Waterloo, Iowa. And he got the Grand Ole Opry. So he could pick up country music, and also get blues music from Chicago and places like Memphis.

We became instant friends. I mean, we were close to the same age, we were both Jewish, and we even looked alike. We were the same height. It was just one of those things that clicked, within 10 seconds—we were friends. He could tell that I thought he was extraordinary. We talked, and after that we just started hanging out.

Early on, I had an old tape recorder and a little microphone. I suggested recording him, so he could hear himself and make corrections. And so we just got into this practice of recording. Around that time, I think, we started smoking pot a little bit. We would sit around smoking it and turn on the tape recorder and have these little exploratory sessions.

Michael took lessons from Frank Hamilton, who was a guitar player and a banjo player—a major senior instructor at the Old Town School of Folk Music. Michael would go to Frank's home. And if you were taking lessons from a guy like Frank Hamilton, he would expose you to all the best American folk music, because Frank was this really brilliant guy. I mean, he was a contemporary of Pete Seeger and Woody Guthrie.

Another person Michael got his musicology from, and his access to all these different styles and sources, was Pete Welding. He would have heard a lot from Pete Welding's record collection. Pete had an enormous record collection. He was the assistant editor of *Downbeat* magazine, a little bit older, and he knew more about musicology than I did. And more than Michael, too. He would play anything we wanted. Michael and I would go over there and spend a whole evening, and he would play records for us and comment on them: "If you like that, listen to this." "You think this is cool? Wait 'til you see where he got that from." That's what it was all about.

You could find Pete all over Chicago. In his capacity as a music critic and reviewer, he was always out in the clubs. For jazz, and for whatever else was happening in Chicago. Plus, he knew all the old blues players, and he was gathering them together to record them for Testament. So it's conceivable that Michael knew Pete Welding through me, because Pete lived at 58th and Blackstone and I remember meeting him in Hyde Park.

The first time I saw Michael was in the Fret Shop in Hyde Park. The University of Chicago is on the South Side, and it's located in the middle of this huge black ghetto. The university is right in the middle of Hyde Park, which is right in the middle of the South Side, which is right in the middle of the ghetto. When we would go to get a can of beer, we would walk over to 63rd and Cottage Grove, which is right in the heart of the blackest part of Chicago. And the blues was a very big presence for everybody who wasn't blind, deaf, and dumb. You'd walk down the street on a hot summer night, and it would be playing. Sounds would be coming out of bars, and people would be sitting on their front stoops with old guitars. It was like a movie or something, and you were in it.

I came to Chicago in 1958, from New York, to go to school. When I went to the University of Chicago, I was pretty much a *wunderkind*. I went at the age of 16 and a half, on a full scholarship. The University of Chicago, at that time, was a very radical place—politically radical. The curriculum was very advanced. You didn't have to take classes or show up. You had to take these eight-hour comprehensive exams in which you had to demonstrate mastery of a subject. I loved it as an environment. It was intellectually challenging, and it had amazing people. We had people on the faculty like Saul Bellow, the novelist. Hannah Arendt. Harold Rosenberg, the art critic. James Dewey Watson, the Nobel Prize winner in biology who discovered DNA, was my bio teacher.

It was an extraordinary environment. And I loved it. It was a very electrically charged time and place, and one of the things was the music that was all around it. So you had these two things going on: you had this vibrant intellectual environment, and you had these really off-the-wall students. I mean, the people who wound up in Chicago were just not ordinary in any way. Many of them immediately responded to the environment around them in a way that other students wouldn't have. Others might have been more protective of themselves, might not have stepped out. But these were times when the culture was saying that anything was possible. You could be anything. You could do anything. There was no overwhelming pragmatic or economic or business ethic.

And this extraordinary place was surrounded by this rich culture of black people who found a mode of self-expression that had migrated up from the South—everybody knows the history of how the blues got to Chicago—and now this was the center of it. It was all around us in those days, and we felt like we could relate to it. There was this enormous cultural permission to relate to it. And the people who were there, were there for special reasons. So it was a unique formula.

Nick Gravenites was living in Hyde Park at that time, as was Paul Butterfield. And Elvin Bishop, who was about Michael's age. He was two years younger than me, and he was a student at the University of Chicago. We were in the same sociology class. And Mark Naftalin was there. He was a music student at the University of Chicago, and his father was the mayor of Minneapolis.

Mark Naftalin I started fooling around with the piano back in grade school, augmenting my lessons with things I picked up by ear. Later on, I played with a band in Minneapolis, Johnny & The Galaxies. We played rock'n'roll and some blues. This was 1959 and 1960. When I got to Chicago, in 1961, I was on the lookout for musical opportunities. I heard there was a guy named Elvin Bishop around who played blues, so I tracked him down and we got together in a dormitory basement where there was a piano. And we jammed.

Norman Dayron Elvin likes to pretend that he's this sort of natural hillbilly, but he was a National Merit Scholar. And even in those days, the University of Chicago was one of the top universities in the country. You couldn't get in unless you had a very, very high grade-point average. So Elvin was this very bright guy from Oklahoma.

Elvin Bishop I grew up in Tulsa, Oklahoma. I started out on a farm in Iowa 'til I was about 10, and then we moved to Tulsa. That's where I got interested in blues, when I was about 14. We heard it on the radio from Del Rio, Texas, and Shreveport, Louisiana, and Nashville, Tennessee. And they had a blues show in Tulsa, too.

I didn't have a very sophisticated ear, I guess. I liked the one-guy-with-a-guitar stuff, the real basic stuff like John Lee Hooker and Lightnin' Hopkins. And I kind of went up to Muddy Waters and Jimmy Reed from there. I remember that B.B. King sounded like jazz the first time I heard him, with the horns and everything.

I tried to pick up the guitar two or three times before I stuck with it. Nobody in my family played an instrument, and it hurt my fingers and everything. I didn't know anybody that really played it, so I didn't have any clues. Finally, I just wanted to do it bad enough and stuck with it. When I got to Chicago in the 1960s, when things really busted loose, I met the blues play-

Michael and Roy Ruby near North Side Art
Fair, Summer 1961.

ers and went out in the ghetto and hung out with them and, basically, lived there for a few years.

I started at the University of Chicago when I was 16, maybe 17. I got a scholarship. But the reason I went to Chicago was because I knew that's where the blues was. I kind of wanted to do the school thing, too, because I was the only person in my family, in generations of farmers, that got a chance. My folks came up in the Depression and education had a big capital "E" on it, to them. But it wasn't meant to be, evidently. I started out in physics, and then I switched to English, and then I just went all the way on the music.

At the University of Chicago, in the cafeteria, there would be some black guys that were blues fans, and I heard somebody playing a harp or something. I gradually got with them. These were young black guys from the South, and they were into blues. I got to be friends with them, and we would play together. Some of them knew a little guitar, some of them knew a little harp, some of them knew how to sing, and some of them were actually almost semi-professional—a couple of them.

I ended up going to clubs with them. They'd take me around and show me the ropes and introduce me to musicians. Even after I got out of school, I still hung out with those guys. The University of Chicago is like an island in the middle of the South Side ghetto, so I stayed in the neighborhood. I wasn't making much money at first, and some of these guys would help me out with food out of the cafeteria and stuff like that.

I met Bloomers at a pawnshop on Clark Street in Chicago. He worked at his uncle's pawnshop. He was trying to sell me some old guitar. And he was a hotshot guitar player. I guess he'd been playing in bands since he was an early teenager, and he was a very accomplished guitarist when I barely knew a few chords.

The first time I ever laid eyes on Paul Butterfield, I was just walking around the neighborhood, and I saw a guy sitting on some steps drinking beer and playing a guitar. That was him. I was fooling with a harp at the time, and he was a little bit more into guitar. I guess he had started on harp. We used to play together at parties and stuff, and he gradually switched over to harp. Within about six months, he was almost as good as he was gonna get. He was great. He just had a natural thing for it.

Michael Bloomfield Paul was the real thing. It fascinated me and yet it intimidated me, too. The cat just went down there, went in the baddest black ghettos, and was as bad as the baddest cats down there. He wouldn't take no jive from nobody. And he held his own. God, did he hold his own.

I learned that was the secret. If you wanted to play with some authority, you had to go down and prove yourself. You had to burn. You had to be up on the stage with Buddy Guy or Little Smokey Smothers or Freddie King, if you're a guitar player. Paul would get up there with Little Walter or Shakey Horton, and hold his own. It was like the James Brown song "It's a Man's World." You had to be a man up there, or you'd blow your whole scene. You'd never get out of it right. You'd be lost.

It was very important to do that, and y'know I really tried to do it. It took a long time to get that way socially—I mean, confident that my music was a man's music, no longer a kid's music.

Elvin'd be down there; Paul'd be down there; Nick "The Greek" Gravenites, he'd be down there. Harvey Mandel, by God, he'd be down there in the baddest places, down on the West Side. We were probably the only ones that were playing. There was some other guys from the U. of C. that would hang out down there, but we were the ones that was going there and playing.

Elvin Bishop Paul and I played together in a lot of different combinations. A lot of times we would just play acoustic. The two of us would play at parties, for beer and food and stuff. Nick Gravenites knew Butter before I did—he was also a Chicago native.

Bob Koester Nick Gravenites was the first of that bunch of Hyde Park white blues kids that I heard. I heard him in a place off 55th Street, or possibly 57th, in Hyde Park. It was called Cellar Boheme. It was, I suspect, a mob joint. It was an illegal bar and, for all I know, they were dealing other shit.

They had Bebop Sam Thomas, a local modern jazz guitar player, playing upstairs. And in the basement, Nick Gravenites. That was the first time I met him, and it was pretty early—'59 or '60. I remember he had his foot in a cast. He'd gotten in a fight or something, I don't know. You were always hearing these stories of what a violent guy Nick was, but he never seemed to be violent to me.

Nick Gravenites We were an immigrant family from Greece. I don't remember my father too much, because he died when I was about 11. My mother really didn't have any education whatsoever. She was raised in a very isolated part of Greece. Essentially, her concepts were from the Dark Ages—superstitions and not too much education. She kept her Greek ways, her country ways. She used to go out foraging for food in the forest preserves and the parks. We'd go out and pick greens, and slaughter sheep in the basement. It was country in many ways. The music we listened to was Greek music, very ethnic.

Once I started to get into my early teens, I became a real problem. I started running around with the local guys and getting into a bunch of trouble. Cutting school. My mother decided it was best to send me away to school, so I went to a military academy: St. John's Military Academy in Doublefield, Wisconsin. I spent three-and-a-half years there and had mixed feelings about the experience. As with everything in life, it's never totally one thing.

I hated a lot about it—mostly the intimidation. They wear uniforms and try to get you all to act the same. A lot of hazing and that sort of thing. At the same time, it got me into sports, I lost a lot of weight, and I got stronger. I got a classic WASP high school education: languages, science, math, English—the basic stuff. I was there from the time I was 13 until I was 17 and a half.

I was expelled. I got into a fight with somebody, and he hurt himself accidentally—hit his head on a wall. So I was expelled for disciplinary reasons. I wound up going back to Chicago, where I went to Central Day YMCA High School in the Loop. That school was mainly for people trying to finish up high school, and for disciplinary problems. Mike Bloomfield and Barry Goldberg also went there.

Fred Glaser After prep school, Mike came back and tried to go to New Trier again to graduate. I don't remember what he did, exactly, but—oh, we all came to school drunk, and they threw us all out. None of us were allowed to graduate. Then he went to the YMCA—the Central YMCA had a school where all the bad kids went. Barry Goldberg went there, too.

Barry Goldberg I was born in Chicago in 1942. I started out on drums, and then I started playing piano. My mother is a pianist and singer. She used to be on the Yiddish stage in Chicago, and she played all the parts that Molly Picon played in New York. She was a child actress. She's quite an accomplished barrelhouse piano player. She taught me a little bit about it, and I basically picked it up by ear.

In high school, I had listened to the blues, although I was more into rhythm & blues and rock & roll. But I also listened to "Jam with Sam" on the radio. He was the last station on the dial, and he had a show at 12 o'clock midnight. Little Walter's "Blue Light" was the theme song. He'd say, "We're gonna go down to the basement now and turn on this blue light, sit down on this orange crate, and just dig some blues." And I thought, "This is some amazing shit."

They were conjuring up the spirits. And I was just 15 or 16 years old, listening to this show in my building on the North Side—which had an elevator man, and a guy polishing the brass everyday—and I'm listening to this shit on my little transistor radio. No one knew I was listening to it. It was these weird and scary sounds. These things would be unleashed in the music, and I could feel the excitement. I couldn't really tell—it was wild and uncontrollable, it was very mystical. These sounds—Muddy Waters, Howlin' Wolf, Little Walter, all those guys.

All during high school, Michael and I had rival bands on the North Side. He had a really hot rock & roll band with a piano player. We were always competitive, playing for Sweet 16 parties and everything, and we would bump into each other. I remember his piano player, a guy named George Demus. I had to play the piano after he played it, and he used to put Vaseline on the keyboard so he could do his Jerry Lee Lewis thing.

Eventually both Michael and I were thrown out of our respective high schools, and we wound up at Central Day YMCA High School downtown. We would see each other in the hallway and say hello and talk about the music scene.

Nick Gravenites The first time I met Mike was when I went to a folk-music shop called the Fret Shop. I walked in and Michael was sitting there. He pulled out a guitar and started playing.

He was playing the right chords and the right fingerpicking styles. It's easy to fool around with that and approximate it, but it's extremely difficult to get down. Michael had a certain facility, at a very young age, to have it sound the way you think it's supposed to sound. He was an authentic player. In folk-music circles that's very important, because part of the whole folk-music thrust was to learn this music the way it's supposed to be played. This was part of keeping the tradition alive, because that's the only way that, 30 years later, you could teach it to someone and teach it the way it was done 60 years ago. Not sort of, but the exact way.

Michael was really into that part of the folk tradition. I mean, after a while, you go out on your own career and develop your own personality. You can do what you want. But in folk music it was really important to do it the way it was done, because it helped to perpetuate the tradition. And Michael was part of that tradition.

So here's this guy, this young wise-ass punk, this smart-ass Jewish kid, playing this blues—not an approximation, but playing it the way it should have been played, the way I heard it on the records and stuff.

It was kind of funny, but I had a certain reputation at that time. I wasn't a junkie, but I sure enough was crazy. I was a pistol-packin' tough guy, and I had a reputation. Michael had heard about that reputation and knew about me, because he was a blues guy and knew about that. He knew that I had been in the clubs in the late '50s and been all around the South Side and different places. Not too much the West Side or the North Side, but the South Side was my turf. I used to go to Smitty's Corners and Frader's Jukebox Lounge and the 708 Club and the Blue Flame Lounge and Theresa's. And there was Pepper's. Those were my South Side joints.

I used to take people to black blues clubs, because at that time I was like a hoodlum. I was a tough guy, and I was armed. I had friends in the ghetto, people I copped reefers from or traded pills with. I had an underground reputation. Nick the Greek, this outside guy.

I never had any problems. Years later I thought about it a lot, and I realized that the black people in Chicago at that time considered me dangerous because I was white. They knew that I didn't know any of the culture. You'd go into a black club, and there might be an argument or a fight, there might be knives and guns drawn. But, Jesus, the guns were shot at the ceiling. There was just a whole lot of woofing going on. But to them white people were crazy. White people'd kill you. You fuck with white people, and they'd pull out the gun, and they wouldn't shoot at the ceiling. They'd kill you with it.

Also, it was pre-civil rights, and if you shot a black person in a club in Chicago, you could get off. You could walk scot-free, with connections and payoffs. But if a black person shot me in a club in Chicago, he'd get the electric chair. So all the while I thought it was dangerous for me to go down to the ghetto and hang out in these black clubs, it turns out that I was the dangerous guy, because I had immunity of being white.

They handled me with kid gloves. They figured I was dangerous, and they knew that if they messed with me and got arrested, they'd go to jail and I wouldn't. So it was totally the opposite of what I was conceiving it as being. It's certainly not that way now, but at that time, it was.

In the '50s, I took Butterfield to his first black blues club. I had most of my early musical experiences with Paul Butterfield. My Butterfield days and my days as a folk singer—that happened in the late '50s, early '60s. I didn't really get to know Michael until later, when I started hanging out on the near North Side.

Norman Dayron I introduced Mike to Paul Butterfield, who was not really a friend. I mean, Paul was hard to be friends with. But he was somebody that I knew.

Paul had been going to the University of Chicago Laboratory School, which was referred to as the Lab School and was like a high school. But it was a very advanced high school run by the university. The teachers were university professors. Paul had been playing flute, and he had just taken up the harmonica and immediately showed tremendous ability with it. I knew he was a great blues musician, and I felt that he could play with Michael. I introduced them, and Paul did not like Michael at all. He thought he was just this fat little Jew, this disgusting person.

Paul was very quiet and defensive and hard-edged. He was this tough Irish Catholic, kind of a hard guy. He would walk around in black shirts and sunglasses, dark shades and dark jackets. And Michael never cared what he wore. Michael was this sort of soft guy, Jewish and very civilized. One part of him was, anyway—another part of him was like a wild animal. I mean, he used to tell me stories. But Michael moved in a circle of young men who were, if you will, inheritors. They were all sons of wealthy industrialists or people who had made their mark in the capital world, and all of them had a little trust fund or an allowance or at least the security of knowing that they had all this to fall back on.

Paul had this hard Irish kind of cool—you don't say much. Michael was always exuberant and always talking and always flamboyant and always playing and saying what he thought. And Michael was an amazing liar. He did it mostly just to find out who people were. It wasn't that he was trying to impress you or do anything with you. It's kind of like he was playing this game, and he wanted to see how you would respond.

I remember when Michael told Susan before they were married that he was a Mouseketeer. I'm sure he told her all kinds of things that weren't true. But when you're 19 or so, your life moves pretty quickly, and your interests and commitments change. So I don't know what more I could say about that, other than that she was in for a roller-coaster ride. I don't know how much of that she was aware of when she got started with it. She certainly got hip to it later.

Susan Beuhler I met Michael in the spring of 1961. I met him at his grandfather's pawnshop, which was called Uncle Max's. It was owned by his grandfather, Max Klein, and it was on Clark Street in Chicago. Uncle Max

Courtesy Susan Beuhler

Uncle Max's Pawnshop, owned by Max Klein, Michael's maternal grandfather, 1916.

was Grandpa Max. Michael helped out on Saturdays. My girlfriend was looking for a guitar, and she said that was how to get a guitar. And there he was.

He was totally unlike anyone I had ever met before. First of all, he told me this crazy story about how he'd been a Mouseketeer. I believed it for a long time. He was always a very good talker. He could talk like nobody I'd ever met.

When I went out with him, the very first time, he said, "Well, I have to go play in these clubs." I didn't even know what he was talking about. He had his guitar and a big, heavy amplifier. I'd never even seen an amplifier before. So we went to a bunch of places, and he sat in with these people. And the battery kept dying on the car. Every time we'd stop the car, we'd have to get somebody to start it. And Mike knew nothing about cars. We had to get somebody to start it every single time, and then we'd have to pick up that heavy amplifier and move it in, and then move it out and get in the car and have somebody start it and go somewhere else. This was the strangest thing I'd ever experienced in my life. I didn't know what was going on. I didn't know what he was. He was an odd guy.

Michael played in a band when I first met him. That's what we'd do—I'd go to gigs with him. I don't even know what this band was called. Mark Schinderman was in the band, and he played saxophone, and it was when the Twist was big. They used to have these dance parties at the University of Chicago, and they'd go and play for free, and everybody would do the Twist in my girlfriend's dormitory.

Elvin Bishop They used to have what they called Wednesday Night Twist Parties. They would hire a jazz band or sort of a blues band or a rock band. They'd have different musicians. We put together a thing for that we called the Southside Olympic Blues Team, and it would include shifting personnel—whoever was available. Butter and I were in that. Little Walter played with us one time, and a bunch of local guys. We played several different combinations.

Mark Naftalin The Twist Party started out with a few people playing records in one of the dormitory lounges, and somehow it became an institutionalized thing. It began to grow, and more people became involved. It became a kind of happening. At some point musicians began to appear, with instruments.

Mike Bloomfield showed up on at least one occasion, with a band. I remember my interchange with him. I didn't know him; I was just sort of hanging around. And he was playing some of the fastest licks I'd ever heard in my life. So I said to him, "How come you play so fast?" And he said, "Because I practice a lot." Years later, when we got to be friends, I recalled that to him, and he said, "Oh, that was a lie."

At this moment, I don't know if it was in fact a lie or an accurate reflection of what he did and how he explained what he did. In any case, one doesn't play with that kind of fluidity without first practicing a lot—that's obvious.

Susan Beuhler We were kids. I had just finished high school. He'd gotten kicked out of New Trier, so he was finishing up high school at the YMCA.

Allen Bloomfield I'll never forget Mike's high school graduation. There were my father and my mother, all dressed up in their finest. And the kids strolled up the aisle to pick up their diplomas. You know, they actually did the Stroll—the dance. It was 80 percent black, 10 percent Hispanic, and the rest were like Michael. They strolled up the aisle, man, snatched those diplomas, high-fived, and that was it.

Denver and Marriage

Fred Glaser Mike and I took a Greyhound bus out to Denver, Colorado, in the summer of 1962. I was trying to dodge getting married. I had just knocked this girl up. She wanted me to marry her, and I didn't want to. He just wanted to get out of Chicago, to go somewhere and chase around a little bit.

He knew some kid in Denver, somehow—just barely knew him. So we went to his house and made him let us stay there for a couple of days. We met this black guy who took us around Denver and showed us a drink called shake-'em-ups. You take a package of frozen lemonade and put it in a big decanter of wine, and you shake up the wine and lemonade. That's what the blacks were all drinking back then.

We'd sit around in this black neighborhood in Denver—Five Points, it was called. We'd sit around in the bars there, drinking these shake-'em-ups, sitting on the sidewalks, me and Michael and random old black people who were just sitting around.

This was our first stab at being independent adults, going out on our own without our parents, without any money, and just seeing what we could do. Finally, the mother of the guy we were staying with threw us out.

We had heard about Boulder—there had been some event like a sit-in or something there—and it was becoming a hip kind of underground scene. So we hitchhiked up there. There was a guy there who had started a hip student newspaper that summer, and we met him somehow, and he moved us into this house. We just drank wine all day long and smoked pot and got high.

He put a band together. There was two bars in town. One of them was a place where all the college kids went, and they had, like, a Beach Boys, white, rock & roll band that played there. And there was another place called the Sink, at the other end of the street. They were trying to make it and couldn't figure out how.

We met this guy who was the son of Happy Logan, who had a string of music stores all around Denver and Boulder. So we put a band together, and we all went to Happy Logan's store. I played harmonica a little bit, so I had a harp. Michael got a guitar. Logan's son played drums. We got a black saxophone player and a couple of other people, and we put together a real heavy R&B band to play in this place called the Sink.

We played there on a couple of weekends, and we took all the crowd away from the other club. We had all these people standing in line in Boulder, in this real hip underground town. We created a little scene there in Boulder for, like, three months during the summer of '62.

We stayed there for the whole summer, in this little cheap apartment. And we met Judy Collins there. She was playing folk music in a coffee house. She let Mike sit in a couple of times, like on Monday nights when they would have an open mike. She would let him play.

Then we hitchhiked back. We didn't have any money. I remember being in Kansas City, panhandling money and thinking, "Boy, this is a crazy life. What are we doing out here, sitting on a street corner with no food and a dime in our pocket?" But it was fun to be out on our own, meeting people and traveling, and not having to be responsible for anything.

Mike always had a guitar with him wherever he was. He had some kind of an old acoustic in a beat-up, taped-up, cardboard case. He was carrying that around on the bus. People would stop to talk to us for that reason. We were two poor, young kids—hippies on the road, seeing what life was about out there.

Then we came back, and I had to get married. I don't know why, I just did. I thought I ought to do it. Bloomfield came with me to my wedding. I married my wife, Bobbie, in the City Hall in Glen Ellyn, this real conservative white town west of Chicago. Bloomfield was there, and my parents and her parents.

Michael was like my guardian angel, my protector, because her parents hated me, my parents hated her, and none of us wanted any of this to happen at all. So I kept ducking into doorways and ducking down the alley or getting back into my car, and Michael would come and get me and say, "No, come on. You got to." I said, "Michael, I don't want to go." "No," he said, "You got to go. You got to get married. You knocked her up. You got to go."

He kept dragging me down the street, and he finally forced me to go into the City Hall and get married. Michael was the best man at the wedding, meaning he basically prevented her father from beating me up and my parents from screaming at me too much.

The instant the ceremony was over, me, Bobbie, and Michael got in my car. Instead of going out to dinner with our parents like they wanted us to, we ducked out of there and went back up to this bar in Highwood, where he was playing. We sat around there all night, on our wedding night. Then we all went back to his house, and he let us take his bedroom. His parents were off somewhere on vacation, and he slept in this extra room in the maid's quarters. He let us sleep in his bed, and that's where my wife and I celebrated our wedding night.

A couple of months after I got married, Mike and Susan decided to get married. We got in the car and drove to New Buffalo, Michigan, which is now a real fancy resort town. But then it was just sort of a black backwater town. You only had to be 18 to get married there. In Illinois it was 21, so we drove to Michigan and they got married in the courthouse there. Bobbie and I were the maid of honor and the best man, the witnesses, for their marriage.

Then they wanted to do something, so we found some place where we could rent a boat and go out on the lake. We got a little rowboat and went out rowing on Lake Michigan. Susan had some barbecued chicken that Big Joe Williams had made as a wedding gift. We had met him through Bob Koester. So on the way to Michigan we stopped at Big Joe's house and picked up a whole bag full of barbecued chicken that he had made. We had this chicken, and we bought a couple bottles of Thunderbird wine, and we sat out in the boat all day on Lake Michigan, drinking wine and eating Big Joe's barbecued chicken and smoking pot and floating away into the distance in our boat.

Dorothy Shinderman Michael was living on the South Side, and then he came home one night and told his father and me that he was married. His father started beating him up, and the kid ran away. I told my husband, "You better have a cocktail party and introduce this girl to our friends, or you'll lose a son." So we had a cocktail party and introduced them, and they got an apartment. I loved Susie.

Susan Beuhler I was 19 when Michael and I were married. The wedding was a nice little civic ceremony in this little town. We were both 19, and we had to go up there one day to get the license, and then we had to go back. It was September 4, 1962. I even have the old marriage certificate. We got married because I'd screwed around that year in school, and I would have had a hard time going through a second year. I felt like, Oh my God, I got to do something. So I said, "We got to get married," and he said, "Okay." And we did it.

I'd blown my status as a student, and it was the next step—I didn't know what else to do. Our marriage was a secret for a couple weeks. We didn't tell anybody at first. We each went to our respective homes, but we spent a lot of time together.

We didn't plan it. We didn't even think, really. We just did it one step at a time. But then Fred, the husband of Bernice—the woman who kept Michael's parents' house—found out, and he called Mike's parents, who were out of town. They got mad, my parents got mad, and then we got an apartment and everybody was happy.

My not being Jewish was a big deal for Michael's parents at that time. But it wasn't for me, because I'd grown up in Jewish neighborhoods and always wanted to be Jewish. I was always an outsider. So it was nice to marry a Jew and finally be almost a Jew, because I'd always felt left out. When I had gone to school on Jewish holidays, there would be three kids in class. I'm not kidding. It was a very Jewish neighborhood.

Fred Glaser Susan was from a real conservative white family, and they hated the fact that she even knew a Jew, let alone that she would marry a Jew. That was, like, unheard of—it was unimaginable.

Allen Bloomfield That was a real rough one. It was hard on my parents when they found out about it. Very brutal. Very bad. Very negative. Very explosive and unpleasant. Michael was still living at home for a while, even after they were married. I don't think they had a place to live in, and, quite frankly, they didn't have the wherewithal to put it all together. Susie had some job in an insurance company, and they didn't have enough money. And then, finally, the thing was reevaluated. I don't remember all the nuances of it, but financially they got a little additional support. And they ended up living in Sandburg Terraces.

At this point, Michael and I were quite polarized. I was going to school and working every summer in the factory—I was doing the dutiful thing. The only interactions that we had were late at night. He'd be up, I'd come in, and we'd shoot the shit. He'd try to explain the stuff he was getting into, and I'd try to listen and try to understand it a bit, and I tried to tell him what I was about. There'd been so much sibling rivalry—it had created a certain strange dynamic. There was also an enormous affection that we had always had, since we were kids. On occasion, if the conditions were right, the walls went down and there was a reaffirmation of love. Under other conditions, it was very polarized.

I was working in my dad's factory in Cicero, Illinois, on the southwest side. It was about six acres of factory. It manufactured over a thousand products and employed 750 people. It wasn't a little place.

While others might look at us as a family and think we were prosperous, we didn't really look at it that way. If anything, it always looked to Michael and me as if it was pretty onerous to have a lot of money. Nobody looked real happy owning a lot of money. We didn't feel a lot of happiness out of that. In fact, we saw a lot of misery. We saw a lot of people that had to suffer. We saw a lot of anguish. We saw a lot of anger. We saw a lot of tough stuff. It was not what you might expect. And we never felt any sense of it as something to take for granted—as a matter of fact, it was like something that could be ripped away in a second.

We were around other people that were relatively affluent, so there was a commonality. When Christmas vacation came around and you went to Florida, you went to the Bahamas, you went to Hawaii or to Tucson, it was kind of like a common thing. It wasn't unusual.

We were never spoiled—let's put it that way. Never, in any way, were we indulged. I don't think that Michael wanted to distance himself from the money as much as what he looked at as the price you have to pay to make the money—the toll that it takes on you.

It never looked to me like there was a lot of fun in making money. It looked like it was tough, hard, arduous, demanding. I mean, we had a father who was out of the house at quarter to seven in the morning, and he wasn't home until nine at night. Six days a week. That didn't look like fun. And when he did come home, he was grumpy. So I'd have to say that he never really had a chance to enjoy the fruit of his labors. But I think that has to be couched in the fact that he saw it as an investment made in financial security that was, in some way, a panacea. His father had achieved significant success, but he got wiped out three times. The possibility of going from riches to rags always loomed in the backdrop. You could never let your guard down. There's always the Continentals and the Cadillacs and the big house and the big parties and all that stuff, but the underpinning of the whole thing is the worry that was constant. The anguish, the bullshit—how to keep on keeping on. How to make it move forward. Always the pressure. It was a big price to pay.

It never looked pleasant, and neither Michael nor I ever felt, in any way, that we lived in the lap of luxury. We were never indulged. We never got cars. The Raleigh and the Schwinn were as far as it went in gifts, and the big *bar mitzvah*, which was really a show for them, not for us.

I was close to my father. I was tight with him. I was tighter than Michael only because I was more willing to, you know, go that route. Michael didn't enjoy it as much because he wasn't capable of compromising. I don't even think it was a compromise—I just think our natures were different. We had different sensibilities.

Susan Beuhler We lived in a part of the North Side that I had never known. It was in a neighborhood that's now called New Town, and it was close to the lake. We could walk to the lake. We paid $50 a month, and our landlord was named Saul. He was a sweet old Jewish man. We liked him. First we lived in that place, and then we went to Carl Sandburg Village, and then we moved back up north again. That's when he started playing with Barry Goldberg, I think, a little bit.

Barry Goldberg Michael and Susan were the youngest couple I had ever met with their own apartment. I thought that was so cool. We'd listen to records and turn each other on to some sounds. We'd sit around playing records: "Listen to this one … listen to the reverb on this record … listen to this guy sing." I can remember listening to "Shake Your Moneymaker," the original Elmore James things, all the Otis Rush records that came out on Cobra. All that stuff was beautiful. And we'd try to—not cop it, but to do our version of it.

The first time I jammed at a club with Mike was when I was 17 or 18. He borrowed his mother's car, and we pulled up in front of this place on the West Side. I think it was Silvio's or Pepper's—one of those places. He said, "Just follow me." And I was thinking, "This guy is crazy."

We walked right into the club, and Howlin' Wolf was playing. And he had a piano. He immediately recognized Michael, and a stir, like a hush, came over the crowd. This was a really bad-ass crowd. Scary. I wasn't scared, though, because I had just come to play. We were bold and cocky. I followed Michael up there. Wolf sort of smiled and introduced us, and then he started playing "Killing Floor." The people started going nuts. Wolf was really mean at first, and then he started smiling afterwards. That happened a lot. I really went crazy. I said, "This is amazing."

I got to sit in with Muddy Waters a lot of times. His piano player, Otis Spann, was my idol. And when Otis saw me, it was like a signal for him to take a break. Not because he thought I was good or anything—he just wanted to take a break. The piano was always on the floor. The stage was above it.

Muddy would be on the stage and singing, and in the middle of the song Otis would switch with me. At first Muddy always scowled, and then one time he smiled—he looked down at me and smiled. That was the most beautiful thing. I thought my time had come.

Susan Beuhler When we first started living together, he got a job. For a while he worked in a shoe store, I think. Can you imagine that? I mean, we took a stab at being normal. The way it ended up is that I got a normal job, about a block or so away, at Kemper Insurance. I supported us. I did that for a long time. Because he wanted to be a musician, so he was going to make it as a musician.

And then he was carrying around a book door-to-door. He did that kind of thing. Maybe he never actually was a shoe salesman—maybe be just talked about doing that—but I know he had this door-to-door thing. He had this big book and a leather case that he had to carry around. Maybe these things lasted a day, you know. When we were kids, it seemed like forever. Then I got the job, so he wouldn't have to worry about that and we could pay the rent.

Also, you know what we used to do? This is a terrible thing. I had my charge cards and charged things to my parents, and then we'd go back and return them and get the money. We did that quite a bit. Or we'd go and charge meals at Marshall Fields. They had everything: You could get your hair cut. You could go to a lot of restaurants. You could buy any kind of thing. We spent a lot of time there, even after we were married, just hanging out. They had a fabulous book department, a fabulous toy department.

And we haunted music stores. They were real music stores. Do they still have those anywhere? You could go look at instruments and listen to records in the booths. And then there was Bob Koester's record store. There was a lot to do. It was fun, and we had a wonderful time.

We walked a lot. We didn't have a car. We lived on the North Side, and then we moved to the near North Side, which was close to all these places, so we could walk. You'd go out at night and walk all over the place. There were certain places you'd visit and hang out. We hung out, and it was fun.

In the fall, I went to school at the Art Institute of Chicago, and he went to Roosevelt University. They were sort of across the street from each other. But we didn't go to school very much. Michael didn't do a whole lot, you know. But he always played, and he was always interested in music. He didn't feel it was necessary to go out and make money, because we always sort of scraped by. We'd get up in the morning and go swimming, and then I'd work all day and stay up half the night. It didn't bother me—I was young. And he was always grateful. For long periods of time, he didn't work at all.

Fred Glaser He was the godfather of my two daughters. One of them, Gabrielle, was born in December of '62, when I was 18. My wife's water broke, and we called the cops, and they came and picked us up in a paddy wagon and raced us to the hospital. Michael lived a block away from the hospital, so I called him up as soon as we got there, and he came over.

He brought me a pair of socks. I had run out of the house with shoes on, but no socks. It was the middle of winter, and my feet were freezing. I said, "Michael, bring me a pair of socks. Whatever you do, don't forget the socks." So he came over to the hospital, and he was waving these socks in the air and running, and they weren't going to let him in. He said, "I've got to bring my friend his socks. He needs his socks."

They said, "It's only baby people." And he said, "Well, I got to bring him his socks. I don't care about the baby." He forced his way in and ran in through the doors waving my socks. Then we just paced around and waited. He had brought a couple of joints with him, and this was in an era when nobody but nobody smoked pot or took drugs. We snuck out in the stairway at the hospital and smoked some pot, and then we sat around in the waiting room all night 'til my daughter was born.

I made him her godfather on the night she was born. He gave her some old blues records. He gave them to me, to give to her when she was older—a couple of old Robert Johnson 78s and a Peetie Wheatstraw 78, as a present for Gigi.

So here we are. I was married at 18 and had a daughter already, and he was married, and we were outlaws. We did everything wrong that you could possibly do. We had found these two girls, Bobbie and Susan, who were like us, who were willing to hook up with wild guys like us. We were a quartet, getting married and screwing and drinking wine and smoking pot and hanging out with black people and going down to the South Side. Basically doing everything you weren't supposed to do.

Susan Beuhler He lied all the time. But it wasn't lying—he'd just tell stories, and he liked to tell people what they wanted to hear. He would tell elaborate stories, and people would believe him. But I've never thought of him as a dishonest person. I don't know if other people do, but I would never say he was a dishonest person. He just told stories.

It was much more like storytelling than lying. They were outrageous stories. If someone believed him, it was their fault, because the stories were usually pretty crazy. He had a creative imagination, but I would never say he was a dishonest person. I thought he had pretty good standards and morals.

You have to remember, too, that he was ahead of his time. When I think about how he impressed me then, it doesn't seem like very much now, but I was 17. We were kids, and he just wasn't like anybody I'd ever met before. I don't think there were too many people like him.

He could be hurtful to other people, saying things that hurt them. I think some people, later on, felt that he manipulated people and put them at each other's throats, but I can say that Michael always respected me. I think that's why we stayed close friends for a long time, because he couldn't bullshit me. I usually knew if he was bullshitting, and I never took it very seriously.

I think he liked that. He needed somebody who knew that about him, somebody who really knew him and wasn't taking him externally. I think that was the function I had in Michael's life. I always felt that we were in many ways like brother and sister. It almost wasn't even romantic. We needed each other very much at the time.

The wealth in Michael's family had some bearing on the situation. You know how people were in those days—the repressed '50s—and both of us needed to get away from that. I know my father used to think Michael was really stupid and pretentious because he wanted to know about eating beans, or he wanted to know about being poor. My father used to yell at me, laugh at me, for singing Pete Seeger union songs. My father was a steelworker and he was in the union, and he used to think that our point of view was really stupid—that it wasn't real.

But we were children. Our hearts were in the right place, and Michael was not a phony. He really did want to know about a funkier side of life. And he was a funky guy. It's hard to know what he was fighting against. Everything was so awful back then for everybody, and we were all trying to get out of it.

There were some other things that were personal problems with his family. He had a very screwed-up family. Michael's father was real mean to him. I wasn't there when he was little, but Michael was overweight and non-athletic. His father was an athletic tough guy. Michael was an intellectual, a musician—he wanted to play guitar. When he found the radio stations late at night, I think that gave him something he needed, something that he wasn't getting—or wasn't even supposed to want—from the way he'd been raised.

It's not unusual stuff. Any of us who grew up with that kind of parents, as nice as some of them were—I'm just glad that time is gone. I'm real glad that my kids don't even know anything about then. You didn't do things.

You didn't say things. It was crazy. It was awful, and he needed to get away from that. Michael had a smothering mother, but she's a very wonderful woman. She, I think, was also pretty rejected by her husband, and maybe she was too close to the boys. Maybe they answered some need in her that she didn't get from her husband. He was a very mean man, and he stayed a mean man. He never really got nice, ever. He was one of the meanest men I've ever known in my life. Slimy and hard and cold and mean. He was never mean to me, but he was mean to everybody in his family.

He was the boss. He ruled with an iron fist, and everything had to be his way. He had the same damn dinner every night, he sat at the same place, and it was horrible. He was an awful man, and he treated his family terribly.

Mike and I were young, and we wanted to get out of our homes. At that time you didn't live together, so we got married. It wasn't serious—I mean, it was and yet it wasn't. We were children, we were playing, but it was wonderful fun. Wonderful fun.

The Fickle Pickle

5

Norman Dayron The Jazz Record Mart was at 7 West Grand. It was Bob Koester's record store, and he had this huge collection of everything. Michael hung out there, so he would have heard a lot of blues music there. Big Joe Williams lived in the basement, and Charlie Musselwhite moved in with him. Charlie worked in the record store.

Bob Koester Mike and his buddy Jim Schwall would come in. We got acquainted there. I remember Michael had a cute wife, a very cute little blonde girl. They were going out to clubs I didn't know existed. They knew about places that I hadn't even heard about. I don't think Bloomfield told me about Theresa's, but he did tell me about the Blue Flame. He might have told me about Pepper's. I have to admit that Bloomfield did get me a little bit more appreciative of some of the modern Chicago stuff, the real modern things.

Charlie Musselwhite was around. He got there pretty early. Charlie wasn't that good a harp player at first, not as good as he later became.

Charlie Musselwhite I was born in Mississippi, in a town called Kosciusko, and moved to Memphis at an early age and grew up there. I always liked music. I listened to blues on the radio, and I would follow around street singers in Memphis and watch how they played and everything. I was learning to play just because I loved the music. I got to know blues singers and would hang around their homes.

There was also rockabilly guys around—Johnny Burnett lived across the street, and Slim Rhodes lived a couple blocks away. So this music was all over the place. My home there, in those days, was kind of on the edge of town, and you could hear people singing work songs in the fields.

I went to Chicago looking for a job. Friends of mine would leave Memphis and go up to Chicago in an old jalopy, and the next Christmas vacation they'd come back in a new car. This appealed to me. I didn't know nothing about Chicago. All I knew about it was it was a big town up north, and there was lots of jobs that paid a lot of money with benefits. That's why I went up there. I didn't know about blues up there.

So I got up there, and the job I got was as a driver for an exterminator. I would see posters and pass by bars with signs in the windows, and they would say stuff like: Elmore James is playing here. Or Muddy's playing at this place. Sonny Boy Williamson. Little Walter. This was great—to find all these people in Chicago. I'd heard all of them on the radio, and I had their records. I'd seen Muddy in Memphis at least once. But here, they were all there in bars.

I was big for my age. I was 18, but I could go into any bar. I had a suit I'd wear, and I never had a problem. I just started hanging out, because there was nothing better to me than to be right there in front of the band, listening to my favorite artists and having a good time. I was out to have a good time. And I was having one, you know.

I'd already learned how to play harmonica and guitar, just for myself, not with any plans of doing anything professionally. One night this waitress I'd gotten to know pretty good told Muddy that I played harmonica and he ought to get me to sit in. I didn't have any desire to be on the stage. I wasn't even interested in that. He called me up there, and it was pretty scary. But I sat in.

If Muddy calls you, you go. And he would always call me up. Other people found out I played, and they started inviting me to sit in. It was a helluva lot of fun. And then I started getting offered work. I thought, Damn, how good can it get? I'm 18, I don't have any responsibilities, and I'm being paid to play this music that I love. I thought, Well, this is my ticket out of the spraying-for-roaches business.

One day I was standing at the corner of Grand and State, waiting for a bus, and there was a record shop there called the Jazz Record Mart. That was Bob Koester's place. I'd never seen so many blues records in a store window before. I got to hanging around there and got to know those people and ended up getting a job there, selling records and boxing them up to sell mail order. And I ended up living there in the basement. That's where I got to know Mike, because he would come in. We just started hanging out together. I'd be there all day, and he'd come in and hang out.

Mike and I, our humor seemed to match. We did a lot of laughing. He was one of the funniest people I ever knew. The two of us would be in tears laughing, gasping for breath, our ribs about to break. We became real good friends. We were real tight. After a while, I guess we were hanging out every day.

But he could be different and strange, too. He didn't really respect other people's property. I had all these records that I would buy when I could afford to, and a lot of rare records that I brought with me from Memphis, mostly blues records. He would just take anything of mine he wanted to take and never say anything to me about it. I would find my records in other people's homes. I'd say, "You know, this is mine. I don't remember bringing it here. How did it get here?" "Oh, Mike brought that over." Or, "Mike gave that to me." He gave away my records, and that kind of rubbed me the wrong way.

I always figured that because he came from a family with lots of money his view of things was just different from mine. I mean, his view of being in music was different from mine, too. I remember him telling me that, to him, there was nothing better than being in a room full of people and all of them looking at him—being the center of attention. To me that was a staggering thought, because I hated attention. That was one of the reasons I never thought about being in music, because I didn't want to be on any stage. So that was another real difference in how we were thinking about things.

And Mike never let the truth get in the way of a good story, that's for sure. Sometimes I would tell him some story and then, at some point later, he'd be telling the story to somebody else or telling it back to me and not realize that I was the one that first told it to him. Only now he's the center of the story—like it happened to him.

Then there's that story where he's talking about how this guy walked into a bar with a bag that had his wife's head in it, and he plopped it down on the bar and said, "Hey, bartender, give this bitch a beer," or something like that. That never happened. That's a folk tale in Chicago. I've heard that over and over and over from different people—different versions of it, you know.

Bob Koester In 1964 Olle Helander from Swedish Radio came to town, and he wanted to do some taping. He had a little money to pay. It wasn't like record money, but it was okay money to pay some blues artists. He negotiated for the use of the Sutherland Hotel's ballroom out at 47th and Drexel. This was a major modern jazz venue. It was where Miles Davis and Art Blakey and cats like that would play when they were in town.

So one weekday a bunch of us went out there. Bloomfield, Blind John Davis, and I forget who else. Ransom Knowling. We figured with Bloomfield, Ransom, Blind John, and Washboard Sam, we could do a Washboard Sam

*Charlie Musselwhite, Michael, unknown, and Paul
Butterfield at Pepper's Lounge, December 13, 1963.*

thing. That did get broadcast over Swedish Radio, and it was probably the first time Bloomfield was heard in Europe in any way, shape, or form.

Around that time, Bloomfield was on two Delmark albums. The first occasion, we actually used Bloomfield's apartment—we recorded it with my old Crown tape recorder in his apartment. We got about half an album down. I don't think Bloomfield played on those sessions; he just offered us the use of the apartment.

To finish the session, Sleepy John Estes and Hammie Nixon and Yank Rachell were supposed to meet me at the Jazz Record Mart. Big Joe Williams was living in the basement. Joe carried a key to my store, so whenever he was in town he'd have a place to stay. He'd stay on this little bed we had in the basement.

Joe wanted to come along to the record taping and hear the guys play. This was set up as Yank Rachell's album, with Yank playing mandolin or guitar, Hammie doubling jug and harmonica, and John playing second guitar. We waited and waited, and Yank and Hammie and John never showed up. I left a note on the door with the address and the phone number for the guys to call. So we went and started to record just Joe with Mike Bloomfield.

As soon as we got set up, Yank and Hammie and John showed up. So we had this marvelous five-piece band. The record had some really great shit on it. It's got one of my favorite Big Joe Williams things, "Move Your

Hand." It's just a marvelous thing. So Bloomfield was on about half that record, and later he came to the studio to help with Sleepy John's record that had Hammie and Yank on it.

To bring in John and Yank and do some more recording, we had some sessions at a place called the Fickle Pickle. The Fickle Pickle was a little basement—it was not a coffee house in the hippie sense; it was more a juice bar than a coffee house, a place for kids to come and hear rock bands. I thought this would be ideal. Let's get the kids in there and pump them full of blues. And it was the same scene—it was Big Joe every week, and either a piano player or another guitar player. I remember we had a lot of good people at those sessions. Washboard did one, Jazz Gillum did one, Walter Vincent did one. And we used Ransom on bass more often than not. Then I decided to hell with this, I'm losing too much money. See, at the Fickle Pickle you couldn't drink, and a lot of people didn't want to come to a place where they couldn't drink.

I quit, and Bloomfield continued the series, very much with my blessing, with the aid of George Mitchell, who was more or less an expert on Georgia blues. He had come up from Georgia and was working for me. I said, "Man, God bless you. I'll even come and pay the dollar." And I usually did.

George Mitchell I met Michael shortly after I got to Chicago. I had gone to Chicago to work with Koester. His was about the only company that was starting to reissue old-time blues. When I was in college I went to see Koester for an interview, and after I finished my next semester I went up there to work for him.

Koester had started a series of blues concerts at the Fickle Pickle, which was on Rush Street. They weren't working out too well for him, and the night I got there was his last night of doing them. Mike and I decided that we would try to keep these concerts going. Rather than bringing in people from Indianapolis, like Yank Rachell, and having to pay them, we would find people in Chicago that hadn't played in a long time. I remember that when we found Kokomo Arnold, Bloomfield gave him a guitar.

Susan Beuhler We used to go and find these blues guys and give them jobs. We never made any money, and a lot of my money went to help them out or feed them. It was what we did.

George Mitchell I was getting paid something like $40 a week, working six days a week for Koester in his shop. Bloomfield's only source of income at the time was with a band in a nightclub. But we decided that we would, the two of us, form a partnership and keep the Fickle Pickle thing going. In the meantime, Bloomfield loses his gig in the nightclub.

Barry Goldberg I had a gig in a topless nightclub, and I brought Mike into this band. During the break he got me to go with him to a drugstore to buy two little squirt guns, and we would squirt the chicks in the boobs as they were dancing around, facing us. They didn't know where it was coming from, and it would drive them crazy. One night we were caught, and we were chased out of the club and into the street.

Mike was also playing in the funky places in Old Town, in the blues clubs. And he was managing the Fickle Pickle—he'd be the MC and he'd book all these far-out shows, people like Big Joe Williams. Mike would be introducing all these amazing blues guys to these college kids and high school kids and their dates. He'd also do some one-liners, like a Henny Youngman routine. He was quite the personality. He could run a show. He loved to do these things, and I thought it was phenomenal.

At the same time I started playing on Rush Street, which was like the Bourbon Street of Chicago—nightclubs with red velvet. It was a really plush club with Playboy-bunny-type waitresses. I played with a New York-based band that came to Chicago and caused a sensation during the Twist era. They had come from the Peppermint Lounge in New York, and they were called Robbie & the Troubadours. We'd have different colored uniforms and dye our hair different colors every night.

Finally, Michael said, "Man, this is not the scene you should be in." He said, "You have to come down to Old Town with me." And we'd go down to the South Side and the West Side. Eventually he won me over. I said, "Man, you're right." So I became a beatnik. I went from the continental suits on Rush Street to being this beatnik in Old Town. It changed my whole life.

George Mitchell Mike and I had decided to keep these Fickle Pickle concerts going, even though he had no source of income and I had $40 a week. And we had to pay the musicians a minimum. They would get a percentage of the take at the door, but there had to be a minimum of something, like $20. Not a lot, but enough where it's half my salary.

And Bloomfield wasn't making anything. His job was handling publicity for these things, and my job was to find the musicians. At first, we were doing it just on Tuesday nights. The manager of the club would just give us the place, and we'd have to pay the waitress and everything. It was rough. I had to take money out of my $40 to pay people, because at first we weren't doing all that great. Bloomfield was sitting out on the street in dark glasses, playing, to get his share of the money to pay the minimum. He looked pretty blind. It was funny.

Ron Butkovich I met Michael in '63, when I was still in high school. He had a lot of street smarts and had been around a little. I was a young kid from a Catholic school and hadn't been exposed to as much as he had. He was running this club called the Fickle Pickle, and I met him over there. I met him and Ira Kamin at the same time. They had a little bluegrass band, and they used to play in the hallway of the Fickle Pickle. I remember walking in there one day, and there was Michael playing guitar, Ira playing banjo, and Michael Melford playing mandolin.

Michael could play a lot of styles of guitar. He could play some good piano stuff, too. He was really knowledgeable about music. He was really an astounding musician, in the sense that he had so many styles he could do, folk styles and other styles. He was a master at what he did, a master American musician. He knew so much about it.

Ira Kamin I met him when I was 16 or 17 in a music store—it may have been the Fret Shop. We were both playing instruments. We were just jamming around, and we became friends immediately. He was already living with Susan; they had an apartment near where I was living with my parents. I used to go over and play music and talk and listen to music—that kind of stuff. We became friends and enjoyed each other's company. We enjoyed playing music together.

We both liked folk music and that's where it started, with bluegrass and folk music. He liked improvisational music and so did I—jazz and Indian music. So we just started stretching out. He was really fascinated with blues and the musicians who played the blues. He interviewed Muddy Waters for *Downbeat* magazine when he was about 18. It was a cover story. He was very respectful of blues musicians and idolized them. And they sort of adopted him as a son, you know.

He had a real devotion, like a musicologist's approach to blues. He really brought those people forward and traveled with them. It was a big effort to get those people heard by white people. And he was helpful.

George Mitchell He was just turned 20. I was big into blues, and I knew something good when I heard it. We're talking about on acoustic guitar. He was wonderful. He could play in virtually anybody's style. It was phenomenal. It always astounded me.

Michael interviewing Muddy Waters at his
home, January 9, 1964.

Mike and I hung out together a lot. I knew his wife and everything, and we worked together two nights a week. I came up there a Southern boy— I wasn't cool Chicago at all, and I didn't dress in the style of the times. I guess I dressed kind of frugally. Michael was always trying to change my dress style, my wardrobe. He was real good-natured about that kind of thing. He always referred to me as the lush, because I would drink a good bit while he'd be smoking pot, which everybody did back then. But it was new to me, even seeing people do that.

He was a funny guy. He was an entertainer even when he wasn't being paid to entertain. It was fun being around Bloomfield—he was always joking around and everything.

My greatest source for finding musicians to play at the Fickle Pickle was Big Joe Williams. He helped a lot, and Sunnyland Slim helped a lot—they were the two primary ones that got me going with finding these people. Big Joe was a wealth of information. He knew everybody, and his memory was absolutely astounding. Sunnyland did a lot, too—he would drive me around to find these people. Bloomfield was publicizing the hell out of the things, and we got pretty successful to where we were packing the place every Tuesday night with two different acts. We had a long table in the back of the place where Chicago blues musicians of all types would just hang out. The cover charge was something like a dollar.

And then the guy gave us Monday nights, too. So we brought in Big Joe for the main act every Monday night and got in one other person. During the time I was in Chicago, which was that spring and summer—about seven months—Bloomfield and I worked together and hung out a lot together.

Michael Bloomfield As I got to know Big Joe better, we became more and more friendly, and soon he began to carry me to see old friends of his. I'd say, "Listen, Joe, d'you know where Tampa Red's living?" And Joe'd say, "Sure, I know where Tampa's at—I'll take you by right now." And we'd go. Tampa, by the time I met him, was just a frail, wizened little man whose hands shook uncontrollably. He had an expensive Gibson in a case beneath his bed, but all he could do was show it to us—his hands wouldn't let him play.

Another singer Joe took me to see was Kokomo Arnold. He told me I was the first one to ask about his music since the early '50s, when some people from a jazz magazine in Belgium had come to see him. The next time I saw him was in a hospital, where I'd gone to visit him with Charlie Musselwhite. Kokomo'd had to have much of his insides cut out, and he was just a shadow of the man I'd seen with Joe.

Joe also carried me to see Tommy McClennan. We visited him in Cook County Hospital, where he was dying of TB. He was just a skeleton, but his eyes were like hot coals burning at you. His music was like that, too—it had a savage, searing sound. He was a fierce man.

And there was Jazz Gillum, who was just about the craziest man I'd ever met. Joe took me to see him on a very uncomfortable summer day, with both the temperature and humidity up in the 90s—the kind of day when doing nothing makes you sweat, when dirt forms under your fingernails for no reason at all. We drove out to the West Side and stopped in front of a tiny frame house—just a shanty, really. When we walked into the place, I thought I'd hit Hell City—as hot as it was outside, it was insufferably worse within. All the windows were shut down tight. Clad in a huge brown overcoat and sweating profusely, Gillum stood beside a wood stove, stoking a raging fire.

He was extremely paranoid. He'd written the very successful "Key to the Highway" and had never gotten the publishing money for it, and he was afraid I'd come to steal his other tunes. We didn't stay long enough to change his mind.

On the Road with Big Joe

Michael Bloomfield I had gone with Big Joe Williams to East St. Louis once and had just a really crazy experience with him there. He got really nasty drunk and stabbed me with a penknife. This is when we had a real fight, man, a real argument.

It started because Joe wanted to visit some of his people in St. Louis. Koester thought it was a fine idea. "Yeah, Joe," he said. "You go down there and be a talent scout. Take a tape recorder along and say you represent my company. Record some people, see what kind of deal we can make, and bring back some tapes."

St. Louis was new territory for me, and I knew there were supposed to be some famous old bluesmen living down there. So I said I'd set up the trip, and I called up another pal of mine, George Mitchell, and asked him to join us.

The drive to St. Louis was real nice—wonderful, in fact. Joe talked about things from 30 years ago as though they'd happened that morning. He reminisced about Robert Johnson and Willie McTell and Blind Boy Fuller; he told how Sunnyland Slim had helped Muddy Waters get a record contract; he explained how Big Bill had gotten rich.

It was the Fourth of July weekend. It was real hot. And, man, if you think the Gary and Chicago slums are squalid, you can't believe where Joe's family lived in East St. Louis.

George Mitchell It was me, Bloomfield, Big Joe, and another guy named Mike, who had a car. He was our transportation. I had asked Big Joe to take me to St. Louis. He said that Walter Davis and Henry Townsend were in St. Louis. I wanted to meet them and get some pictures of them, because I had it in my mind to put together a book of pictures of blues singers. So Big Joe agreed that he would take us there and introduce me to Walter Davis and Henry Townsend.

On the way to St. Louis I asked Big Joe a question, just to see if he claimed he knew somebody who didn't exist. I said, "Big Joe, do you know Hickory City Simpson?" He looked at me and said, "No, I don't believe I ever heard of him." So then I believed Big Joe completely, believed that he knew all these people.

That was certainly a trip to remember. Because, see, when Big Joe would get drunk, he would get pretty obnoxious sometimes. And actually not be able to recognize people—you know, he'd get confused. He'd get drunk to the point of confusion.

Bloomfield and I decided that we would get Big Joe to agree—and we did—that he would not drink on the trip to St. Louis. And he didn't. I remember the funniest thing riding down there: he wants us to stop out in the middle of the country so he can take a shit. I said, "Big Joe, you know, we'll be at a service station sometime." And Big Joe said, no, he wanted to shit outside. He said, "There's nothing like a good country shit." That's one of my main memories of riding down there.

But he did not get drunk. We ended up at some relatives of his—he's got relatives all over St. Louis—and it was hot as hell. It was pretty late when we got in there. We went over to some relative's house. I believe it was his cousin and her husband, and there was a whole lot of kids. And Big Joe proceeded to make up for what he didn't drink on the way down. He drank, as I recall, a case of beer and a fifth of bourbon and a half-pint of vodka. This is one person.

Michael Bloomfield It was nightfall when we got to St. Louis, and it was hot—Lord, was it hot. The first place we stopped was the home of Joe's sister or sister-in-law or step-sister or something. When we walked in, there were kids sleeping on every available surface, so we all went into the kitchen and sat down.

"Now, you know I play the guitar," Joe said to his relatives, "and this boy Michael do too, so we'll play some while we visit." He brought out his guitar, and with it a bottle of schnapps. I took George aside and said, "Man, we better not let this guy start drinking."

But Joe was set on drinking. And when he said, "Michael, why don't you have a little taste?" I went ahead and put some down. I figured if Joe was going to get drunk and crazy, I was going to get drunk and crazy right along with him. So I drank as much gin and schnapps and beer and wine as I could get in me that night, and I sat with Joe and played the blues.

And, man, I got sick. For the first time in my life I got king-hill, shit-faced, tore-up drunk. I puked in the hall, I puked on the sofa and on the wall. I was just rolling in puke. I was sick, sick, sick.

I woke up on a bed the next morning to find Joe standing over me. He had stayed up all night drinking, and he was more than just drunk—he was on a bender. His nostrils were flared, and his eyes were red and runny. He had a barbecue fork in his hand and on it was a pig nose, and hot grease from the nose was dripping on my chest. He opened his mouth, and his schnapps breath hit me in a wave.

"Snoots, snoots!" he shouted. "I promised you barbecue, an' fine snoots is what we got!" My head was throbbing and my stomach was still queasy, and when I looked up and saw this horribly fat and greasy pig nose an inch from my face, I lurched out of bed and threw up again. Joe began to curse me. "Man, you done puked all damn night and into the mornin', an' now you pukin' up again! Can't you hold that stomach down?"

Raeburn Flerlage

Michael and Big Joe Williams at the Chicago Folk Festival, January 31, 1964.

George Mitchell Bloomfield and I decided he had to get into some air conditioning and get a Coke. Big Joe was drunk as hell somewhere. And Mike, the guy with the car, was asleep. So we just took his key and drove two blocks to a drugstore and sat there at the soda fountain, to cool off, and came back in about 20 minutes.

Big Joe was standing out there in a fucking rage. He pressed a knife into my belly—another quarter of an inch would have punctured my stomach. It would have gone in. He was in a fucking rage, saying that we had stolen that guy's car. I said, "We did not steal his goddamn car. We borrowed it. He's our friend, anyway." So, finally, he moved the knife.

The rest of that day was terrible, because it was hot as hell. Big Joe talked to Walter Davis, on a pay phone, and then he was going to take us over to see Walter. But he wasn't taking us—he was just driving us all the fuck over St. Louis for no damn reason. This is going on and on, hour after hour. I said, "Big Joe, where is Walter Davis? Why aren't we going there?" He turned around and started calling me a racist, which he'd never done before. He says, "If you say another goddamn word"—he was shaking his fist in my face—"I'm going to knock your fucking teeth down your throat."

Michael Bloomfield I was looking for this piano player named Walter Davis and this singer named Mary Johnson. He said he knew where they lived. But he didn't know where they were—nothing like it, man. All he wanted to do was visit his kin. It was a stone burn job. And I got hip to it in the middle of the thing, man. All day long, I was saying, "Man, we're leaving. I'm going to go." He just wouldn't let me go. So we trucked around, man, to a hundred different relatives.

George Mitchell We were driving hour after hour, and Joe wouldn't take us to see Walter Davis. Then, finally, he took us to some fiddle player's house, and we recorded them playing together.

Michael Bloomfield I was ill all day. And then it's getting towards evening, man—it's dusky now. Finally, Joe directs us to a place that didn't even have front steps. They'd all just rotted away. We walked around behind the building to try the rear stairs, and in the backyard was a mountainous collection of refuse. Every kind of filth imaginable was back there. There were old moldering mattresses, shredded and stained, with the springs sticking out; there were pieces that had rusted and reddened from years of exposure. And I don't think the garbage from the tenants had ever been collected. I believe they'd been throwing it in the yard ever since the apartment was built, and from the looks of the building that had been a long time ago.

We climb up these three flights of stairs. It's incredibly hot. And sitting up there on the third flight of stairs is this girl around 14 years old, weighing about 600 pounds. Man, so fat she has never left. Since she's been a child, she has been living on the third floor of this horrible slum. She was a freak. She can't get down the stairs or in the house. She was dipping spareribs in an old jar of mayonnaise that looked like Unguentine, man. A 600-pound, 14-year-old imbecile fat woman, sitting outside on this old broken-down couch, eating old spareribs, dipping them into ancient hot mayonnaise. She was wearing a garment made out of sack cloth, made out of sewn-together sacks—wheat sacks and grain sacks and stuff like that.

My stomach started roiling again, and I was sure I was going to be sick. I asked the woman of the house where the toilet was, and she led me to a door at the end of the hallway. I opened the door and found not a toilet, but a closet. There was nothing in the closet but a few sheets of newspaper and a hole—a hole, about two feet in diameter, in the floor. I turned and looked at the woman. "Our daughter have a little trouble with her weight," she said. "She too big, don't you know. The regular seat in the bathroom, it ain't right for her, so we done fix up this here place."

I tried to stammer out a question, but the woman just waved at the hole. "Don't worry none," she said. "No one livin' down 'neath us now. Ain't been no one for months." She walked away, and I got down on my hands and knees and got sick with no trouble at all. But I faced away from the hole. There was just no way I could look down that thing.

George Mitchell Finally, at some point, Bloomfield and Mike and I got the car—we got out of Big Joe's hearing—and decided we couldn't stand it any more. We decided we were going to say that one of us was sick or something and that we were going back to Chicago. We were supposed to stay there another day, but it was just horrible. Big Joe was threatening and he was drunk, we weren't getting anywhere, and we were just miserable. I think Bloomfield might have told him, because he'd told me he was going to knock my teeth down my throat if I said another word. So I think Bloomfield broke the news to him.

Michael Bloomfield Man, I had to leave. I was slummed out. I just had to leave. It was so sad. It so shocked me and so appalled me, man, I had to leave. And Joe wasn't about to leave. We had a huge fight. I said, "Man, I'm leaving. I'm leaving you here in East St. Louis. I'm going back to Chicago."

Joe wouldn't let me leave. He grabbed me by the arm. I snatched my arm back and said, "I'm leaving, man." He went downstairs carrying this real heavy tape recorder and his amplifier and guitar. And he got in the car.

I said, "We're going back to Chicago." He says, "No!" And we got in this huge argument.

He said, "No! We going to visit my people. My people are here." Like that, man. I said, "Okay, man, listen, then get out of the car. I'm going back to Chicago. You get the motherfuck out of the car, man. You just get out of the car." He pulled out a little penknife and went [*sound of slapping hand*] like that into my hand.

Then he pulled it out, and I got insanely furious, man. Kicked him hard as I could in the side of his stomach. And he punched me in the leg. And then we looked at each other. We both felt real bad. Real bad. It was like hitting my father or something. And he was real sad for getting so drunk and hurting me.

He got out of the car. And the last thing I saw, as we drove away, was this old man walking down a dusty road with his guitar and his amplifier— just walking down a dusty road back towards East St. Louis.

George Mitchell I'll never forget it. Big Joe got out of the car. He had his nine-string guitar and his old beat-up case and his amplifier. He started to walk down the street, and then he came back and said, "Mitch, give me that tape—the tape with the fiddle player." So I gave it to him. And then I said, "Big Joe, are you going to be at the Fickle Pickle Monday night?" Shook his head. "Well," he said, "no." He wasn't going to fuck with us. He wasn't going to be there.

Then he starts walking down the street with the beat-up guitar and amplifier and that tape. He looked so pathetic. We all felt kind of sorry for him. And then he turns around and comes back and gives me the tape. So he actually did a nice thing there—he gave me the tape back.

So the three of us came back to Chicago, and I hired Little Brother Montgomery in Big Joe's place that Monday night. And then he shows up about six o'clock that evening, ready to play. I said, "Big Joe, you said that you weren't doing it anymore. I hired somebody else." And he said, "Well, you know, people going to be upset because they come to see me." And indeed they were. They were upset Big Joe wasn't there. So we hired him back.

Michael Bloomfield I saw him about three weeks later. And you know he has to be real embarrassed. He used to get this real boyish, bashful look on his face. He said, "We sure had some times in St. Louis, didn't we, man?" That's what he said to me. I said, "Yeah, man, we sure had us a time." And he meant, like, I'm sorry, you know, and everything. And I was sorry, too. It was all cool then.

Okay. Now tell about going to see J.B. Lenoir's big band and Lightning

Hopkins, with Musselwhite, and Big Joe Williams. Tell them how the evening ended up for you.

Roy Ruby Willie Dixon is a great songwriter. He's written all these great songs, and he's a very intelligent man. He's also a promoter, and he promoted this show—there's Lightning Hopkins, Big Joe Williams, J.B. Lenoir. So Charlie, Mike, and I drove out to Gary, Indiana, with Big Joe.

The show was held at a roadhouse in Gary. A roadhouse is a place which is out in the country. It's a large nightclub in the midst of—well, it's hard to call it the country, but it's where there's factories and oil fields and shit. Imagine a nightclub for Texas rednecks, set out in an oil field, where the only people that come are Texas rednecks who work on the oil rigs. These are rough guys that work hard all day and drink hard all night, man. This is the same thing—only it's in a black area, but it's the same type of deal. Steel mills, coal fields, you know, miners. God knows what.

Michael Bloomfield This place could have been in Mississippi, man, or Tuscaloosa, Alabama. It was just so funky.

Roy Ruby It's a gigantic room, like an auditorium almost, with a cement floor. Metal chairs and metal tables with Formica tops. This is the blues circuit—this is where Jimmy Reed plays, people like that. For this reason, there's this radio show broadcasting from there.

So we're out there, and Lightning Hopkins and Big Joe sat at a table by themselves the whole night and drank two or three bottles of whiskey. God knows. They're just washing it down, and they get drunker and drunker. After the show, Michael drove back with Willie Dixon. He had a big car there. Michael knew better than to stay.

Michael Bloomfield Right. And you were left with Joe and Charlie.

Roy Ruby Right. And you see, to me, at that time, Big Joe was like a folksinger. My concept of what was happening was: this is a folksinger, a Negro folksinger. But I learned.

I'm out there with Charlie, and Charlie lives with him. And Michael knows him—everyone knows him. They're sort of giggling behind my back. I don't know what I'm getting into. So I'm left with Joe and Charlie. I didn't know Big Joe too well. When he was sober, I could understand him some of the time. But when he was drunk, I couldn't understand him at all. And when he was drunk he'd get real hostile and irate and sullen.

I'm the type of guy that doesn't like drunks, because you get to a point with them where you can't communicate. It's like being in a room with this completely insane person. No matter what you do or say, it's hopeless.

Big Joe's about 60 years old at this time, and all his life he's loved to fight. He has scars, man, a lump on his head. My God. And this guy's powerful.

We're driving back after the show—I'm driving my mother's car—and Big Joe's sitting next to me. All the way back he's giving me these directions, very cursory directions, like, "Left ... garbled drunken mumble." And I was embarrassed to ask him what he meant, because I felt like I was denigrating the Negro dialect by asking him over and over again what he was saying. He had no teeth, and he was drunk. I couldn't understand him, and every time I'd ask him, he'd get more and more angry. He'd say, "Garbled drunken mumble ... said *left*, man." And sometimes I'd disagree with him—I'd say, "But I think we went *this* way when we came."

Now, the thing I have to make you understand is that Charlie got into the car and crawled into the back seat and pretended to be asleep. He left me there, dealing with Big Joe by myself. So we're driving down the road to Chicago, and it should take about two hours to get back. We started out at about two in the morning, and I'm real anxious to get home because I feel very insecure.

Charlie goes to sleep—but he isn't really asleep, because he knows what's going to happen. He's lived with Joe, and he doesn't want to deal with it. When Joe would get drunk like that, Charlie'd leave. But here he's stuck in the car. And somebody has to be the butt of Joe's hostility. I kept turning around and punching Charlie. I'd say, "Hey, motherfucker, get up. Hey, Charlie." It was like I wanted Charlie to mediate. I would say, "Charlie, tell me what he's saying, please." I thought Joe was physically threatening my life. And I wanted to ask Charlie, "Is he threatening my life? Should I get out of the car and run? What should I do?"

At a certain point I got the courage to say, "But Joe, this isn't where we came." And he'd say, when I could sort of understand what he was saying, "Fuck you. Don't tell me what to do. Turn left."

We're going further and further out into the country. And I'm getting more and more weirded out—I just don't know where I am or what's going on. I'm out past my bedtime with my mother's car. And this crazy old man is just so drunk, and he exudes this incredible force and power.

We ended up in a place I can't even describe. Imagine the most decrepit—not a housing project, but like the kind of place in Chicago, on the South Side, where you have little alleyways going through mazes of wooden buildings, with wooden stairs going up three or four flights. Shingle sides and shingle roofs. Hundreds of little apartments in a labyrinth of places, like the most incredible slum transplanted somewhere out in the country for some reason. You get to this place and begin walking through, and it's a huge area, like a city block of houses built up in this weird way. Stairs would be broken, and they'd build another stair around it.

This is where he stopped. He said, "Here's where we're coming. Stop here." This confirmed all my fears—I mean, I had this sneaking suspicion that we weren't going back to Chicago. Here I was, man, and I was like someone who had taken sleeping pills every night and finds himself one night without any sleeping pills. No liquor, no sleeping pills, nothing. You face the prospect of an entire night, just a horror of nervousness and up-tightness and not being able to sleep, not being able to rest, not being able to fall into your cubbyhole.

So we're out there, and Charlie's still in the back. He doesn't move an inch. Big Joe tells me to come along, so I come along. What else can I do? I was more scared to sit out there alone in the car, even with Charlie—I know he's not going to help me. So off I go with Big Joe. It turns out we're going to see his long-lost sister and his brother-in-law, or something like that. It was about 12 people. He went where he wanted to go. He knew where he was going all the time.

They hadn't seen him in two years or something, and they're very surprised. Everyone climbs out of bed, and there's about four or five families living in this apartment. He woke everybody up, and everyone is super friendly to me, just super friendly. No big thing. No big deal about it. They get me a glass of beer and a chair. And they're rapping with Joe. They say, "Where you been, man?" Joe says, "You know." "Where you been?" Joe says, "Well, I've been around, man." They say, "Why didn't you ever come by?" And Joe says, "Well, I'm here now."

He wants to drink. He says, "Where's something to drink?" They pour him drinks of beer, which is all they had. And they just sat around in the kitchen for a couple hours and rapped. I was immediately aware that everything was cool.

You can't imagine what I thought, being led into this labyrinth. I mean, it seems insane to feel like, what—is he going to rob me? You know, he's a 60-year-old artist, a great musician, a historical figure in American music. I'm aware of this part of it, you know. But what is he going to do to me? What in God's name? With the hostility that I felt. Just the orneriness—orneriness is what it is. I felt an aura of physical power and danger emanating from the man, in the way he was being so gruff with me. Now I understand—he's that way with everybody when he's drunk. It's the way he is, that's all. But I didn't know that.

It's a beautiful, friendly, family scene. They're rapping, "You remember so and so, and so and so, and where's so and so?" This goes on. Things cool down, and then finally Joe says, "Let's go." He's still pretty drunk, but he's sort of mellowed.

He was pissed at me for being scared, you see. He could feel that I was scared, and that pissed him off. Because he really felt like he was protecting me. He was taking care of me. He was going to do me the favor of taking me to see his family.

We left the relatives' house and started driving back. It's more or less cool. And I realize that finally we are going toward Chicago. We get into Chicago when it's just barely beginning to get light. It's not quite light yet when we pull up along the street where Koester's store is, West Grand.

Big Joe gets out of the car, and I get out of the car. Big Joe walks over to the store and goes in. At this moment, Charlie peeks his head out. He looks over the seat, looks around to make sure Joe isn't still there, and then slowly crawls out of the car. I'm so pissed, man. Charlie and I had this tremendous argument. I blamed everything that happened on him: "This whole night—it's all your fault!" I told him all the horrible details of how bad I felt, how scared I was, and he just laughed at me.

When I'd completely exhausted myself with vituperation against Charlie, that was the end of that. We took a long, long walk through Chicago. Charlie and I had this wonderful discussion, like one of those things you have with a close friend. We were walking on State Street. We looked at the little houses and looked in the little yards and had some kind of philosophical discussion on the meaning of life. One of those beautiful moments with one of your closest friends.

In the end, when I knew Big Joe a little better, I understood that he was full of love, too. He has great love, and he wants to help people. It was so wonderful to him that people would be interested in him, and come to him and want to learn, because he thinks he's a genius. He realizes that he's great. He knows that. When people would come to him and say, "Teach me this, teach me that," he accepted it. He knows that's where it should be at. That's where a part of his bitterness comes from, because he knows he's a great genius.

This was a real old-time Southern bluesman, man. Like Jack Kerouac, *On the Road*—those guys were young white fellows who went on the road for a few years. They were taking it in, having a good time, and laughing it up. Big Joe's been on the road since he was a child, and he's been having knife fights and gun fights and scrapes with the law. He's a real tough guy, man. The real thing.

And his style—see, he had a nine-string guitar. He had these three extra strings strung below the other strings, and he would tune them differently for different songs. And he had this weird little contraption that looked like it was glued on. He said he had patented it. He always insisted that it was his invention. I asked him once why he did that, and he told me because he was sick of people asking him to play his guitar.

He did it to mess up other guitar players. They'd say, "Let me play your guitar." Joe would say, "Okay, man." He'd give them the guitar, and they would get fucked up trying to play his nine-string guitar. That was his big thing.

He'd tell you, "I invented this. I invented that. All these people stole my songs. And all those people copied from me." It's all true. Big Joe Williams was one of the greats—one of the most powerful, original blues singers. A great genius. You have to understand—he's a drunken old man, which he is, but he's a great genius.

Michael Bloomfield Being with Joe was being with a history of the blues—you could see him as a man, and you could see him as a legend. He couldn't read or write a word of English, but he had America memorized. From 40 years of hiking roads and riding rails he was wise to every highway and byway and roadbed in the country, and wise to every city and county and township that they led to. Joe was part of a rare and vanishing breed—he was a wanderer and a hobo and a blues singer. He was an awesome man.

The Real Thing
at Big John's

7

Norman Dayron In 1963 Mike and I worked on a film called *And This Is Free*. It was one of the first *cinema verité* pieces. The Maysles Brothers had done this thing on Bible salesmen called *Salesmen*, which was out about that time, and Pennebaker was starting to work on the Dylan film. These movies were using the same technique—the idea of being able to take a "slice of life."

Today, anybody can go out and shoot a documentary. But in those days, if you were going to do it seriously, you had to use 16-millimeter cameras. And there wasn't even sound synchronization. It had just happened where you could use a Nagra tape recorder, and we had to make a device that would put a thousand-cycle tone on the tape. You know, like a slate for synching up the sound and the picture.

How it happened was this: Mike Shea was a still photographer, a pro, for the Chicago newspapers. And he had this ambition to make the transition from being a still photographer to making films. Somehow, Mike Bloomfield had run into Mike Shea. So Michael calls me up and says, "You know, I'd like to do a film with this guy Mike Shea. It'll be a documentary about the music—the blues and gospel music on Maxwell Street."

Michael was familiar with Maxwell Street and knew the performers, because he would go down there to hang out and sit in. It was like this huge flea market, and Michael and I had both gone down there almost every Sunday to hear the music and eat Polish sausage, which was real cheap. There was always something happening on Maxwell Street.

Mike Shea was this short, powerful guy—all muscle, but about 300 pounds, maybe five-seven. Stocky. Shea could walk through the streets with a heavy camera rig on and a drunk could fall into him, and the camera wouldn't shake. Shea was a liquid-filled dolly. And he was a damned good photographer. We had a couple of other students from the University of Chicago with us, helping out.

We filmed Robert Nighthawk, the great guitar player who taught Muddy Waters how to play and who was this rare figure that nobody ever saw. But Nighthawk would appear on Maxwell Street. The Robert Nighthawk sequence was shot on the back porch of a tenement building that had a dirt yard where people would come and dance.

That Nagra was covered up with black friction tape so people wouldn't know it was a tape recorder. You couldn't even see the reels turning. And Michael was making our presence there acceptable to the musicians, so they wouldn't get hostile and would cooperate with us.

We did everything out of the love of doing it. We were not at all into being paid for what we did. And it never occurred to us to pay the musicians, although I think we did give several of the performers some money from Mike Shea's thing.

In many cases, the people weren't even sure what we were doing. We used to go down there every Sunday for about a year. We'd get there at five in the morning and set up cameras, sometimes on the roofs of tenements using long lenses. Mostly we were just walking through the streets, filming all the musicians and gospel singers, black and white, that were down there.

At this time I was a student, but I was also working for Chess Records part-time as a janitor. I did a lot of different jobs there, and finally worked my way up to being a recording engineer and then a record producer.

The Chess brothers were very funny. Here I was, a Jewish kid who was a student and who a year or two later became a professor, or at least an instructor, in the college. They thought it was novel to have somebody of that educational level running the elevator and cleaning up after recording sessions. But it gave me a chance to learn a great deal and to be in the environment that I loved, with all these blues players.

Other than going to school and working for Chess, the rest of my time was spent hanging out with Michael. We would do projects and have these adventures. We stole a piano from the Bear, which was a defunct nightclub, and we took it all the way to Carl Sandburg Village, where he and Susie were living.

Michael was a natural piano player. He could just sit down and play Chicago barrelhouse blues—but he had no piano. And he was complaining that he had no money. So one day he calls me up and says, "I want you to come down. We need to get me a piano. I know where there's one that's owed to me—it's my piano."

I don't remember the exact story, but Michael had an interpretation that he was owed some money by Howard Alk for some work he had done. And that Howard had said, "Well, I don't have any money, but you can take one of the pianos out of the Bear." To be honest, I didn't know how true this was. But I borrowed a station wagon from one of the faculty members at the university and drove down to Carl Sandburg Village. And we decided we were going to have this adventure. We drove up to the Bear with the intention to take the piano and put it in his apartment in Carl Sandburg Village.

We went to the side door and noticed that it was locked, but not very well, so we just shook on the door until the lock fell off. We broke and entered. We went cruising through the Bear and saw any number of pianos, none of which could be moved by two young Jewish men who weren't in great shape. But we did find a little piano in a back storage place. It was one of those three-quarter pianos or miniature pianos—I don't know what it was. But it wasn't so heavy that we couldn't move it. So we grunted and groaned and by an absolutely Herculean effort got that piano out of the Bear and into the back of my borrowed station wagon. It was an enormous effort, because even the smallest piano must weigh five, six hundred pounds. We had no dolly. We had no levers. This was just two people using their hands to move that piano out of the Bear and into the back of the station wagon.

We were confident that we would not get caught. We were so ballsy that we took it in broad daylight. We took it up the elevator into Carl Sandburg Village and put it in his apartment. Michael's sitting there playing the thing, and he's just a natural. He's playing blues, and it sounds wonderful. And then the phone rings.

Susie picks up the phone and says, "It's for you guys." It was the police. We were busted. We had been observed committing this robbery. I don't know why they waited until we got it back to his house—it was this huge effort. It took us all day to get it up there. They said, "Look, we have this report that you've committed a robbery." You'd think they would break down the door or something, but they just phoned.

I can't tell you why the police would have his phone number and just call him up. Mike gets off the phone and says, "Well, we have to take the piano back. The deal is: If we put it back where we found it and promise to be good boys, they won't arrest us." It was a gray area—I mean, we really didn't believe that we were committing robbery. We thought there was some righteous thing there, that he was owed it. The police must have thought so, too—they must have known there was some dispute.

Apparently, we had been observed by a private security operation, and they had reported it to the police. And there must have been some doubt whether or not we had the right to be there or not. After all, who in their right mind would break in in broad daylight like that? No honorable thief in Chicago would be that stupid.

George Mitchell I left Chicago in the fall of '63. But those Fickle Pickle concerts became rather legendary, and Norm Dayron recorded almost all of them. Bloomfield and I brought him in on the deal, to tape all the concerts, but the Fickle Pickle things didn't continue that much longer after I left.

● ● ●

Nick Gravenites I'd spent a long time out on the West Coast. Eventually, around the end of 1963 or the beginning of '64, I left San Francisco under trying circumstances. I left my wife and my baby boy. I took off back to Chicago to play blues, because I was just getting tired of not playing it. Everybody I knew back in Chicago was really getting into electric music and blues, Chicago blues. Out on the West Coast it was still folk music, and I missed a lot of my buddies back there. So I left.

I went back to Hyde Park. I got a job at the steel mill, the U.S. Steel South Works, on the southeast side of Chicago. I started hanging with Butterfield again and wound up living in this rooming house, with Butterfield next to me in one room and a crazy artist named Karen Stern in another.

This was '64. Butter was working as an illustrator, a graphic artist, and playing blues. He'd been playing blues while I was gone, hanging out with the blues guys on the South Side, and playing with various people. Playing with a guy named Smokey Smothers. He did a lot of sitting in with various bands, and he was part of a revue at a joint called the Blue Flame Lounge. That became our club. The Blue Flame was a great place, and it was there that Paul really honed his skills. We had a great time there.

Sam Lay I met Paul when I was playing with Little Smokey Smothers at the Blue Flame over on 39th Street. Butterfield come in there one night, and he came up and played the harmonica. Every weekend we would play there, he would come back. Finally, he started getting a following over there.

Now, it was a black-owned club in a black area, right? But Butterfield had a few friends that came over. Those friends went and got somebody else, and then there were people coming from the North Side—a lot of whites started coming. So they had a good mixed audience, and the people that's coming in there is spending money. The club owner, Roy Marshall, would make good money, because Butterfield was drawing the whites from the North Side. The Blue Flame became one of the most popular spots in town.

*Michael and Nick Gravenites at a North Side
club in Chicago, Fall 1964.*

Michael Bloomfield   Paul, by that time, was a specialty act. They had him booked in this club, the Blue Flame, and it was like a freak show—our white star. Irish white guy plays the blues. But he held his own. My God, man, he'd walk in a place, and Little Walter and Junior Wells would put down their harmonicas. They'd put 'em down and get that cat up there. I knew Paul, and I was scared of him, because he was so accepted—he was so a part of that scene. I would sit at a table with Muddy Waters and James Cotton, and they'd be looking at Paul and just be beaming at him, like, "That's my boy." That's what their eyes were just shining out and saying.

Nick Gravenites   At the Blue Flame Lounge, we were there with our contingent, and we had a ball. But mainly it was the black people. They were tired of the same old blues guys. They were tired of Junior Wells and all these other people. They were glad to see a fresh face come up that really could play. It wasn't the white people that got Butterfield really accepted—it was blacks. They loved him and thought he was great.

Norman Dayron   One of the first recordings that Michael was on that became public, although limited in distribution, was on Out of Sight Records.

It was a 45 RPM of Nick Gravenites singing "My Baby's Got a Whole Lot of Soul" and "Drunken Boat." After Rimbaud, the French poet—it was a very bohemian, artistic thing.

The record was financed by a close friend of Nick's, Jeff Spitz. Nick was on vocals, and he had written both songs. Michael and Paul Butterfield and a number of other musicians played on it. It was the most extraordinary band—and an extraordinary performance. It was recorded in Mike Shea's film studio. He had this small room, and we crammed all those guys in it and recorded. We made, I think, a thousand copies of that record. It's a very rare record.

Ron Butkovich There were two record shops we used to hang around in: Koester's Jazz Record Mart and the Old Wells Record Shop. For some reason, Bloomfield was eventually banned from the Jazz Record Mart. Koester was the kind of a guy who, for some reason, irritated everyone. Everyone had a run-in with him. Everyone ended up hating him or punching him out.

Charlie Musselwhite I beat up Bob Koester one day. He just pissed me off one time too many. I would usually just kind of brush it off. I didn't pay any attention to him—he was like some little dog barking. But one day I just wasn't in the mood. I came around the corner there and started slapping him around. Then I left and went to work at another record store, where I could live there, too. It was in Old Town, at the corner of Schiller and Wells—a place called the Old Wells Record Shop. I lived in a room in the back. Big Joe Williams had been living in Koester's place, but when I moved Joe left and went with me over there. But that was good, because it put me about two blocks from Mike's place.

Ron Butkovich The Old Wells Record Shop was run by an old guy, half black, half Indian, named Bill Shavers. It was sort of a funny situation. On weekends, there'd be a lot of traffic in the Old Town area, and he'd have it sort of open and sort of not open. There'd be a bunch of guys in there hanging out, drinking beer, and watching TV. If somebody would come to the door and it would be, like, a good-lookin' woman, he'd go and let her in. But if it was just an ordinary customer, he didn't have any use for 'em. We'd all hang out there, and Bill Shavers had nicknames for everyone. He called me "Rudy" for some reason. He called Michael "Melonious Thunk." He gave Applejack his nickname—his name is Jack Walroth, but Bill called him "Applejack."

We were all hanging out there, and Michael was, like, a tremendously forceful personality. He was already a star at that time. Nobody knew about him, but he was a legend around Chicago as a guitar player and a personality—a maniac. He had an amazing presence and way about him. His charisma was overwhelming.

Applejack I was living in a very low-rent hotel room on Clark Street. Michael's record player broke down, so he wanted my turntable. The only possessions I had were some records and a record player, right? And about three pairs of socks. So we made this arrangement where I loaned him the record player for a week or two, until he could get another one, and he was going to give me any two albums out of his collection. The two albums I picked were this Big Maceo French import record and a Arthur Cruddup record, *On Fire*, which was a pretty cool album at the time. Who knows what I would have chosen if I went back and looked at that collection today—I don't know. But it was like: you only do that for somebody who's a friend.

One time we went to South State Street, and he was looking at guitars. I remember being impressed because he could read the code on the pawn tickets and called the pawn broker a *meshuggener* and stuff like that. He said, "What do you mean? This guitar is not worth $25." It was like a Fender Strat with scrapings on it that said "Guitar King" or something, hanging up on the wall. Then he sat down and plugged it in. The owner of the store was just blown away, because Mike played this amazing amount of incredible music in a very short amount of time. That was his test for the guitar. He put it down and said, "How much you want for it? No, that's too much." And we left.

Michael lived in Sandburg Village, and I first met his wife, Susan, there. I used to go over there in the snow and listen to Muddy Waters records and hang out. It was a circle of people like Roy Ruby and Charlie Musselwhite. When I first met Charlie, we went to Clark Street and watched horror movies and drank wine. That was entertainment.

Charlie Musselwhite Mike and Susie were living at the Carl Sandburg apartments. That was close to the record store, so every day Mike was over there. We'd be playing records, and I'd be drinking a good bit. Mike didn't drink. I don't think he drank at all back then. We were just having a good time, hanging out. A lot of different musicians would come by—Homesick James would come by, and Joe was there a lot. We'd sit on the front steps or something. It was just real serious hanging out, you know.

Down the street there was a neighborhood bar called Big John's. They knew that Joe was some sort of folk singer. They weren't sure exactly what it was he did, but they knew he had a guitar. They invited him down there to play, and he had me come play harp with him. They had an old piano in there, and Mike came and started playing the piano. So it was piano, harp, and guitar. What happened was: business was so good that night that the bar asked Joe to stay, to keep playing there every night.

But Joe never could stay in one place too long. He'd be coming and going. When it was time for him to go again, Mike and I decided to stay and keep the gig going. Mike switched over to guitar and I kept playing harp, and we got a drummer and a bass player. The money got better, and I could buy an amp one day. We were having a ball.

Norman Mayell In Chicago, there were a couple of places to go if you were looking for girls and parties. One was Rush Street, and one was Old Town. I was in Old Town one day, and I walked into Big John's and heard somebody playing blues guitar. And as a Chicago boy living in the area, I used to listen to all the South Side blues stations.

Michael was standing there, and Big Joe Williams was packing up and leaving. I started talking to Michael about the blues, and he said, "I got to start a band. If I get a band, I could play here." I said, "Well, I play the drums." And he said, "Well, get some. We'll get a band together quick." It was just that casual. So I went downtown and rented a set of blue-and-silver Slingerland drums and brought them back to Old Town. And it seemed like the minute we had the drums set up this guy called Gap—because he had gapped teeth—was playing rhythm guitar.

Charlie Musselwhite, Michael, Norm Mayell, (drums) and Mike "Gap" Johnson at Big John's, Fall 1964

Mike Johnson. We called him Gap—or I did. He seemed to appear out of nowhere. He was no lead guitar player, but he knew the rhythms and could play the blues stuff behind Michael. And then Silver Sid Warner popped up and said, "Sure, I can play bass."

Sid had a jewelry shop in Old Town, and he had played with Roy Rogers—that was the story. He knew all the standards. He was older than us, and he was a nice guy. I really liked Silver Sid. He was a blues guy. He had played Vegas, in the desert showrooms and stuff. It didn't matter what key you were in, he knew exactly what to do. He played fairly standard blues riffs on the bass, but he knew them. And he could walk it. He could push it along really well. He didn't even have to think about it.

The original band was called the Group. At that point, we had four guys. I think we rehearsed a few times in a garage or a small studio. And then Charlie Musselwhite showed up. He was a friend of Michael's. He was pretty much a country boy, and he didn't say a damn thing. He just smiled a lot. He wouldn't even go on the stage. He sat at the side of the stage with a microphone and his harmonicas and a glass of water, and he wouldn't get on the stage with the band. In case he didn't know the number, he wasn't going to play.

When I met Michael, he and Susan were living in Sandburg Village. I couldn't figure that out. Well, I guess he's independently wealthy, I thought. He must be a star already and I don't know it. He was certainly hot. I'd never played with anybody that had that kind of power.

We played Big John's for almost a year and packed them in. We played one night a week, and then it was two, and then they wanted us to play three. During the summer, I remember playing Thursday, Friday, Saturday, and Sunday.

While we were at Big John's, Butterfield and Bishop were playing somewhere on the South Side. Occasionally, when they weren't working, they would come up and watch, which was kind of interesting. In would come Sam Lay with some kind of metallic blue or silver shoes on. And then Jerome Arnold would show up, and Butterfield would come in. Elvin came occasionally. And I remember Naftalin coming in, sometimes to play.

We were all just starting, and we were high on dope, and the house was crazy, and Michael was off the top of his head. It was very intense. Michael was so strong.

None of us had the slightest idea what we were going to play when we went onstage. We always knew that we would close with "Mojo"—it seemed to be one of the things we did. The rest was any combination of shuffles and/or blues songs. Some of them were instrumentals. Charlie would play a solo, Michael would play a solo. If the keyboard was in, he'd play a solo.

If Michael knew blues lyrics, he sang them. There was one song we did called "Satin Lady," which is sort of a jazz song—that was to appease Mike Johnson. He always got to do one of those where he got to play lead, since he was studying guitar and trying to learn to play lead. It would make him feel all right. Of course, it was nowhere on the level that Michael was putting out, but it was there nonetheless. Some nights we were very great, I think. Other nights we were probably terrible.

Big John's had a pool hall, and people used to sell Panama Red in little matchboxes for $5. It was the main staple. The drugs brought us together onstage, but I think it set us apart socially. I remember smoking dope with Mike and other people late at night and having strange conversations, because all of us were from completely different backgrounds. We weren't brothers and we didn't grow up in the same part of the city.

Gap didn't socialize with any of us. He always seemed to be gone when it was over. I lived in Old Town, so then I could go places. It was my first experience with marijuana, and many a night I had my mind totally blown out—like, what in the hell just happened? I had no idea.

That club probably could hold only 120 people. It was not very big. If they filled up the pool room and had guys standing out in the street to get in, then it looked like there was a couple of hundred people there in a very small club.

The scene in Chicago was sort of like a pub revolution. The folk scene was the dominant scene in Old Town, and the fact that there was an electric blues band in Big John's was a novelty. No one saw it as the future.

Charlie Musselwhite Until then, the only blues played on the North Side— the white area—was just like folk music. And in Old Town, there was some folk clubs. Mama Blues or something—Mother Blues—places like that. And there was jazz. The only blues that was available was folk—acoustic blues. But what me and Mike were doing was electric. Plus, we told this club, "You ought to have people like Otis Rush playing in here," and stuff like that. That was the first club, to my knowledge, that would have electric blues bands coming in and playing.

Norman Dayron To be honest, the quality of the band wasn't that good. They could barely keep up with Mike. But it was enough. He broke open that place, and pretty soon there were lines around the block. You couldn't get in. There'd be 200 people waiting outside, and the place was packed every night. Because it was the real thing.

Blues at Magoo's

Charlie Musselwhite Every once in a while, Mike and I would take off and ride the bus, or get a ride from somebody, just to go hang out in New York City and try to get in on the scene. We'd go to parties and jam sessions. One time we met John Hammond, and he happened to be recording. So he asked us to join him. Mike played on that, and I played harmonica with the band.

John Hammond Jr. I'd met Michael in 1960. There was a blues festival at the University of Chicago, and I went up there. We hit it off right away. We were both blues fanatics. I was just starting out, but Michael could really play.

When I came back through Chicago in '62, he took me down to the South Side to hear some music. He said, "Man, you've got to meet Muddy." So we go to Pepper's Lounge, and Michael walked right up to the bandstand and said, "Hey, Muddy." Muddy says, "Hey, Michael, how're you doing?" And Michael says, "I'd like you to meet my friend John Hammond." I felt like I was going to fall down. And then, in the middle of Muddy's show, he calls Michael up to play with him. I was mind-boggled. And Michael was great. He knew all the details of cool stuff. He was a wonderful guy. I valued his friendship more than I can ever say. He was just a terrific person.

The thing that Michael liked about me, I think, was that I wasn't afraid to get up and sing my ass off. Michael was always a little awkward about his singing and preferred to be the lead guitar player instead. But Michael could sing. He didn't have the greatest voice, but you could feel it. He really was phenomenal.

I saw a lot of him in '63 and '64. I had recorded my first album, and it had been released. Michael was totally on the scene—he was playing gigs and building up his chops. He was jamming with everybody. He introduced me to Howlin' Wolf and Butterfield. And Nick Gravenites, who really impressed me. He knew everybody in Chicago.

I got Michael to record on an album I made in '64, called *So Many Roads*. I had been playing with a band up in Toronto called Levon & the Hawks, and I got everybody together to record this album. We had one day to record it. It was so intense, it was magical. It's one of my favorites, too, I must admit after 32 years.

That was such a dynamic time. The Village in New York, at that time, was just a hotbed. Everybody was coming from all over the country to play in New York and make the scene, and blues was being included in the folk scene.

Charlie Musselwhite Those guys stayed friends of ours, and when they would come to Chicago, they'd look us up. One time they called up—I think Levon Helm called Mike, and he wanted to get some reefer. They went all around town looking for reefer. Mike got the bright idea to go to Paul's place, only Paul wasn't there. But Mike could really talk. He told this girl, who was the apartment manager or something, that he was Paul's best friend and to open the door.

He got her to do that, and as soon as they went in, he saw that Levon knew just what to do. He started going through drawers and everything looking for the reefer—the stash. And they found it. I don't know if they took it all or what, but they got loaded. They took part of it or all of it and left, and then went somewhere else and smoked it up.

And then Mike got real paranoid. He called me and wanted to know what he should do. Because he thought Paul was going to beat him up. I said, "Well, there's only one thing you can do. Get some more reefer and take it to him and apologize." And I think that's what he did.

● ● ●

Norman Mayell We played in Big John's for close to a year. And then we went north, of all things, to another club, because the club offered us more money.

Charlie Musselwhite We had a piano player, Brian Friedman, by this time, too. And Nick Gravenites was on some of the shows. The business was going well, the other clubs were seeing this, and they wanted to have blues, too.

So we got hired away to another club called Magoo's. Paul Butterfield came in and took our place at Big John's. That started the whole flip-flop from the South Side to the North Side, because none of the clubs on the South Side could outmatch in money these North Side clubs. And people loved it. They didn't want to go to the South Side. They were afraid, or they didn't know where to go. That was sort of where it really began—it planted the seed for a lot of people to learn about modern Chicago electric blues. It might have gone up and down since then, but that was where the corner was turned.

Paul was playing with Elvin, Sam Lay, and Jerome Arnold. They were playing around the University of Chicago area. They took our place at Big John's, and we went to Magoo's. We were playing seven sets a night—we'd start at nine and go to four in the morning, 45 on and 15 off, Wednesday through Sunday. Twenty-five bucks a night. I thought I had something.

Nick Gravenites At Big John's, they remembered Butterfield from when he used to come down there, occasionally, and sit in with Michael. Called him up and asked him if he wanted a gig. Butterfield, at that time, wasn't quite sure whether he wanted to do that. Paul didn't have a band. He had just gotten this job offer as a graphic illustrator, and it looked like he was going to follow that career.

But he made some phone calls to Sam Lay, the drummer, and Jerome Arnold, bass player—they were Howlin' Wolf's rhythm section. He remembered playing with them in the blues clubs when he was hanging out. So he called to see if they were interested in playing with him, which they were. Various reasons, you know. I mean, they liked him. They thought he had a lot of talent. They enjoyed playing with him. But primarily it was the money.

Sam Lay I was in Wolf's band. Then Wolf got Jerome Arnold from Otis Rush to play with us. Then myself and Jerome Arnold left Wolf's band together to go work with Butterfield. We was looking at the money part of it. The money was better. We had a guaranteed four nights a week in one place, didn't have to go nowhere. And the money was, like, 20 bucks a night, man—that was a lot of money then. Because I have worked from nine o'clock at night to five in the morning for $8. Working with Wolf we was getting, like, $12.50 a night, and we were working just on the weekends.

Without a doubt it wasn't just the money, but I will tell you this, and I have to be honest about it: I wasn't used to playing all the time for a white audience. And it was unbelievable the way that they accepted us—they danced and everything. If I ain't mistaken, we might have been one of the first mixed bands.

Nick Gravenites Playing for black blues guys in Chicago was not a way to make money. The guy who kept the money was the band leader. You were lucky to get paid. But white guys didn't have that sensibility—they'd get the money at the end of the night and split it up. This was a radical concept for most blues guys in Chicago. So they said, Yeah, they'd like to do that. And then Butter asked Elvin to join him as rhythm guitarist in this venture at Big John's.

That was the beginning of the white blues explosion right there—'64 in Chicago. Paul started playing there a couple nights a week, on the weekends, and I think he played there for eight or nine months straight. By the end of that time, he was playing there four nights a week, sometimes five. And the joint would fill up every night.

Charlie Musselwhite We're playing at this place, Magoo's, and it's just a terrible place. The people that hang out there—I don't know how to explain them. Sort of a criminal type, you know, a lot of guys that are going in and out of the joint. And it's all kind of lightweight stuff. They're not really Mafia types, but they'd have loved to have been in the Mafia. They're just real unpleasant people. No sense of humor. I don't mind the criminal element. I've been involved with that sort of people a lot, but if there's no sense of humor, what's the point? It gets pretty bleak if there's no humor in there.

Mike, more than anybody, hated playing there. I think he hated the audiences. Because you're playing to these people, and they're thinking they're hip and they're in, and you know they don't have a clue. You look at these big empty eyes, and you know that behind those eyes there's just nothing. There's nothing to talk about with these people. There's nothing to relate to. It's just horrible. And you have to act like you like them, which really is hard.

Norman Mayell I think there was a move to go there to get some money, 'cause it was a larger club. it was strong at first, and then it turned out not to be cool. It started to trail off because people weren't interested. That's when we did the Columbia sessions. John Hammond Sr. from Columbia Records came to see us and put us in the studio.

Allen Bloomfield Michael's rabbi was very good friends with John Hammond Sr. The rabbi was a jazz aficionado. When John recognized Michael's talent, he went to see this rabbi and said, "I found this guy, this kid Bloomfield, and he's just a hotshot on a guitar." And the rabbi said, "Michael Bloomfield? I was the guy who *bar mitzvahed* him."

Norman Mayell We did the Columbia recordings as though maybe something would happen. It was sort of, "Wow, we're making records. John

Hammond Sr. This is amazing." As I recall, they didn't have any idea what white guys were doing with this music. There was no hotshot guy coming up and saying, "Man, I know how to make this sound great."

I had the feeling they were demo sessions. I don't believe we did any of the songs more than once or twice. It was just a question of whether we could get everyone to start and end together. The vocals were done live—everything was. There were no overdubs. Michael had a vocal mike, and he sang and played.

Those tracks on the *Essential Blues* CD, I think that pretty much caught it right there. I recall it maybe being stronger in nightclubs, but it isn't all that bad of an idea of what we were doing. When I listen to it, I can see how Michael is still undeveloped—raw talent overflowing and still not sure how he was going to resolve and make his licks the way they were. Trying to figure it out.

And then it was sort of like—well, there's the tracks. No one talked about it. Nothing happened. And it seemed as though when nothing happened, that was it. The band was done with.

Charlie Musselwhite I remember something happened where we found out that the bass player, Silver Sid, was somehow getting double paid by the bar. I don't remember how that worked out. I think he was getting the money and splitting it up—oh, it's been too long. There was a lot of stuff going on there, and it was all negative.

So one night me and Mike were sitting in his apartment, and it was getting time to go to work, and he just said, "Fuck it, I ain't going." And we just didn't go. But after a while we drove by, just to see what was going on. The door was open, and we could see Sid was up there. He had switched over to guitar and was leading the band. We just kept on driving and never went back.

When we were at Big John's, it was like a regular gig. We were there every weekend. And at Magoo's it was five nights a week. We were the house band. All of a sudden, we were playing only one night here, two nights there. And we were off for long periods of time.

Susie was working, and Mike had some sort of trust fund from his parents, so they had money. They didn't really have to worry about money. But I didn't have any money. So I started gigging around with other people. Mike kept talking about all these irons he had in the fire, but nothing was happening.

Nick Gravenites Big John's became a real hotspot. People would come down to hear Butter's band, and the place would fill up all the time. It was like blues heaven. And at that time in Chicago, people started to congregate—all the young white blues people started to congregate there. They'd go to hang out at Big John's. I mean, it became, like, *the* place. That was the heyday of the white blues people in Chicago. Butter played there for eight or nine months, and by the end of that time the place was hopping all the time. It was a great club.

Charlie Musselwhite At this point, I was living in an apartment with Roy Ruby. We were sitting there talking one day, and Mike comes up the stairs and says, "I got a gig coming up at such-and-such a place." By this time Roy's got a little group, and I'm working with Roy. And Roy says, "Oh, well, we've already got a gig."

I could tell that that really pissed off Mike. Because then he started talking kind of fast and nervous about this horn section he had lined up. I just knew that it wasn't true. Then he left, and I really never heard from him again. I mean, our paths would cross, but I think he felt that I had let him down. It wasn't long after that he joined Paul Butterfield's band. We stayed friends, but it never was the same after that.

II

1965 to 1968

I Was Scared of Paul

Michael Bloomfield I was scared to work with Butterfield. He was a bad guy. He carried pistols. He was down there on the South Side, holding his own. I was scared to death of that cat. Always scared of him. Elektra brought me into the picture. It wasn't Paul's choice. I didn't like him, and he didn't like me. It was the record company's choice—Rothchild wanted me.

Nick Gravenites Back in 1963, when I was in California, Butterfield came out to visit. This was before he put the band together. He was traveling around. He had a girlfriend who lived down near L.A. We played in a coffee house in Berkeley called the Cabale Creamery.

Paul Rothchild I met Paul Butterfield at the Cabale Creamery in Berkeley. I was staying at Jim and Suzie West's with Bobby Neuwirth. We went down to the club because Neuwirth would do an odd little set once in a while. Butterfield came and sat in. I had never heard him. And I had never heard harmonica played that way, except on old records. I told him, "You're great! Are you going to put a band together?" He said, "I don't know."

Fritz Richmond Paul Rothchild was on the board of directors of the Club 47 in Cambridge, which was a folk club. And I was the house bass player. Rothchild started producing records of some of the acts that were big draws in the Club 47: the Charles River Valley Boys, the Keith & Rudy Bluegrass Band, Geoff Muldaur, Eric Von Schmidt, Mitch Greenhill, Tom Rush—quite a line of performers, most of whom he signed to Prestige Records. He went to work for Prestige as a producer, then he got a job with Jac Holzman at Elektra Records.

Paul Rothchild I was at a party at John Cooke's in Cambridge, and I got a call from Fritz. "We're in Chicago, and we just heard Paul Butterfield's new band. It's the greatest thing you've ever heard. Get on a plane right now and go to Chicago." So I left Cooke's party and flew to Chicago.

I walked into Big John's and heard the most amazing thing I'd ever heard in my life. It was the same rush I'd had the first time I heard bluegrass. I said to myself, "Here is the beginning of another era. This is another turning point in American music's direction."

We went next door to a pizza joint, and I talked to Butterfield. I told him I wanted him to record for Elektra. He was going for it. He was totally, magnificently jive. Beautiful. I loved him. Chicago street hustler. And here's this hotshot from New York telling him he wants to make records. I'd shined up my act a little bit, so I was pretty good at it by that time—talking to artists about making records.

After I finished talking with Paul and the band—which was Elvin Bishop, Jerome Arnold, and Sam Lay—somebody said, "Let's go over and catch this other band at an after-hours joint." So I heard Mike Bloomfield's band for the first time. When they came off, I leaned over to Paul and said, "Hey, Paul, let's get this guy into your band." He said, "No. He's got his band and I've got mine. He'll never leave his band. Anyway, I've got a guitar player."

I said, "Can you imagine two guitars in your band!" He said, "Well, you can ask him." So I leaned over to Bloomfield and said, "How would you like to join the Butterfield Band? We're making a record, blah, blah, blah." We talked for about 20 minutes, and he finally said, "Yeah!" He leaned across the table and said to his band, "I quit!" And we were off.

Michael Bloomfield It took lot of persuasion to get me to play with Paul, because he was such a personally intimidating guy. I was scared to even work with him. For a while he thought I was a turkey, and then, when he realized I was not a turkey, he gave me utter freedom to do what I wanted to do. And it worked fine. The thing became a real good act, and I added a lot to the band. The band added a huge amount to me—it made me a pro, because Paul was such a professional.

Charlie Musselwhite I know that Mike was afraid of Paul, and I never could understand why. But I do remember seeing Paul hit Elvin onstage. He would wear a sport coat, and he kind of—I don't know if it's from hearing about it or if I actually remember seeing this—but I have this picture of seeing him in Big John's going over to Elvin and, with his back turned to the audience, hitting Elvin in the side, with his right fist. With his coat sort of hiding it.

The Butterfield Blues Band at Big John's: unidentified drummer, Mark Naftalin, Michael, Paul Butterfield, and Jerome Arnold. December 1965.

And I remember seeing Paul shaking his finger in Elvin's face and hollering at him. He would do it at Sam, too. One time he felt Sam's time was off, so he stood right in front of him and was stomping on the edge of the stage with his foot. "Here's the right time," you know. He could be kind of a bully.

Elvin Bishop One time we were playing a place called Poor Richard's in Chicago, and there was a dressing room that was just marked off with a curtain. It wasn't really a wall partition or anything. And me and Paul got to arguing. I don't know what it was about, but I remember we rolled out under the curtain, out where the people were, and kind of shocked everybody pretty good.

As for my feelings about Michael joining the Butterfield Band, I don't think I can quite put myself back in that state of mind, but I can give some pretty good educated guesses. I imagine there was a little part of me that resented it. But for the most part it took a load off of me. I was trying to do more than I was able to do at the time, as far as playing leads and keeping up enough rhythm at the same time. I was green, and I knew it.

It was good for my development. I learned quite a bit from Michael, in odd ways. Not so much anything that would ever make me sound like him, but he had a lot more experience playing in bands and entertaining than I did at the time. Bloomers was always this brash, out-front professional—

kind of a sophisticated, experienced guy. When I first started out with Butter, I was so shy I would stand behind the bass player. Paul didn't let me do too much, you know.

You've got to give it to Paul, because he was a real serious musician. He and everybody else in the group were always more concerned about the respect of the real blues musicians than we were about a lot of popular acceptance.

Norman Dayron I think Paul really wanted Michael on the record. He was concerned about how the band would sound. It's one thing to knock people's socks off in a nightclub. It's another thing when you sit down and listen to a record, listen to what's happening on it. If Elvin was going to be the only guitar player on there, I don't know that Paul had the confidence in Elvin's playing to think that it was going to make for a good recording. And he knew that Michael could add to that.

They didn't have the distinction of, like, "I'm going to hire you just to work on the record." We were all very young, and it was all very personal. I think Paul had to have him be in the band. You can't make music—I mean, not really—out of rivalry. It can help to spark things, maybe. But I think they truly enjoyed playing off one another. They found that common sympathy with one another.

And then the rest of the band—it was a very good rhythm section. Jerome Arnold was a very good bass player. Elvin filled in on rhythm, mostly. And Sam Lay was one of the best blues drummers. He played like two trains running—I mean, he was a freight train on the loose.

Sam Lay Well, I'll tell you one thing I thought about Mike's guitar playing. If I had to be on a show with him, I'm glad I was a drummer instead of a damn guitar player. I got a feeling I would have just walked to the window and opened it and threw my guitar out, trying to compete with that cat. He could play any kind of style, not just blues. He was just a damn heavy guitar player in general. He was getting better and better. I don't care what he was, his father being a multi-millionaire. I look back at that cat playing guitar, and I'm tickled to death that I was a drummer.

When Bloomfield started to playing with us, man—the recording was okay, but to play live onstage—I can't say I hated him, but I hated his guitar playing. I mean, then. I had come from a band such as Howlin' Wolf and Little Walter and other people, and I wasn't used to no guitar player playing that loud, turning that volume up all the way like that. It seemed like, to me, Bloomfield was the loudest thing on the stage, and it used to

Jerome Arnold, Michael, and Paul Butterfield at Big John's, December 1965.

piss me off—Bloomfield playing his goddamned guitar like it's got a turbine engine in it or something. I finally got used to it.

Norman Dayron It was very powerful. And the truth of the matter is that Paul and Michael really loved one another. Because they had that harmonic sympathy. When they played, they used to do this call-and-response stuff. Paul would play a phrase on the harmonica, and Michael would respond on the guitar, imitating it. And then he would set up a phrase, and Paul would try to match it. So it was like—I wouldn't say a battle of the instruments, because it was much more cooperative. But they kept creating and generating together in this call-and-response manner.

It was a pretty amazing experience. When they used to play at Big John's, people would go completely berserk. They had never seen anything like it. And I believe that it had legitimacy, not just because it was this mixed band of white and black, but because they were doing a very vibrant, alive kind of original blues playing. And they were very, very, very good. Butterfield was certainly one of the best improvisational blues harmonica players you'd ever hear. And, you know, him and Michael blended, and it just caught fire.

Paul Rothchild Jac Holzman had come up with this idea of putting out sampler LPs for $1.98. On this sampler *Folk Song '65*, there were a number of new acts that I had brought to the label—Tom Rush was on it, and Dick Rosmini and Judy Collins. And "Born in Chicago" by the Butterfield Band.

Up until this point, he had sold maybe 20,000 or 30,000 of these samplers, which was great for then. But this sampler sold 200,000 copies! In a three-month period. Jac said, "What's going on?" And I kept saying to him, "This tune is going on: 'Born in Chicago.' Jac, we have a hit band on our hands."

Nick Gravenites It was Bloomfield that talked Butterfield into doing "Born in Chicago," which is my tune. Butter didn't want to do it. He just couldn't figure it out. But Michael insisted, taught them how to do it, and they recorded it. It was a big hit for them. And then they were off and running.

Paul Rothchild I played manager for them for a little while. I got them gigs at the Philadelphia Folk Festival and Club 47. They played the Cafe Au Go Go in New York. They looked really shoddy. At that time, the British bands were all wearing suits. So we went down to the lower East Side to one of those really sleazy suit places and got them all brown suits. Except for Butterfield, who got a green one.

We finished recording what we thought was going to be the first Butterfield Blues Band album [later released as *The Original Lost Elektra Sessions*]. Edited it, which took a month. I finally completed it, and it was sitting in boxes, ready to be shipped, when Jac Holzman and I flew up to Martha's Vineyard to visit Tom Rush for a few days and eat zucchini. While I had him up in the plane I said, "Jac, I want to scrap the Butterfield album."

I thought he was going to have a cardiac arrest right then and there. He wanted to know why. I said, "Because I haven't captured the band. 'Born in Chicago' is the only good cut. The rest of it sucks." He got really upset. "We've spent more on this album than we've ever spent before, and you want to scrap it? What do you want to do?" And I said, "I want to record them live. I want to capture that live feeling." By the time we landed he had agreed, and that's when we set up the gig at the Cafe Au Go Go.

We brought in a recording truck, and we discovered how much it cost to record at union rates in New York City. We recorded four nights—miles of tape. I listened back to the tapes for two weeks with Butterfield, and we didn't have 30 consecutive seconds of good music. We had nothing, absolutely nothing.

During that time, I called George Wein and asked him to put them on at the Newport Folk Festival that summer. I called Albert Grossman and told him I had a band that was way beyond my capabilities and asked if he would consider managing them. He came down and heard them and said, "I'll see them at Newport."

Drivin' Bob Dylan

Ron Butkovich Things were happening at a quick pace. All of a sudden, Michael was a pretty famous guy. It accelerated very quickly. Michael and Susie lived up on the North Side, and I'd come over every once in a while. He'd give me a lesson, or we'd just hang out.

One day, he said, "Look, I got a call." For some reason he ran it by me. He said, "Ron, what do you think of this? I got a call from this guy Bob Dylan. He wants me to play on his album." And I said, "Wow, it sounds great." But Michael says, "Look, this guy's terrible. He can't sing. He really can't sing. Do you think I should do it?" And I said, "Of course you should do it."

I don't know why he would even question it. It was Michael's way of thinking. He said, "God, this guy can't sing. He can't play guitar, either. But I might give it a shot. The bread's good."

Michael Bloomfield I had heard the first Dylan album when it came out. I thought it was just terrible music. I couldn't believe this guy was so well touted. I went down to see him when he played in Chicago. I wanted to meet him, cut him, get up there and blow him off the stage. He couldn't really sing, y'know. But to my surprise he was enchanting. I don't know what he had, but he got over.

Bob Dylan I was playing in a club in Chicago, and I was sitting in a restaurant—I think it was probably across the street or maybe it was even a part of the club, I'm not sure—but a guy came down and said that he played guitar. He had his guitar with him, and I said, "Well, what can you play?" And he played all kinds of things—Big Bill Broonzy, Sonny Boy Williamson, that type of thing. He just played circles around anything I could play, and I always remembered that.

Michael Bloomfield He could get over better than anybody I ever saw. I thought Jack Elliott was the best single guy, for just a man with a guitar, for getting over, I mean—winning you. But Bob got over better than anyone I'd ever seen in my whole life. Anyway, we jammed that day, and way later he phoned me up. He remembered me, and he asked me to come play on his record.

Bob Dylan We were back in New York, and I needed a guitar player on a session I was doing. I called him up, and he came in and recorded an album. At that time he was working in the Paul Butterfield Blues Band.

Michael Bloomfield Dylan picked me up at the airport, and we passed this big, huge mansion with this old *kocker* sitting out front who looked vaguely familiar to me. This Benjamin Franklin guy. I said, "Who's that?" and Dylan said, "Oh, that's Albert." That's when I met Grossman and got to know him a little. He's very hard to get to know pretty well.

You wouldn't believe what those sessions were like. There was no concept. No one knew what they wanted to play, no one knew what the music was supposed to sound like—other than Bob, who had the chords and the words and the melody. But as far as saying, "We're gonna make folk-rock records" or whatever, no one had any idea what to do. None. They had the best studio drummer. They had a bass player, a terrific guy, Russ Savakus. It was his first day playing electric bass, and he was scared about that. No one understood nothing.

Al Kooper The first time I met Michael was at the Dylan session for "Like a Rolling Stone." No one knew who he was. He was in the Butter Band, but they had no records out. They weren't known outside of Chicago. The first time I heard about Bloomfield was when I read about him in *Sing Out* magazine. There was a picture of him that really didn't—I mean, when I met him, I knew that the picture was off a lot. They had a picture of him and a little blurb about him—this is the hotshot guitar player from Chicago. So when I met him, I had that as my only reference.

It's pretty funny—it was in New York, and he came into the studio with his Telecaster, without a case. He had it on his shoulder like some guy in a platoon or Johnny Appleseed or something. It was all wet, because it was raining out. He just wiped it off with a towel, plugged it in, let's go—you know, that kind of thing. So he endeared himself to me right away, with that stunt.

He was very funny. He cracked me up. He had a great sense of humor. And he was very primitive. He could tell a story pretty darn good. He certainly could tell a lot of lies, but they were—they made great stories, anyway. And what difference did it make? I mean, he could tell a story so good, you didn't care. The primitiveness and the humor were the key things for me.

Michael Bloomfield The producer was a non-producer—Tom Wilson. He didn't know what was happening. I think they wanted rock & roll. We did 20 alternate takes of every song, and it got ridiculous. These were long songs, and poor Dylan was cranking out these versions of "Desolation Row," doing it three times and finally saying, "Do you guys realize this is a 10-minute song? And you're making me do it three times?"

It was never like, "Here's one of the tunes, and we're gonna learn it and work out the arrangement." That just wasn't done. The thing just sort of fell together in this haphazard, half-assed way. It was like a jam session.

The album was astutely mixed. I believe it was mixed by Dylan. He had a sound in his mind, because he had heard records by the Byrds that knocked him out. He wanted me to play like McGuinn. That's what he was shooting for. It was even discussed. He said, "I don't want any of that B.B. King shit, man."

Michael Ochs Archives

Bob Dylan and Michael, 1965.

Dylan would play me Cher's versions of his songs. And different English versions, Animals' versions, but the Byrds' sound was what he wanted to get in his sessions. I don't think he was into getting a producer and letting himself rest in the producer's hands. He didn't want to log the studio time that someone like the Beatles or the Stones had, so that your records sound good—or if they don't sound good, at least you can drive for a certain kind of sound. He never wanted to log that time. And it's a pity.

Al Kooper We had lunch on break at one of the sessions, and Bloomfield assumed that I would go on and play live with Dylan. He said, "Yeah, you're going to make all kinds of money, and get chicks, and have a great time. But I would never leave Butterfield's band. I'm a blues guy. You're going to be on the cover of *Time* magazine. And I'm going to be in Chicago, playing the blues with Butterfield."

●　●　●

Nick Gravenites In July of 1965, the Butterfield Band was going to play the Newport Folk Festival. After the festival, they were going to record in New York. So Paul, of course, was very excited and ready to go. But he was also real nervous and apprehensive. He asked his friends to go with him—you know, like the support group. And a bunch of us did. We all got in our cars and drove back east to Newport; a whole gang of us went out east for that trip.

I participated a little bit in some of the workshops that they had at Newport. I sat in with Butter at one. I did a few of my numbers. It was a pretty exciting time. See, the vested interests of folk music—the people who owned it, essentially—didn't want to see these new people come in.

When Butterfield's band was introduced, it was almost an insulting introduction by Alan Lomax. I mean, he insulted them onstage. It was something like, "Well, they've got this band from Chicago. Some people feel that white people can't play the blues, and some people feel they can—you make up your own mind. Here they are." It was like—why didn't you just say "fuck you" while you're at it? And then Butterfield came up and did his routine. That whole folk festival, there was really a lot of turmoil going on. And that Butterfield introduction—I know that Albert Grossman and Alan Lomax got into a fight backstage. They were rolling around in the dirt. Grossman didn't like what he did to his guy, you know. Butter was his guy then.

Michael Bloomfield Alan Lomax, the great folklorist and musicologist, gave us some sort of introduction that I didn't even hear, but Albert found it offensive. And Albert went upside his head. The next thing we knew, right in the middle of our show, Lomax and Grossman were kicking ass on the floor in the middle of thousands of people at the Newport Folk Festival. Tearing each others' clothes off. We had to pull 'em apart. We figured, "Albert, man, now there's a manager!" We used to call him "Cumulus Nimbus"—he was such a vague guy. It was so hard to understand what he was saying. The Gray Cloud.

Eric Von Schmidt I can tell you a little bit about the '65 festival at Newport. I was the guy they chose to run the blues workshop—they called it "Bluesville" that year. It was run pretty loose at that time. They had a list of people, and the guy that was listed as the closer was Mike Bloomfield. Just his name. I'd never heard of him. I asked Geoff Muldaur, "You ever heard of Mike Bloomfield?" He said, "Oh, he's a great guitar player." That was all I knew. I had no idea who he was, and there was no introduction or anything like that.

It was a long afternoon, and it was getting quite windy, and somebody— I guess it was one of the musicians or maybe it was one of the roadies—said, "Well, can we set up here for the band?" I didn't even realize that this was going to be a band playing, but I didn't care—that sounded fine with me. I said, "Sure, go ahead and set up." This was back when no one was plugging in all that much. People were playing acoustic, so for the most part it was just a question of setting up some mikes. But here these guys come with amps and drums. And it took them maybe half an hour to set up.

I was waiting around, and Alan Lomax came up to me and said, "Eric, would it be okay if I introduced the group?" By this time, I'd found out it was Paul Butterfield and his band. I said, "Sure, it's okay with me." I figured, Well, I'll get a chance to just kick back and listen. So I walked away as Alan started off on what turned out to be a diatribe about white boys playing the blues. It wasn't just that they were electric. It was that they were white. Because by that time, Chicago was totally electric. Muddy and all the people that he had championed were electric. But this was white kids playing electric blues.

I didn't really hear it all. I walked off. I kind of got the gist of it and thought, I don't need to listen to this shit, because I don't agree with it. And I was tired. I'd had a few sips and was just feeling like hanging out. I thought, I'll wait 'til the band starts and hear the music. I don't have to listen to Alan Lomax. Actually, I respect Alan in many ways, and I think that book, *The Land Where the Blues Began*, is pretty damn good. It's got some great stuff in it.

So I walked off, and then I wandered back when they finally kicked it off. I don't know how long Alan rattled on, but I do know Albert Grossman and Lomax had a fist fight. Grossman sought out Alan and said, "That's the worst introduction I've ever heard in my fuckin' life." That was what started it. And the classic moment was—see, they're both pretty hefty guys. And they both threw roundhouse punches at the same time and missed and fell down, both of them, in huge clouds of dust. That kind of broke it up. They didn't need anybody to come in there and break it up. I think by the time they got erect again and dusted themselves off, they realized they'd made total fools of themselves, so they'd better quit. At any rate, that was one of the events of the '65 festival.

Maria Muldaur When the Butterfield Blues Band started playing Chicago-style blues music with amplified instruments, a lot of the old guard was passing judgment and deciding it wasn't true folk music. But it was not something contrived. The natural evolution of blues music in Chicago was to plug in. And the Butterfield Band was one of the best examples of that. Of course, they had grown up in Chicago and learned from the masters.

They were just so truly electrifying, no pun intended. I loved it. I was dancing, that was my reaction to it. I was jumping out of my skin. Everybody I was hanging with thought it was just incredible. So that was a very memorable moment in the music scene.

Fritz Richmond For the Butterfield set, I was standing right in front—over on one side, but right up against the fence. It was shaped like an orchestra pit, and right in front was an area that was full of photographers. Performers could get in the next section back from that without any problems, so that's where I stood.

I had not seen Mike Bloomfield play until the Newport Folk Festival. I just loved the way he looked. He was so into it, so fidgety. He was all over the guitar—he wouldn't let it alone for an instant, and he shook it all around. It was like he was in a fight with it all the time. It was marvelous to watch. He was hunched over it. And you didn't get the impression that he really had to look at it, like an amateur player. He was just staring it down. It was beautiful. I'd never seen anybody who was so visual playing an instrument. He would have made great television.

Eric Von Schmidt The reaction of the crowd to the Butterfield Blues Band set was very positive. I didn't notice anybody getting up or walking out on that thing. It was a big crowd. As I say, the wind was kicking up, and the sun was going down, and the people were loving it. People were dancing. There was no doubt about how they felt about it all. It was very positive. Then I found out that Dylan was going to use the band, and I thought, "Well, that ought to be interesting."

Nick Gravenites It was just a spur-of-the-moment thing. When they were putting the band together, there was a meeting at a big house in Newport—George Wein's house. Michael was there with Dylan and Dylan's sidekick, Bobby Neuwirth, and Albert Grossman and a few other people.

Michael was brilliant as a guitarist and as a musician. He knew how to do stuff. People would come in, and he knew what Dylan's stuff was going to be like. He knew all the chord changes and stuff. And he'd waltz people through the chord changes. If they could cut them, they'd be part of the band. If they couldn't—"Next." They got the band together that way. Michael was, essentially, the leader. He's the guy that selected the band. He figured that these guys could cut it and do it.

Al Kooper Michael and I had already recorded some things with Bob. The 45 of "Like a Rolling Stone" was released two weeks before the Newport festival, so people were walking around singing it at the festival before Dylan even played. I went to the Newport festival as a concert-goer. I had played on the record and a week had gone by, and then my wife and I went up to Massachusetts and visited some relatives—like a vacation. I bought tickets, and we went to the festival. I used to go to the festival every year.

The first day, I ran into Albert Grossman. He said, "You know, Bob's looking for you." He gave me some passes, and I sold my tickets. Bloomfield was playing there with the Butterfield Band, so they decided to have the Butterfield Band back up Dylan with me. The rehearsal was in some millionaire's mansion, and it was all night. Paul Rothchild put it together. And it was pretty fun—I mean, it was a good rehearsal. It was a lot better than the show was. Michael got Barry Goldberg to play, also.

Barry Goldberg I got to play with Dylan quite by accident. Michael and Paul had asked me to go to Newport to play with the Butterfield Band. I was their first keyboard player. I would sit in with them all the time. I said I'd love to, so I went with them. When we got there, Paul Rothchild was really obstinate and rude. He said, "Absolutely no organ." He didn't want that element—he just wanted the five pieces. Paul and Michael tried to talk to him, but he was really against it. So I had nowhere to go. I was stuck there, a long way from Chicago.

One night we were just sitting around, and Bob showed up and said, "The keyboard player isn't here yet." Michael said, "There's a great keyboard player here—Barry." Bob said, "You want to come to the sound check?" And I said, "Sure." That's how I got to do it, and it worked out great.

Michael was playing guitar, and he used Sam Lay on drums and Jerome Arnold on bass and myself on keyboards. And then Kooper came in, later, from New York. That was the band. That was Bob's first electric concert performance. So I didn't get to play with Paul, but I got to play with Dylan. I was really fortunate, as it turned out. It turned an unpleasant experience into a great one.

Nick Gravenites On the way to the festival that evening for Dylan's show, I was part of the entourage. Albert asked me to drive one of the cars, and the guy I drove to the gig was Bob Dylan. So I was his chauffeur. He didn't say a word. But I could just imagine the pressure he was under. It was that kind of an affair. Later on in the evening, when Dylan came out and played electric, the people went nuts. They were booing him. The whole folk festival became a really crazy affair.

Maria Muldaur I was sitting with my friend Betsy Siggins, who helped run the Club 47. We were very excited. We both knew Dylan, and we'd already decided we were fans of the Butterfield Band, so we thought this was going to be great. The guys came out and plugged in, and that sent a ripple of reaction through the crowd.

They started to play and it was very loud. Back in those days nobody even had monitors, as far as I know, and the guys hired to work the sound system hadn't had a lot of experience with loud, electric music. But what really blew my mind was the negative reaction of the crowd. A third of them booed, a third of them cheered, and the other third didn't know what to do.

Betsy and I turned to each other in amazement, because every other time we'd seen Dylan perform it was like he was God and could do no wrong. And this was a very unexpected reaction.

Barry Goldberg We went on that night, and Michael just went nuts. He rammed it right down their throats. He loved those kind of things. I thought it was an amazingly brave and bold move—Dylan plugging in. And the old folk crowd, the old guard, was standing fast. They felt so threatened that a new thing was happening—out with the old and in with the new.

But it was more about a new frontier of music called folk-rock. And electric blues was happening. So many people got turned on by it. Unfortunately, the majority of the crowd there was die-hard folkies who didn't want to accept this no matter what. They wanted to make their presence

Michael, Bob Dylan, Elvin Bishop (behind Bob Dylan),Sam Lay, Jerome Arnold, and Barry Goldberg at the Newport Folk Festival, July 25,1965.

known and make a statement, so a lot of people booed. But I remember a lot of people cheering, too. It was probably 60 percent booing and 40 percent cheering. I remember Michael counting it off and saying, "Let's go!" and it was like POW!—we went into this whirlwind. Bob was like a warrior, and we were all on this mission.

Michael Bloomfield When I played with Dylan, I thought they loved us— but they were booing. I heard a noise. I thought it was, "Yeah, great band!" But they were booing. I said, "Well, Bob, we knocked their asses in the dirt." And he said, "I thought it was boos, man."

Eric Von Schmidt Dylan got up there playing electric with a band that was vaguely in control. I was one of the first people that started hollering, "Turn up Dylan's mike, turn down the guitar." The first number, "Maggie's Farm"— I mean, I knew some of the words and I could occasionally hear something. But there was no way of stopping Bloomfield in the midst of that thing. It was atrocious.

It was obvious that Bloomfield was out to kill. He had his guitar turned up as loud as he could possibly turn it up, and he was playing as many notes as he could possibly play. I thought it was terrible. I thought, "Well, this is music, not just a fuckin' bunch of notes." I admire his music, but at that moment he was just a note machine. And I was wishing they would turn him off. "Maggie's Farm" was one of my favorite Dylan songs, but Bloomfield couldn't have cared less whether they were playing "Maggie's Farm" or "Old McDonald Had a Farm." It was just his moment to scream. It was like a little kid in the middle of the floor kicking his heels: Me, me, me, me, let's hear how many notes I can play.

They finally got it a little bit under control. Rothchild went up there and turned down Mike and tried to get a balance where Dylan could be heard. But by that time things were pretty much out of control, and people were shouting that they couldn't hear Dylan—you know, to turn up Dylan's mike.

Farther back in the crowd, other things were happening. I know that some people were booing. Some people walked out in a huff. There were people that were thinking that Dylan had sold out. To me, it was just music. I wanted to hear the music, and I wanted to be able to hear the singer. In the case of "Maggie's Farm," Dylan wrote it—and who's this kid playing the screaming goddamned guitar? I didn't really get into the politics of it, but I guess there were people who did.

Sam Lay At Newport when we played with Bob Dylan, they kind of booed us. They didn't boo us because it was us. They didn't want Bob Dylan playing with electrical instruments.

Al Kooper No, that's not true. At Newport—the legend is just not true. I was there. I understand exactly what happened. I would have booed myself, if I was in the audience. What happened is that they had paid top dollar to see Dylan. No matter who was on the show that night, Bob Dylan was advertised as playing. He came out and played three songs and said, "Thank you very much. Good night." And people went nuts. A lot of them had sat through three days of music that they didn't understand or care about just to hear their idol play. And then he sang three songs and took a hike. They were angry. They were in disbelief—"What do you mean? Three songs? That's it?"

We had stayed up all night the night before rehearsing, and we only got three songs together. I'm not so sure Dylan wanted to play more than that. That's why they were booing. They didn't boo until that particular moment. There's a film, and I defy you to point out a boo to me until the last song is over and he says, "That's it" and leaves. There *was* booing, but it wasn't for that reason. And then people wrote, "Oh, they booed them off the stage," which couldn't be further from the truth.

Michael's playing that night was pretty wild. It was raw. Again, I keep coming back to that primitive thing. The whole set was not really great. In the middle of "Maggie's Farm," the beat got turned around. I was embarrassed by that—half the band was playing on *one* and *three*, and half the band was playing on *two* and *four*. That was weird. We came off, and Sam Lay really felt bad, because he was the drummer. It was pretty brutal. I thought it was a dreadful performance, myself. I didn't think it was historic.

Peter Yarrow was screaming at Dylan, "Go out and play some more!" Bob said, "We only rehearsed three songs." So Peter said, "Well, go out and play acoustic." They gave him a guitar, and he went out and played. I thought it was pretty funny—he played "It's All Over Now, Baby Blue." I thought that was the key thing, more than the booing. That was the thing they should have talked about, but it was always swept under the carpet. He played three burning electric tunes, and then he came out and said, "It's all over now, baby blue." I mean, that's the thing they should have paid attention to, not that stupid booing thing.

● ● ●

Al Kooper After Newport, we came back to New York and finished the *Highway 61* album. They wanted the band that was on the record to be the band that went out live, but Michael really wasn't interested. There was nothing they could dangle in his face to make him do it.

Harvey Brooks After the sessions, we had a discussion. Dylan had some gigs coming up—we were going to do Forest Hills and the Hollywood Bowl. But Michael was going to stay with Butterfield, because he felt that was his obligation and that's what he should do. That's what he felt was best for him. He said we'd go on and be stars and everything, but he was going to play the blues.

Michael Bloomfield Since Grossman managed both Butterfield and Dylan, I figured he would say, "Well, I think you'd be most effective *here*. Or most effective *there*." I probably would have bowed to his judgment, even against the wishes and dictates of my own soul. My own soul told me to play with Paul.

I could see even then that Bob was real thrilling, but idolatry and charisma and all like that was almost becoming more important. I just thought I wouldn't get a chance to play enough music, enough licks. Seriously, to move my fingers enough—I don't care if I'm moving 'em in the back.

Nick Gravenites It wasn't so much playing with Paul. He wanted to play blues. He loved Bob Dylan. Bob Dylan was a *landsman*, which in Yiddish is a compatriot. He was a good guy. I met him a few times back in those days, and he was just an ordinary, nice person. "Hello, how are you," you know—that sort of thing. Formal courtesies. This wasn't a weird, freaky guy. It takes a little time in this business before they turn you into a fuckin' monster. A lot of times you get trapped in your persona—you're supposed to be Bob Dylan, so you're Bob Dylan, you know.

Michael Bloomfield With Bob, I'd have had no identity. I didn't even know that—all I knew was that I didn't understand what was happening. At the same time, I was being offered a gig as the guitar player on a TV show called *Shindig*. I was supposed to be in the Shindogs. They had set it all up. The idea of going to LA and being a Shindog instead of being a bluesman was just crazy.

I told Albert, "Man, I'm a bluesman. I'll go with Butterfield." So I played with Butter and didn't play with Dylan, and we were cookin'. We wailed from then on.

Butterfield
Adds an Organ

Mark Naftalin I was going to school in New York City, at the Mannes College of Music, when the Paul Butterfield Blues Band showed up. They were recording again with Rothchild. The recordings they had made earlier in the summer, when Mike was new in the group, had been rejected as a first album. Listening to them now, I can understand why. To me, the band doesn't sound gelled yet as five pieces. Whatever their reasons were, they were back in the studio, trying again.

I dropped by the session, hoping for a chance to sit in on organ, which was the only keyboard on the scene. Someone, probably Paul Rothchild, said that they might try organ later in the session. I was too impatient to hang around. I went home and came back the next day, sometime in the mid-to-late afternoon. On this occasion Elvin was late for the session. This was four-track recording, so they put me on his channel, and we played an instrumental.

I had never played a Hammond organ before, so my sound is not what you might call "informed." But they threw it over to me for a solo, and I made it through. They seemed to like the track, so they invited me to stay on organ. When Elvin came, I shared his track, continuing to play as the session stretched to nine hours. If Elvin minded sharing his track with me, he didn't say anything about it.

During the session, Paul asked if I could join the band and go on the road with them that weekend to the Philadelphia Folk Festival. I said that I could. As things turned out, of the 11 songs on the first Butterfield album eight are from that session. The instrumental that we started with is included, called "Thank You Mr. Poobah."

Mike later told me that during the session he told Paul something to the effect of, "You didn't hire Barry"—referring to Barry Goldberg—"so you'd better hire this guy"—referring to me. I never tried to verify it with Paul. In any case, it was nice that Mike wanted to take credit.

The engineers had trouble getting a good recording of Sam Lay's vocal on "Got My Mojo Working," because of all the leakage of the drum sound into the vocal mike. For that reason, his vocal on that song was over-dubbed. Other than that, there are no overdubs on the album. Nor do I recall any attempts at repairing or altering parts by punching in. In other words, what you hear on the record is nothing more than a mixed version of what was played live in the studio.

That day, September 9, 1965, was one of the happiest of my life.

Carlos Santana The first time that I heard the Paul Butterfield Blues Band, friends of mine turned me on to it. We were in Mission High School. That left an incredible impact on my mind about a new kind of blues, different than what I was used to hearing. It didn't sound dated. It didn't sound like something that was done in the '30s or '40s or '50s. It didn't sound like an old stove where you burn logs. It sounded like a new stove where you burn with electricity. In other words, the electricity of the blues. It had a different electricity than Muddy Waters, although it came from all those people.

That album, to this day, is something that should not be ignored, because it was a great contribution to bringing back the blues into the mainstream. All of a sudden, everybody that I knew, they were playing "Born in Chicago." And if you couldn't play "Born in Chicago," you just couldn't cut it. That was the thing.

Fritz Richmond *The Paul Butterfield Blues Band.* That first album. It's one of the great albums. When that album came out, I was on the road with the Kweskin band. We had a certain routine when we would hit a strange city, or even a city we'd been in before. We couldn't afford to stay in public accommodations, so we always stayed with people we knew or people that we would meet when we got to town. And one of the things we would always try to do was organize a party at somebody's house. Anybody in the band who needed a place to stay knew that it was important to go to this party.

The way we would get these parties going was to play records. We would carry around a few records that were very good to serve this purpose, and I carried the Butterfield album. That was worth about two bottles of whiskey, as far as getting a party going. That album and the Junior Walker *Shotgun* album were wonderful for that.

Michael listening to playback during recording of the first Butterfield Blues Band album, A&R Studios, New York, 1965.

I'll tell you one very specific thing. The album was a multi-track recording—I think it may have been three-track or four-track—so there needed to be mixing sessions to combine it down to the left and right for stereo. I was at some of those sessions with Paul Rothchild, who did it essentially all by himself. The band was not present. At one point in "Shake Your Money-Maker" there is a series of slides that Mike Bloomfield does on the bottom string of the guitar. It sort of sounds like a bomber going over. He did that four times—every two bars, at one point in the song. I thought that was the greatest thing. I picked up on that, and I said to Paul Rothchild, "That is a hit lick. We've got to push that." And Paul was a little reluctant to push it up—to make it take the lead at that point.

Well, let me take an aside here and explain to you this business of multi-track recording and electric instruments. Nobody knew how to do that. Even the Chicago bands recorded mono—they weren't on these big-budget folk labels that could afford to go into the best studios. The Chess brothers were cutting every penny just trying to get the records out there. Paul was a very conservative producer and tended not to do sudden shifts of volume of individual instruments. But I kept pulling on his sleeve, and, finally, I kind of got my way. And to this day, I think it sounds great. Everybody that heard it loved it. I think I really helped out that song.

Elvin Bishop Recording an album was just a mind-blower. There was nothing like that in anybody's experience before, anything remotely like it. And it was a heavy thing. The recording was done completely live. Some of it was one take; some of it was 50 takes.

Sam Lay The first few jobs we played after we recorded, Butterfield gave us a little money. Bloomfield didn't like that, and he raised all kinds of hell. Butterfield came back the same night after Bloomfield raised so much hell about it, and he paid us more than double. See, Butterfield told Mike what he was paying us. And that's what pissed him off. It wasn't, "Hey, man, you got to pay me more money." It was, "Hey, Butter, why don't you pay them guys more than what you're paying them?" He wouldn't let nobody take advantage of us.

Michael Bloomfield Paul was a despot, as far as the money was concerned. And I remember when Paul's despotism as far as the money stopped. We went to Elektra one day. We were sitting around the hotel—we always stayed at these rotten hotels, the Albert Hotel and stuff—we were sitting around thinking, and I said, "Paul, y'know, I bet we have some money at Elektra from the Butter album."

He said, "Yeah, I think I'll go down there and get $1,000." And I said, "I think I'm gonna do it, too. I'm gonna go down and get $1,000, too." And he purses up his mouth like a fish. He makes this fish mouth at me and says, "Man, look, I think I'm gonna go down and get $1,000. This is my trip, and maybe some other time you can go down and get $1,000." He said, "I don't want you to blow...."

I said, "You mean, you don't want me to go down and blow your $1,000?" I said, "Listen, Paul, the whole band's going down, and we're getting $6,000." And that's what we did. We went to Jac Holzman and said, "We want $6,000." Which was, I think, pretty cheap, as we had never gotten an advance or nothing. I don't think we even got session pay. And he forked over a check. We said, "Now listen, you gotta help us cash it. Cash it right now. We want green cash money." So he took us to the Chemical Bank of New York and got it cashed.

Mark Naftalin For the performance at the Philadelphia Folk Festival, I was fitted out with a portable organ. It was the prototype of an instrument that the Guild company, in the end, never put into production. I got an instrument to use, and the Guild company got their instrument, with logo emblazoned, pictured on the back cover of the first Butterfield album. That Guild organ was a real drag. Picture me trying to play manly music alongside the likes of Paul Butterfield with an instrument far worse than a Farfisa. I did the best I could with it for months, until I was able to get a Hammond.

After this, the band—now six pieces—went back to Chicago. We played five or six weeks at Big John's on Wells Street on the North Side, which had been the band's home base for a while. During this time, I slept in a sleeping bag on Jerome Arnold's living-room floor and walked to work. The pay for the gig was $100 a week for the musicians. Butterfield, as leader, got $200. This was for five nights, from nine each evening 'til four the next morning, five a.m. on Friday and Saturday nights. I was accumulating money faster than I'd ever been able to, my previous jobs having been in the $2.50 per hour range.

On this gig, Mike and I developed the ritual of walking along a certain route during our set breaks, smoking joints. This we referred to as the "Wells Street Promenade." The door charge at Big John's at this time was, I believe, 50 cents, and may have gone to a dollar. After work we typically went out to breakfast, then home to sleep.

To me the band was a warm family, and I felt altogether accepted, though sometimes musically inadequate. I retain a vivid memory of Paul looking at me over his harp with such an intense expression of what I thought was disapproval that I later sat on the curb and shed private tears. I think he was trying to get me to play right, and God knows I was trying.

From Big John's we went back to the East Coast, for five or six weeks at the Unicorn in Boston. On the way back, Mike and I stayed a night with Sam Lay's family in Cleveland. In the morning, I—not much of a breakfast person in those days—politely, I thought, refused the offered morning meal. Mike later chided me roundly and soundly, mercilessly describing the scene as he saw it, with the younger children of the house, denied, in his version, food—because of me—looking on in envious disbelief.

During the Boston gig, Mike and I stayed in a duplex in Cambridge. The band was sounding great, the crowds were going crazy, and there was much excitement. We were listening to a widening range of music, including Indian classical music, particularly that of Ravi Shankar.

Mike and I had been given some LSD, which was on sugar cubes and represented as being "Leary acid." On one of our nights off, we took it. Early in the trip we ventured outside onto the wintry street, without a destination—without, in fact, the ability to conceive a destination. Perhaps as an alternative to heading in a direction, Mike unzipped his fly and relieved himself in the street. It may have been my attempt at discouraging this behavior that moved him to ask the rhetorical question that was later quoted from time to time: "Can this little lump of flesh offend?"

Later in the evening, Mike sequestered himself for a few hours, of which I remember only the melting paintings flowing down the walls. Around daybreak Mike joined me in the kitchen, and we tried to keep things going by smoking some joints. This was when he told me that he had had a revelation and that he now understood how Indian music worked. On our next gigs, while we were still in Boston, we began performing the improvisation that we called "The Raga" for a while, until it was given a name: "East-West."

This song was based, like Indian music, on a drone. In Western musical terms, it stayed on the "I." Elvin started with a long solo, then retreated to a *tamboura*-like droning role while Mike soloed on a sequence of sections, using a different mode in each section. Some of the modes were more Eastern, some more Western. Paul came in with some bluesy wailing toward the end. I didn't play any solos but tried to stay with the soloists through the moods and modes as they proceeded.

Michael Bloomfield I had been hearing the names of jazz guys for years and years, and I didn't know how it all fit together. And so this guy Pete Welding, from *Downbeat* magazine, started giving me a jazz jam course, just playing me the history of jazz—endless hours and hours of records.

I didn't really draw upon this in my music. The only thing I drew upon was that you could improvise for a long, long, long time on certain modes or themes, and not just play straight blues. You could play a lot of other things, and it would fit, too. That sort of half-assed pseudo-jazz—I didn't really think of it as jazz—that way of playing, became my own personal vehicle for improvisation, coupled with some other things that I'd heard in Indian music, although I didn't play anything that was like pure Indian music.

Mark Naftalin The studio version of "East-West," as heard on the Elektra album of the same name, is 10 or 12 minutes of relatively toned-down playing. On stage, the song was longer and wilder. The climax of the song, at the end of the concluding section, had everybody droning and wailing to beat the band. Later, as the piece developed, I dropped "Joy to the World" into

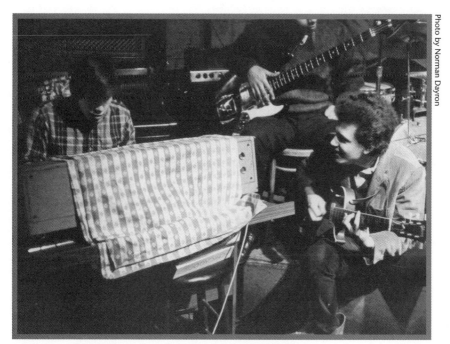

Mark Naftalin, Jerome Arnold, and Michael, December 1965.

that section, with all stops out, in quadruple octaves. The band played "East-West" for over a year, until Mike left the group. After that, we never played it again.

As the Boston gig wound up, Sam Lay became very ill with a condition known as pleural effusion. I believe this happened because he made a practice of coming off the bandstand steaming and going directly into the cold New England air without a jacket. Mike and I visited him in Cook County Hospital in Chicago, where we found him lying in an underlit and uncomfortably crowded ward. He spent some weeks there but emerged in good health.

Sam Lay I left the band when I took sick and was unable to play. Once I got well I wasn't going to play no more, but kind of after all that sickness I started to work with the James Cotton Blues Band. I didn't go back to Paul.

Mark Naftalin Paul had hired Billy Warren, a Chicago drummer, to take Sam's place. It was wrenching when he was sent back to Chicago, deemed unsuitable for the job. I think he had given up steady employment in Chicago to go on the road with us. But it was obvious that it wasn't going to work. I was glad not to be the band leader. Then Paul miraculously turned up the incomparable Billy Davenport to be our drummer, and he was with us when we flew to California over New Year's.

Billy Davenport I knew Mike before I knew Paul. I played with Otis Rush, and I worked with Magic Sam. I also played with Fenton Robinson, and I worked a little while with Corky Siegel during that period. That's when I met Michael—maybe April or May of 1965. I was working with Junior Wells at Theresa's, 48th and Indiana, and Mike would come down and sit in with the band. We was playing the blues, and he was right there, following with no problem. This was a surprise to me. I never did give it too much of a thought, because I had never come across a white fellow who's playing blues guitar. But then it got to me: This guy knew what he was doing. He was playing the blues, but playing it in a different way. But you could still feel what he was doing.

Eventually, Elvin and Paul would come around and sit in, and then they invited me over one time to where they was playing at. I sat in with them one night, and I realized they were gooder than I thought they were.

Then, about October or November '65, Mike came down and sat in and played with the band. I was working with Fenton Robinson. And Mike said, "Man, if I ever need a drummer, I'll give you a call, because I like some stuff that you do there. Playing jazz mixed up with blues." And so about December he called me. He said that Sam was sick and might be leaving the band pretty soon. I told him, "No." I didn't want to go on the road, because I was afraid. I had played with a lot of mixed bands around the Chicago area, but never on the road. It kind of put a little fear in me. I said, "You know, with all the stuff going on, man, I don't know."

He let it go. He got a guy named Bill Warren out of Chicago, but Bill didn't click with the band. They was in Detroit, and I was working Pepper's with Fenton Robinson. I was making $15 a night, which was no money, but it was good in '65. Mike called me on that Friday and said, "Man, we're going to need a drummer. Because the drummer we got, he's going to have to go." I said, "Okay, man, let me know." I didn't know he meant, like, next week. He called me that Saturday about two or three times. He said, "Man, come on." I said, "Well, man, I'm not sure. Because I got a wife and she depend on me and everything, no kids or nothing."

That Sunday, when we was closing out the gig, Mike stayed on that phone for about one hour. I had somebody else play in my place while he was talking. Eventually, Paul got on the phone. And he said, "Man, you come on and go." I said, "Well, I never went out on the road with no mixed band like that. I don't know what might happen." And he said one thing that changed my mind. He said, "Billy, I'll tell you—where you can't go, we won't go." That was it. I said, "Okay." He sounded real serious, which he was.

I said, "Man, I'll be there in the morning." I closed that Sunday night and met them up in Detroit, me and my wife. I had $11 in my pocket. And I went from Detroit to Hollywood, California, with $11 in my pocket. The band helped me out on the way there.

I was fearful about going on the road with a mixed band at that time. I didn't know what was going to happen, so I had told my wife, "Well, I got this drum set I've had about three months. We get to California and it don't work out, we can get a Greyhound and come back home. We'll sell the drums, because I can always get some more drums."

Mark Naftalin In LA, the band settled into the Colonial West Motel on Sunset Strip. Our first engagement was two weeks at the Trip, which was a club in the Playboy building, also on the Strip. For the first week, we co-billed with the Byrds. Our second week at the Trip was a co-bill with Wilson Pickett.

A few weeks later, we moved down the Strip to the Whiskey Au Go Go. During our Whiskey gigs, where we worked with groups like the Leaves and the Grassroots, our routine included walking down the Strip to the club for a high-calorie dinner, then back to the motel to watch *Batman* on TV, then back to the club for the gig, and finally back to the motel.

The California clubs closed hours earlier than Chicago clubs, and during these early days in LA Mike and I spent most nights, after work, holed up in the large closet in my room, smoking joints and rapping for hours. We were in the closet because we thought that would protect us from detection as pot smokers. We kept our stash outside the room, under the stairway carpet. We got to know each other pretty well during this time. And this was when I started to see the seriousness of Mike's sleep disturbance.

Billy Davenport Hollywood was dead for the type of stuff we was playing at that time. We didn't really get started in Hollywood. We went over when we got to the Fillmore in San Francisco.

When we got to the Fillmore, it was frightening. We went onstage and nobody said nothing. The place was packed. They were just standing there looking. And then we played—we opened up with a medley or something—and, man, when we got through, them people was like they went crazy. We were surprised, because up 'til then it seemed that nothing was working. But after we played that one number, man, from there on the Fillmore was our place. I mean, they really gave us a warm welcome there.

Burning Down
the Fillmore

Michael Bloomfield The Butterfield Band made a record, and it did pretty good, and eventually we found ourselves booked in San Francisco in 1966. Of course, we had heard that there was something happening there. Chet Helms and Bill Graham were partners. We played for them and did real good, and Bill thought he could do real good next week, so he broke up his partnership with Chet and rented another hall.

Chet Helms I was managing Big Brother & the Holding Company. At that time, the clubs wouldn't book the long-hair bands, the psychedelic bands. So it kind of fell on people like myself and my partner, John Carpenter, who managed the Great Society with Grace Slick at the time, to create our own venues for these acts.

I know Bill Graham always loved to take the credit for it, but, fundamentally, John Carpenter and I, under the name Family Dog, were the first people to book the Butterfield Blues Band on the West Coast. John had known Bill previously, and we made a deal with him to do four shows in the Fillmore auditorium over about a four-month period. We were supposed to have alternate weekends, but somehow Graham never quite was straight with us about that. We always ended up with our dates being shoved around at his convenience.

We paid more for the Butterfield Blues Band than we could even imagine at that moment, which I don't think was all that great. It was something like 2,500 bucks for the weekend, but that seemed astronomical to us. I think we actually ended up running six or seven thousand people through there that weekend, at two bucks a head.

We fought Graham tooth and nail to do that show. He'd never heard of Butterfield—and, in all candor, I had not heard of him for any great length of time. It was just that he was making a little bit of a word-of-mouth stir among certain of my friends. And people were attracted to certain songs, like "Born in Chicago." At the time that we booked them, we checked with one of the West Coast distributors here. In all of California, they had sold 200 albums.

So John Carpenter and I decided to fly down to LA the weekend before our gig, just to meet Butterfield and all these guys. I have to say, to some degree we were sold on him being handled by Grossman and being part of the whole Joan Baez-Bob Dylan coterie. So we flew down to LA and went to this little jazz club. John and I sat there the whole evening and, basically, there was the band, the bartender, and us. We were pretty scared about it at that point, but we were also pretty committed, because we had really fought Graham to have that show. His only real control over it was that he had the lease on the hall, and at that point he got seven percent of our revenue, plus we paid him for cops and things like that.

Once we went to LA and saw how little they drew there, we kind of panicked. So the way we promoted that show was: John and I had personal phone directories of two or three hundred people, and we just got on the phone and said, "Are you going to be there for the Butterfield show? Who's Butterfield? You don't know who Paul Butterfield is?" And so on and so forth.

We had him for three nights. The first one was a Friday, and we did really well. Bill Graham told a famous story, which he was very fond of telling, about how he got up early—like 6:30 or something—so he could call Grossman on Saturday in New York. And, essentially, he bought the options on the next two or three years of their future dates in the Bay Area: "Hey, we're having a good evening here. We want to repeat this thing." So Graham made a deal with Grossman and locked up the Butterfield Band for the next two or three years in terms of Bay Area performances.

The things that make me angry about that story are: One, he was technically our partner, to the tune of seven percent, and as far as I'm concerned, he had no business going behind our back. Second, I really resent the fact that he laid such weight on the fact that I did not get up early the next day. I was the person—he didn't promote the show; he wasn't even there most of the evening. I promoted the show, I did the work, I was the guy who went home at four o'clock in the morning.

But he had run businesses before. I'd never run a business in my life. He had a number of important people, investors, behind him that he could go to for money. So there's an element of truth to it—that he was a businessman and we weren't.

Michael Bloomfield We realized from the get-go that Chet had no business at all happening for him. But if Bill had made us an offer directly, we probably wouldn't have gone with him. Because no one liked him. God knows what he was doing in San Francisco, in this peaceful, loving, acid scene. He was anti-drug.

I remember Mark Naftalin and me gazing at this insane guy on the stage, just at a sound check, no one in the place, but still freaking out. But I grew to love him in a really short time. It really endeared him to me, because this was a gung-ho crazy who could take care of business, too. As soon as I realized that he wouldn't hit me, that the guy wouldn't get so mad that he'd just jump on me and I'd have to fight him or something, then it was a lot of fun.

Bill Graham I met Mike Bloomfield in 1966, when he was a member of the Butterfield Blues Band out of Chicago. He came to play at the Fillmore. I got to know him better and better as they came back to play the Bay Area more often. And I kept in touch with him from time to time, primarily through music. We weren't socially friendly outside of the gigs, but the gigs were often enough so I had an ongoing relationship with him.

The impact of the Butterfield Blues Band the first time was rather awesome. There was another organization here in the Bay Area that put on dance shows, called the Family Dog. They had some problems getting facilities where they could put on their shows, and I was starting an arrangement where we would do shows together as partners at the Fillmore. The first ones that they brought in, through their awareness of the band—I did not have knowledge of them—was the Butterfield Blues Band. And that first weekend they played for three nights.

They just took the town by storm—the sound and the joy of the music, the Delta-based black roots music coming out of Chicago, and the make-up of the band. Obviously, the sound of a lead harp and a guitar player with Michael's talent and, also, Elvin on rhythm and the whole band—Jerome, Mark, Sam, and later Billy. The sound that came out—it was big-city, good-time, foot-stomping, happy Saturday night music.

Nobody ever played—nobody held the guitar the way Michael did. He cradled it. It was like a child to him, if you ever watched him. When he would get lost, he would just dance with it. And the way he'd move it, his body would surround the guitar. I don't know why or how it came about. Nobody took the guitar into the womb the way Michael did. Michael surrounded the guitar with his body. He became concave, and the guitar sort of fit inside that shape.

He had an extraordinary, big, fat sound. And "East-West"—if I only had one song to play at my wedding, it would be "East-West." To me, that is typical *Yid* wedding music, especially the breaks and the way Michael comes back in.

Michael's a very schmaltzy, very sensual, big-city *Yid,* as I am. And what's the best thing you can say about music—not the lyrical part of music, but music? It moves your senses or it makes you move. It's pelvic music. The Butterfield Blues Band played pelvic music. It made you want to move, made you feel good. You could feel it.

Nick Gravenites Bill Graham was totally freaked out by Bloomfield. Here was a *landsman* who was a brilliant guitarist, a crazy son of a bitch with a crazy sense of humor. They hit it off really well. Michael used to crack up Bill so much. I mean, just make him laugh. It was quite a show.

Bloomfield and Graham, they're both like funky Jews. They appreciate the funk side of existence. The two of them would get together and hold these mock arguments, these mock fights, and the only reason they were doing it was they were both showing off with their mouths. The convoluted arguments they could develop.

They hit it off like two long-lost brothers. I mean, they loved each other. And they were respectful of each other, too. Bill knew that Michael's father was a tough businessman, and Michael knew where Bill was coming from. He knew that Bill was a real tough businessman. Bill had a hot business, was starting to make some money, but he didn't necessarily know too much about the music.

Bill used to ask Michael, "Where the hell did you learn this stuff?" He'd never heard anything like Michael's guitar playing before in his life. And Michael would say, "Hey, I ain't shit. You should hear the guys I learned from." And Michael starts rattling off these names. Particularly, he says, "Well, I learned most of my stuff from the best guitar player alive on earth, named B.B. King." Bill said, "Who the hell's B.B. King?" He'd never heard of him. And Mike says, "He's a black guy. He's very famous in the black community. He's the best blues guitarist on earth."

Michael Bloomfield B.B. King was such an influence. I learned from him, and I know Clapton learned from him. We all learned from this man. He was like the Ravi Shankar, the guru. And he had to be recognized. The world had to know this genius for what he was.

B.B. King Michael was one of those disciples, if you will, that said, "I listened to B.B. King." He was one of those super guitar players that the kids liked. And I think that they felt if Michael Bloomfield said he listened to B.B. King, we'll listen to him, too. So that, to me, was—gosh, when someone is giving you a good representation, how much more could you get?

Nick Gravenites So Bill hired B.B. for the Fillmore, just on Michael's word that this guy was the best. And it was from that point that Bill started to hire blues bands along with the hippie bands. It was, essentially, Michael clueing him that there were all these great bands out there that he could hire. He didn't have to be dependent on the San Francisco talent pool. This expanded Bill's business immeasurably.

It was like payback. We weren't out there saying, "Oh yeah, we're great." We were saying, "Sure, we can play, but the guys who really are good, who taught us—they're the *real* players." And we tried to see if we could help the people that helped us. We were really happy to do that. Michael, I think, was the guy, *the* guy, that got a lot of the black blues bands playing in the major venues.

It was Michael a hundred percent, through his flashy talent, his whole trip with Bill Graham, turning Bill on to the black blues bands, and Bill jumping right in with both feet. So it wasn't a ripoff. It was like, "Thanks," you know.

Bill Graham It was Michael more than anyone. There were other musicians, but Michael was the first one that I befriended and who befriended me. He was a Chicago guy, I'm a New Yorker, and we hit it off, personality-wise. Michael was quick and very witty. And we were able to jabber on easily. He became very important to me. He and just a couple of other people were really my teachers, as far as who influenced their music and who they thought I should bring into the Bay Area, to expose to the predominantly white audience that came to rock & roll shows.

Michael, because of that constant nervous tic that he had, always had somebody that he was pushing. If it wasn't the Staple Singers, it was Albert King or B.B. King or Otis Redding or Howlin' Wolf. He, more than any single musician, kept bringing me records and mentioning groups to me. Prior to 1965, I knew nothing. I wasn't in the rock & roll world. It wasn't part of my private life. I'm a Latin music fan, a jazz fan of sorts, but I never listened to blues much or rock & roll at all.

I think the music industry owes Michael far more than they realize. Besides being a very special musician in what he brought out of the guitar

Paul Butterfield Blues Band, Town Hall concert,
New York City, 1966.

and how he made people feel. I don't know if I would have been that successful early on if it wasn't for Michael, his knowledge and his awareness and his prodding me to bring these artists to the Bay Area. So, as great a guitar player as Michael was, he was really a teacher.

At his prodding, and other people's, I eventually tried to contact some of these people. The Fillmore had gotten the reputation of being a psychedelic place, and for a lot of the blues artists that wasn't a good point. That was a negative point.

Michael Bloomfield We had been turned on to acid in Boston. We had heard—we didn't really know what was going on here, but we knew that it was supposed to have a lot to do with acid. Our consciousness had been changed by being acidheads. We didn't take it every day, but we took it as much as we could manage—several times a week at least. And we loved everybody, sort of—we were very young and receptive.

We got to San Francisco and met all these really nice people. I remember meeting Jorma and Jack of the Jefferson Airplane, and they were extremely friendly, very hospitable to us. Our first gig, I believe, was with the Airplane and Quicksilver.

Chet Helms The Butterfield Band finally played at the Fillmore for the first time. It was fantastic. They hadn't released their second album, *East-West*, yet, but they were working on it and were about to release it. It was quite a fantastic show, I thought.

I personally feel that over all those guys that are compared to him, Michael was *the* guitar player, period. I mean, I like Hendrix and I like Clapton and all that, but Michael was *the* guitar player, as far as I'm concerned.

I remember him being very giggly and just kind of ecstatic. I don't think he'd ever experienced anything like it. He was accustomed, I think, to very repressive kind of Chicago small-club environments. Suddenly, here was a place where not only were musicians respected, they were virtually adored and catered to in pretty much every regard possible. There was a considerable amount more freedom, by what he could witness in the audience. I mean, people running around smoking pot. I remember Michael telling me many times that the thing that blew his mind was watching a couple making love under the stage while they were playing. I remember him being giddy and ecstatic and just kind of bubbling, like, "Oh, you wouldn't believe what's going on!"

I think there were certain affinities that had to do with the fact they were coming out of the blues world rather than the rock & roll world, that allowed them to slide into the San Francisco scene pretty easily. A lot of the big rock & roll bands in the country at that time were costume bands, like the Beach Boys in their blazers and the Beau Brummels. Paul Revere & the Raiders had their elaborate costumes. They were all pretty nattily dressed. But they were coming out of the blues world, where they were accustomed to playing small clubs. And they weren't too fancily dressed. I think there was a certain shock for them, to some degree, in that—at least at the outset—there weren't a lot of spotlights on the band itself. It was more the light show, and I think that was a change for them to have to go through.

Elvin Bishop When we first came to San Francisco, we were wearing continental suits, little skinny ties, Italian shoes, and all that—Chicago style, you know. It took us about a week to get into hippie clothes, though. It was kind of a mind-blower seeing the hippies. We'd seen a few in Chicago, but just to walk down Haight Street was like a circus parade or something. It was amazing. The quality of the audience and the whole atmosphere—the pervasive smell of weed, b.o., and all them hippies, you know.

Michael Bloomfield I didn't like the San Francisco bands. I thought they were amateurish. Some of them weren't—Moby Grape was slick, guys who had paid their dues in the clubs for a long time. It was a strange amalgamation. Jack Casady was a guy who'd played a lot of lounge gigs, who could play anything.

I remember hearing Quicksilver. I remember hearing the Airplane, which we thought was the best arranged, most sophisticated band for what it was at that time. I remember Chet touting Big Brother, and when I first heard them I couldn't believe the amateurishness. Not everybody in the band—Getz could play, Albin could play. Gurley could not play nothing. Sam, to be honest—he was just learning. And Janis wasn't in the band.

Helms was telling me about Gurley as this most far-out musician. It made me distrust Chet's taste in music. But these people were all so sweet—they gave us good grass to smoke, and they gave acid to us. They were so nice and everything, and it was a schism.

Carlos Santana I can see why Michael criticized the musicianship in San Francisco, because at that time I felt the same thing. When I went to a concert, I saw the three main bands—the psychedelic bands from San Francisco—and I was very disappointed also, because I felt that although it was a nice merging of ideals, musically it was a different standard. It was a lower standard. It was kind of like verging on cute versus serious, gutbucket, switchblade music.

At the same time, there was another thing happening in San Francisco. But Michael was right in saying that when he first came here, it was pretty green. It needed some time to ripen, for us to be plugged in on the pop thing. We needed a lot of work, all of us, but I appreciate that he brought that to mind.

Nick Gravenites When Butterfield first played out on the West Coast with Michael and his band, Jesus, people couldn't believe it. I mean—wow, these guys could *play*. They were actually playing these goddamned instruments, not just strumming around. They were shocked. They were really shocked. These guys could *play*. But the thing is that Butterfield and Bloomfield had been playing electric music for many, many years.

Elvin Bishop In Chicago, the bars stayed open until four o'clock in the morning. You would start at nine o'clock, and you played seven shows a night. It was a real good thing for our chops, for all concerned.

Nick Gravenites These people on the West Coast had just started. They had just started to switch over from their acoustic guitars to electric instruments, and they were amateurs. Butterfield was playing electric music all through the early '60s. So was Mike Bloomfield. When they came out west, they already had years and years of electric playing under their belts, where people on the West Coast didn't. This was strange to them.

Bill Graham The San Francisco bands were somewhat haphazard. They may have played off-key sometimes. They also weren't nearly as professional. They hadn't been on the road. They hadn't been together for too long—a year or two. They'd just been put together. And they also lived in an area that sort of let it all hang out. There wasn't a form.

I know for a fact that there was no such thing as a "San Francisco Sound." This is something that people made up. A lot of bands came from here and were successful, so everybody said, "Okay, they all have the 'San Francisco Sound.'" I think what they had in common was that they had unstructured time-space music within the framework of a song. They'd begin a song, and then they would take off. The lead guitarist would go in one direction, and the keyboards would go somewhere else, then they'd eventually get back together again.

But there was no such thing as a "sound," as opposed to the fact that the Butterfield Blues Band may have looked loose, but they had structure to their songs. There were leads in there—harp leads and guitar leads—but there was a strong interplay using rhythm guitars, harmonica, and lead, and interchanging with keyboards. There was freedom within the structure, but the song had structure.

Mark Naftalin Our first appearances at the Fillmore were really eye-opening experiences. We had not been prepared for the fact that we were, at that point, the biggest thing in town. During the next couple of years we were in and out of San Francisco a lot, sharing the Fillmore stage with the emerging San Francisco rock bands as well as with jazz artists like Charles Lloyd and Roland Kirk.

Bill Graham was sensitive to the suggestions of musicians like Paul Butterfield, Mike Bloomfield, and Eric Clapton, who pulled his coat to the forebears of the music we were playing. Soon we found ourselves sharing bills with such blues greats as Muddy Waters and Albert King. I recall looking at the Fillmore marquee one night, seeing our band billed above Muddy Waters, and wondering if they hadn't somehow mounted the marquee upside-down.

Carlos Santana I'll always treasure the first Butterfield Band, because when they came out and played the Fillmore, it was very tight. It was a team. At that time, the chemistry was intact between those cats. It was scary how tight they were. There wasn't a band in San Francisco who wanted to close or open or anything like that.

By the time *East-West* came out, it was like another band. They were playing different variations of "Born in Chicago." By that time they had chewed it every kind of way they could chew it, so they were branching out, just like a tree. And they were outgrowing their own shoes, you know.

We all used to wait for him to take his solos. As much as we loved Paul Butterfield and Elvin, all of us were always anticipating, "What is Michael going to do, man?" Just the way he put his finger on it—you get a chill and it gets you excited, you know.

Country Joe McDonald I was a blues nut. I'd heard some Chicago blues, and I had the Butterfield record. But then we saw them play—Barry Melton and myself and some other members of the then Country Joe & the Fish. We saw the Paul Butterfield Blues Band, the Jefferson Airplane, and a light show. That was very impressive. Barry and I were both on LSD, and we just hung out right on the stage. I mean, we were standing right underneath Michael for the whole entire set.

Blues players will normally trade solos, a verse and a chorus, like that. But they were trading threes that night, Michael and Elvin and Butterfield. So each would play three full verse solos, which added up to nine. It was great for us. Michael was playing a Telecaster, which I'd never seen anybody play before. He used it like a prop. He'd knocked the chrome plate off the bottom, where the strings are from the bridge, and it was very impressive.

Jorma Kaukonen The Butterfield Band was truly unbelievable. I'd never seen anything like it before. Mike and Elvin Bishop played so well together; the whole band, Mark Naftalin, truly unbelievable, just to see that kind of virtuosity and power. I'd heard things like that on records before, but I'd never seen it before. So it was a real epiphany for me. They were the first young virtuosos to come and play here that I'd actually seen. I'd seen the great ones like B.B. King, but this was the first I'd seen of guys who were more or less in my age bracket that were world-class players, and it was really inspirational.

When Michael first came to San Francisco, for some reason, he befriended me. I had just started to play with the Jefferson Airplane, and I'd never played electric guitar before, really. He showed me how to bend notes, and to feedback and sustain things, and I was really thrilled. Because in those days some of the East Coast guitar players were very guarded about their secrets and the way they did stuff. I knew guys who used to turn away from you when they played so you couldn't see how they were doing it. Michael was a really sweet guy and a brilliant guitar player, and he was really instrumental in getting me into being an electric guitar player.

Jack Casady Onstage, when we first saw him, he was one of the earliest guys I knew that didn't seem to be aware that he was even there, you know. Other people, their eyes would be open, and they'd be checking the place out, and Michael's eyes were always squinted shut, perspiration pouring down his face. He'd be holding his guitar up and squeezing his notes out, and really would capture your attention, that this is a man who loves to do what he does.

And he was a good sweet person. We used to have record-playing sessions together, and he gave me a copy he had of the Swan Silvertones, that was very influential to me for vocal harmonies and emotion, and I'll never forget. It still is one of my all time favorite records. He would just show you things like that, share things. We'd have these record sessions, sit around talking, just like folks, and learn a lot and share things.

Bob Weir I became a fan of Michael Bloomfield when that first Butterfield Blues Band record came out. We were all just awestruck. For instance, he could bend a note up and then do vibrato. That seemed way beyond the limits of human ability at the time. No one had even considered the thought that someone could do that. We hadn't discovered B.B. King yet.

Not only did he up the ante for musicianship in the San Francisco scene, he was a heavy influence on that, but he was also sort of a teacher because we'd all go and watch him, and learn how he was doing some of the things that he was doing, making some of those wonderful sounds. Within about six months everybody copped all his licks and stuff like that, so he was certainly a big influence on San Francisco music.

Mark Naftalin The Fillmore was always packed when we played. The floor of the ballroom—as well as the hands, faces, and garments of more than a few of the assembled dancers—was decorated with day-glo designs, made prominent by black lights. The atmosphere was characterized by patchouli. The liquid projections coruscated and throbbed behind us as we played.

From the stage, the scene looked like wall-to-wall joy. It's a wonderful feeling to be adored by an unquestioning audience, and the Fillmore audiences drank in our improvisatory experiments, giving the impression that they may have perceived them as the gateway to Nirvana. "East-West" slowly grew in length, reaching performance times of over an hour at full flower.

Photo by Mark Naftalin

Michael demonstrates his fire eating technique.

At some point, Mike felt that it would be appropriate to add a visual aspect to the presentation, so he ate fire. He had picked up this performance-art technique from Barry Friedman, a creative record producer who had recorded several songs with the band in LA. I remember Mike showing me his fire-eating kit—wand, rags, and white gas—and watching him practice. He said it was easy: all you have to do is keep your lips wet and make sure you keep breathing out.

Elvin Bishop Michael turned them on to his fire-breathing act. He thought it would be the right thing to do when we did that raga-like song, "East-West." And man, it went over huge. It was amazing. Can you imagine people being stoned on acid looking at shit like that? I mean, it was enough of a spectacle to see this weird-looking blues band—and then for a guy to start up doing some stuff like that? It was just—I don't know. They must have had to carry a few people out.

Let the Man
Play the Guitar

13

Mark Naftalin In addition to the Fillmore, the Butterfield Band had certain spots on both coasts that functioned as home bases. In Southern California, it was the Golden Bear, which was operated by a canny businessman named George Nikos. The club was directly across the highway from the ocean in the vacation burg and surf center, Huntington Beach. Our engagements there were usually two or three weeks long, during which time we resided at the Compass Motel, which was walking distance from the club. This was by far the mellowest lifestyle the band ever encountered.

On the East Coast we played fairly regularly at the Club 47 in Cambridge, which was operated by Jim Rooney, who was a musician and a real nice guy. It wasn't a very big place, and we tended to have big crowds who waited for their turn to hear us in lines that wound around the block. To me, there was something about the Club 47 audiences that made the music, and the experience, especially exciting. The Northeast was where the band seemed to have its most concentrated and dedicated following, and I was always glad to get back there.

In New York City, the band's home base was the Cafe Au Go Go, which was operated by Howard Solomon, the brother of Maynard Solomon, the owner of Vanguard Records. I found Howard to be a likable guy, although he came across as a little neurotic. But then who wouldn't be, trying to operate a nightclub where you couldn't serve alcohol. On several occasions we shared a Cafe Au Go Go bill with the Blues Project who had an enjoyable presentation.

Al Kooper There was an intense rivalry between the Butterfield Band and the Blues Project. We were always paired off against each other, either in reviews of the albums or live performance reviews or comparison of personnel—that sort of thing. Once we played the Cafe Au Go Go on a double bill over a weekend for three nights, and it was the only time we ever did that.

It was very tense. But it was remarkable in that if they played a bad set, we'd play a bad set, and if they killed, we killed. It was very evenly balanced. At the end of the weekend, Bloomfield came into the dressing room and said, "You guys are really good. We heard you were shit. But you guys are really good, and it was great working with you."

We had a jam, I think, the last night of the gig. And everybody sat in. I have pictures at home of Bloomfield and Danny Kalb playing together. And Elvin Bishop with Andy Kulberg playing the flute. I think I was playing bass while Andy was playing the flute and Naftalin was playing keyboards.

There was a nice friendship. Personally, I didn't think we had that much in common, except we both had "blues" in the title of our bands. Butterfield was a traditionalist, and he played traditional blues. If he played "Two Trains Running," he played it the way Muddy Waters played it; if he played "Juke," he played it the way Little Walter played it. But when we did other people's songs, we did them with completely different arrangements. We didn't play really traditional—we were more pop-oriented. I think that was probably my influence, because I was not a blues purist at all. I came from being a rock & roll guy. Danny was the blues purist. Andy was a classical musician, and Steve Katz was a folk musician, and Roy Blumenfeld was a jazz guy. So all those things came together.

The other guys in the Butterfield Band, they were all blues guys. They got jazzy as time went by, and more intellectual, musically speaking. But they came from that blues thing. We were more diverse. I mean, they couldn't play "Catch the Wind"—not that that's a great thing to do. But we couldn't play traditional blues anywhere as good as they could. So it was apples and oranges. But we were constantly compared, and as long as we dug each other, it was good. It was okay.

The kids in college wanted to know where the music came from. They saw these white guys playing this music, and the white guys were saying, "Hey, this is a Muddy Waters tune" and "This is a B.B. King tune." And "Hey, I couldn't even play the guitar if it wasn't for Albert King" or "I couldn't play the piano if it wasn't for Otis Spann."

There were some very brave promoters in New York. Howard Solomon had a show at the Cafe Au Go Go called the "Blues Bag" over Thanksgiving weekend in '65. He had the Blues Project, but he also had Bukka White, James Cotton, Muddy Waters, John Lee Hooker, and Big Joe Williams. It was unbelievable—it was a whole potpourri of these acts. And white people hadn't come to see this stuff before. These black guys must have been in shock. They were playing in a club, and there were no black people in the club—just white people. The draw was the Blues Project, and here they were being fed this other stuff. And, of course, it was very exciting to see where it all came from.

Unfortunately, we had to close the show. And it was embarrassing for us. It was like, you know, we were the Great White Hope. So we'd go on after Muddy Waters and close the show. And of course, they'd love it—the white audience. If it'd been a black audience, we'd have been killed. So that's interesting, sociologically.

If Butterfield's band played in front of a black audience, they would probably have been accepted. And they were integrated—they had a black bass player and a black drummer, whereas we weren't. We were all Jewish.

Michael Bloomfield White kids would dig the white imitation. And that's what we were. But I do believe, by that time, Paul and I were playing the blues as good as people can play the blues. We would hold our own. That's all I can say.

When our first record came out, this reviewer, this black cat named Julius Lester, really panned it. He really put it down. He said it was just a watered-down version of the blues. I met him in New York—I made a point of meeting him and saying, "Listen, you don't know how many gigs I've played with black cats. You don't know how many cats have took me to be their protégé." I was enraged. I was furious, 'cause I had paid plenty of dues, man. And I had great respect for my own talents and Paul's talents at that time. He was telling me something that wasn't true.

But you know—he was right. It was a cultural rip-off. It's been one since the history of black music. Joe Turner had "Shake, Rattle and Roll"; Bill Haley had the hit. LaVerne Baker had "Twiddle-Dee-Dee"; Georgia Gibbs had the hit. "Pinetop's Boogie" became the "Dorsey Boogie," and they had a hit on it. And Elvis—constantly.

There was Louis Armstrong, then along comes Biederbecke. Paul Whiteman was crowned the "King of Jazz." It was just an endless cultural rip-off. A lot of these cats didn't give credit where credit was due. And some cats became fanatic about it, like Mezz Mezzrow—he was so fanatic. Or Johnny Otis—he almost became, in his mind, a black man.

And I'll tell you: there was some grief. Billy Davenport, our drummer, had a lot of trouble with black cats that he knew. They'd say, "Man, what're you selling out, working for this white cat, for?" The same thing happened with Sammy Lay. And he'd say, "Listen, man, white, black—Paul plays. Paul plays the blues. I don't care what you say. Paul plays the blues. I'm gonna play with him. Now that Walter"—Little Walter was a little crazy then—"he

Michael and Elvin Bishop, June 1970.

said, 'Paul's just the best I know.' So I'm gonna play with this cat, because he's the main man. Paul holds his own."

Billy Davenport A lot of people asked me things. They'd say, "How did you get along with a mixed band?" Nobody looked at the band as mixed. Everybody looked at everybody else as a musician, playing, regardless of who you are. If you played it right, that was it.

Michael Bloomfield These guys got a lot of trouble from some of the black cats they used to play with because they thought they were selling out, purely on a racial basis. But even those cats had to respect Paul. And after a while I hope they had to respect me, too, for what I was doing.

Paul used to be a pretty savage, torturous kind of guy—right up until the middle of when the Butterfield Band was really cooking, until we had this revolution against Paul. Paul had this old sort of domineering relationship, like Howlin' Wolf would have with his sidemen. He was the stone leader. He took all the bread and all the things. And we were contributing as much as we could. So we had this revolution, and we all quit on him in the middle of this gig in LA. We just quit on the cat. We said, "We're leaving. We're gonna go with the people that manage the New Christy Minstrels and start our own band." Paul got real uptight. He punched me—and I really quit for good then.

I was on my way to the airport, and they pulled me back. We got it together then and made it an equal organization.

Elvin Bishop It was something like the baseball strike, you know. Butter was the owners and we were the players. Butter always had a good, healthy self-regard and was willing to take whatever anybody would give him. Or he could bullshit it out of them, you know. I was making $125 a week with Butterfield. And I don't think we got any royalties—Butterfield got them.

Michael Bloomfield Paul was despotic in weird ways. We had bought a band bus, the Butter bus, and it was this blue Chevy van. It didn't have a back seat, so we put three wooden chairs in it. It didn't have back windows—Chevy vans just had those little vents—but it had front windows that could roll down. And this was what we'd tour in.

It would get so hot in the summer that your skin would sizzle if you touched the side of the van. And Paul would always either drive or sit in that front window. I remember once, at a toll booth in Boston, I just got out. I said, "I'm quitting. Paul either sits in the back and somebody else sits in the front, or I quit. This son of a bitch is gonna swelter like I swelter and sizzle like I sizzle." And gradually the despotism got worn down.

Norman Dayron Mike was a guy that wouldn't fit in with any band for long unless he was running the show. And Paul was definitely the leader of the Paul Butterfield Blues Band. I think Michael was always pushing at the edges of expressing himself or dominating that band. So it was a push-pull kind of relationship. Paul wanted to keep the leadership of his band and guide the direction of it, but Michael was so dynamic. He had so many ideas and was always expressing himself outwardly in that band. It really couldn't last that long with him in it.

Elvin had been the guitar player, but Mike was obviously a much more dynamic player. Elvin got reduced to playing rhythm guitar in the band, which was very difficult, I think, for him to deal with. But Michael's talent and what he contributed to that band was so obvious that that's why everybody went along with it.

Ira Kamin I think Elvin was jealous. And Paul Butterfield was nuts—he abused both Elvin and Michael. He would hit them. Michael was big, but he wasn't a fighter at all. And Paul also fueled that competition between them—between Elvin and Michael.

I liked Paul Butterfield's band before Michael joined it. I used to go to these dances where he and Elvin and the rhythm section would play, and they were great. I thought they were a great band. Then they added Michael, and I thought they were really fantastic.

Michael was this creative genius as a guitar player. Elvin was adequate, and he knew the idiom, but it was two different things. I really don't see them in the same league, musically. I think Michael was really into stretching the music and moving beyond the blues. He had ideas.

Elvin Bishop I didn't feel that Mike and I were really competitive in the band. I would try to do my best, but it was like apples and oranges. It was different things. We just tried to get a good total effect going.

Michael left because he wanted to do his own thing, I guess. I didn't think his leaving left a big gap. By that time we had horns and keyboard and all kinds of stuff, so the sound was still plenty full. And I got to play all the solos. As far as I was concerned, it was all right.

Mark Naftalin Elvin had been with Paul from the beginning. His guitar sound, combined with Paul's playing and singing, was the essence of the band's sound. But from what I saw, Paul didn't allow Elvin much lead space when they were a four-piece group, and when the more flamboyant Mike was hired as lead guitarist, Elvin's role as rhythm guitarist was cemented. It was the axis between Mike's and Paul's lead voices around which, in the eyes of our audience, the band revolved.

Michael stated to me, very directly, that he was uncomfortable being in a position where he felt he was standing in Elvin's way. Mike felt that Elvin was frustrated by insufficient opportunity to shine as long as Mike was there doing it. Mostly, though, I think Mike was eager to step out on his own. He had lots of ideas, obviously. He had some people in mind that he could get together with, and that's what he did.

The last day that he was with the group, we played three college dates in the Boston area. We spent all day and all night going from place to place giving these concerts. I didn't consider it to be particularly a bad thing. I think it was only a coincidence that that was his last day—I mean, that had already been planned. The way I remember it was that it was painted as something of a last straw. You know: This is it, that's enough of that, and whatever.

I wish he'd stayed a little longer, because I believe that if he had, the band would have risen faster and higher in a commercial sense, which would have helped us individually as we went on to separate careers, and might have allowed us to earn more money at the time—although this is questionable, given the fact that the money was controlled by Albert Grossman, who, if the publishing company he set up to represent us as writers is any indication, got over on Paul and the rest of us.

Michael Bloomfield What happened with Paul was this: We were doing a tremendous amount of touring, and the band never sounded better, and, in my opinion, Elvin was really getting fidgety to step out on his own. He'd been playing a long time. He was the original guitar player in the band, before I joined. He and Paul had a great band. I played piano on some early sessions, and Elvin played guitar.

By the time I left, Elvin was champing at the bit to stand out on his own. And I said, "Man, let him. Just let him do it. Let the man play the guitar."

I was interested in getting a band with horns, that played other music. I had all these ideas I had learned about arranging, and making pop records and all that, and I wanted to put them into use.

Groovin' Is Easy

Michael Bloomfield For so many years I had heard Ray Charles records and B.B. King records with horns, not to mention all the R&B I heard—Otis Redding and all the Motown records. That stuff—I wanted to play it. I wanted to hear that sound around me. I wanted to play some B.B. King stuff and hear those horns come in.

Barry Goldberg Mike and I were in New York, at the Albert Hotel. We were doing sessions with Mitch Ryder. And Mike said to me, "Will you help me get a band together? I want an American music band—everything in American music from Stax to Phil Spector to Motown." And, of course, blues. He wanted to cover the whole spectrum of American music. I thought it was a great concept.

Harvey Brooks Michael's back in town, and he's talking to me about this new band they're going to do called the Electric Flag. The thing was—they needed a bass player. Did I want to go to California and hook up with this? I was doing a lot of sessions in New York. I had become a popular session player, and I had an apartment in Manhattan. I was playing. I was doing my thing. I had just gotten a new car. I was doing all right.

But it seemed to me like that was growth. It was getting more in the actual game, which—being an ambitious young man—was what I was after. I didn't realize how basically different I was from these fellows. You know, a lot straighter. Not having had a large majority of the experiences they had already had. My existence was very regular. And, as I was to find out soon, theirs was quite different.

At the time, I had a partner who was managing Murray the K. And we were doing a show with Wilson Pickett—also the Cream and the Who, in their American debuts. The significant part of it is: Buddy Miles was the drummer with Wilson Pickett, and I saw Buddy playing there. When Michael and Barry spoke to me about playing in the band, I told them about this drummer that I had seen who was getting fined left and right by Wilson Pickett and might be ripe to join the Electric Flag. So I brought them down there. They saw him, and, you know, Buddy was an amazing guy at that time. Buddy was young and innocent. I don't know if it was a blessing or not, but we got Buddy.

Nick Gravenites In Wilson Pickett's band, Buddy was way down on the totem pole. He was a young guy. In Wilson Pickett's band—or any other famous black person's band, like James Brown or anybody like that—you were just in the band. You didn't show up the band leader. You didn't try to sing better than him; you didn't try to do any flashy shit with your instrument to detract from him—that sort of thing. So Wilson, essentially, was sitting on Buddy. Wouldn't let him do nothing.

Michael Bloomfield We saw Buddy Miles with Wilson Pickett and said, "What a fabulous drummer, what a great drummer." I was just knocked out. I said, "Jesus, man, if we're gonna get a band together, let's get this guy. He's just tremendous." And I'm wondering, "Can he sing?" We went up to his hotel room with him, and Buddy sang great. We knew he was just dynamite.

Barry Goldberg Our original thought on the drummer was Billy Mundi from the Mothers of Invention. And then we walked into this theater, and the whole theater was rocking to this massive drum beat. We were just mesmerized. It was Buddy Miles, who was Wilson Pickett's drummer. So after he got off the stage, Michael and I went up to him and started talking to him. We invited him back to our room at the Albert Hotel for further conversation.

We bought a box of Oreo cookies, and we kept giving Buddy Oreo cookies and telling him about all the beautiful young girls in San Francisco. Our plan was that he could be the star of San Francisco and have anything he wanted—which is basically what happened. And Buddy said, "Okay, count me in." He left Pickett, and Pickett was pissed off. We heard that he was looking for us for a long time, for stealing his drummer.

Buddy Miles I credit Michael Bloomfield with embellishing all of the glory things that I've ever done in this business. Michael was very, very protective of me when we first started in San Francisco. He was very protective of me because he felt that he had the best drummer in the world, and that really made me very happy.

Michael Bloomfield We got Harvey, and we got Buddy, and then Larry Coryell recommended Marcus Doubleday, the trumpet player. And Peter Strazza, the tenor player, was an old friend of Barry's.

Peter Strazza When I was in high school, I was in a band in Connecticut called Robbie & the Troubadours. And when we got out of school, we went on the road. We wound up in Chicago for a while, and the organ player left to go into the army. Somehow, Barry Goldberg got in the band, and I got to be pretty good friends with him. Then that band broke up, and we parted ways for a while. And then he called me up and said, "We're starting this band. Would you be interested in playing?" I met Barry in New York, and we drove out to San Francisco. That's where the band started.

Barry Goldberg Nick Gravenites, who we'd spoken to, was already living in San Francisco and made arrangements, along with Michael's wife, Susan, for all of us to get houses. That's where we decided to start off this thing, in San Francisco. Because the scene was happening there.

Nick Gravenites I'd gone back and forth from Chicago to San Francisco for many years, and I wound up back in San Francisco in '66. When I came back, a lot of the people that I knew as folk singers were now in bands— Big Brother & the Holding Company and Quicksilver Messenger Service, in particular. Also the Jefferson Airplane. I knew these people from folk music days. And at that time I was living with a guy named Ron Polte, a friend of mine from Chicago who was now managing the Quicksilver Messenger Service.

Barry Goldberg Ron Polte had this flag that started waving when you plugged it into the wall. It was an electric flag. And he actually gave us that name: the Electric Flag. That's where that came from. The flag would sit up on top of the Leslie speaker, and whenever I put the tremolo switch on, it would start waving.

Nick Gravenites San Francisco represented something totally different than Chicago. Most of my memories of Chicago were hard memories, but in San Francisco there weren't that many hoodlums around. People were more open and more relaxed and didn't have that gangster mentality. That's what I was looking for. I was looking for a place to expand, to grow as a person, as a personality.

I really couldn't do it in Chicago. I had to find some other place. Chicago was great for the blues, but stretching out from it—nope. That's why everybody went west. Everybody wound up going to San Francisco, because it wasn't so restricted. You know—chauvinist Chicago and their blues.

Michael called me from New York and told me that he was putting a band together. Albert Grossman was going to back him, and he asked me if I wanted to be the singer. I said, "Sure." He says, "Well, you're out there—go rent a house. I'll start shipping people out to you," which he did.

When he put the Electric Flag together, he tried to get the best people he could—but, at the same time, he also got people that he knew. They were his friends, people he'd feel comfortable with in the band, myself being one of them. He knew me. He felt comfortable with me. I used to play with him and stuff. So I rented a house, waited a couple weeks, and the band started to show up.

Michael Bloomfield We moved in with a bunch of Indians, from India— we all lived in one house. Grossman had booked them into this country. Well, first who moved to my house—before I lived there—was these crazy musicians from Chicago. Jazz players, called the Chicago Art Ensemble. They lived there, and then we lived there.

It was real weird, because our neighbor was a guy named Reutegger, and he wakes up one morning—who knows what he thought of Joseph Jarman and Roscoe Mitchell and Lester Bowie and all them people sitting in that house, on the front lawn playing that music. Then one day he wakes up, and there's all these Indians from India, the Bauls of Bengal, smoking these clay pipes. And Buddy Miles laying on top of an organ that's on wheels while Harvey and Barry Goldberg roll him up and down the driveway. And he was just wearing this bathing suit and a bathing cap. He looked like a boxing glove wearing a cocktail onion.

So we all lived in this house in Mill Valley, and the Bauls had this one guy who we called the talker. He spoke English. We called him the shuck and the talker. He *was* a shuck—a hustling hipster con man. We'd offer him grass, and he'd say, "No, Lucky Strike." He was still in that cigarette-chewing gum mentality. He got along real good with Grossman, though. They were right on the same wavelength.

The first tune we worked out was "Groovin' Is Easy." Nick wrote it, and we worked it out. We worked out all the parts, but we never played it as a band 'til we had every part worked out. Then all of a sudden I said, "Okay,

Peter Strazza, Michael, Susan, and Bauls of Bengal at Michael's house on Wellesley Court in Mill Valley, 1967.

• •

now we're gonna play this song from beginning to end." And the sound just blew our minds. All of a sudden, we knew we had a dynamite band. And, man, it was a fantastic feeling.

Nick Gravenites After a couple of weeks, Albert Grossman came out to sign the deals. At that time, I was still part of the San Francisco crowd. And I was getting to that point where I was going to be forming my own group or putting a group together, because I had the reputation and the desire to do so. When Albert came out, he came out with contracts—contract after contract. He had a recording contract. He had a personal management contract. He had publishing contracts. I was perfectly willing to sign a recording contract and the personal management contract, but then he told me I had to sign over my publishing to him, too.

I got a little quirky. I thought, Man, this guy wants *everything*. What? Why? For the money, of course. I said, "Man, you know, Albert, I don't know about this. I just went through years of having a publishing deal with Elektra, off of Butterfield's first album. I've been waiting for years to get out of that thing, and it's up in about three or four months. I'm not ready to sign another deal. Anyway, even if I was ready to sign another deal, I can't. I'm signed to another company."

Albert says, "No, you either sign or you're out." So I signed, which was a major mistake. Essentially, what Albert got was the publishing—my publishing. But I thought it was the price I had to pay for him personally managing me. I was supposed to get certain percentages and stuff. And not only didn't I ever get the percentages, but the contracts didn't exist for the things I was supposed to be getting paid on. It was a huge mistake. But that didn't really play out until later.

Anyway, the band formed, and our first job was the movie score for *The Trip*. Grossman handled it. That was our first gig together as a band. We got together—bam, right away, a film score. We went to LA to record it. That's where we met Dennis Hopper and Peter Fonda. They were always in the studio with us. And Jack Nicholson was also involved in that. Then, immediately after the film score, we played the Monterey Pop Festival.

Peter Strazza *The Trip*—well, that's good, because we had full control of it. We didn't have anyone else meddling. Mike produced it and mixed it. Because that's before we were signed with Columbia, so Mike got what he wanted on it.

But *The Trip* soundtrack was, in my opinion, a real big mistake, because it separated us from what we should have been doing. We were going to play the Monterey Pop Festival and doing *The Trip* at the same time. But we weren't concentrating enough on the band part. And we were living in and out—we were living in Frisco, and then we went to LA to do the soundtrack, and it sort of diverted our attention from the music that we were supposed to be doing.

See, that's what got messed up. We weren't ready for Monterey. We were ready—but not for 50,000 people. Nobody had ever played in front of 50,000 people at the time. That was the first time a concert had that many people. We didn't have everything down the way we should have, because we were messing around with *The Trip* too much.

Harvey Brooks Monterey was a great experience. It was the first festival of that nature, for one thing. I remember sitting in a room with the guy from the Rolling Stones who passed away, Brian Jones, and Jimi Hendrix and Bloomfield and a few other people. We were just sitting in this room, and everybody was tripping on a little acid and talking about how groovy everything was. That was the whole theme song: how groovy everything was. When we went to the stage they interviewed Michael, and he was on the groovy thing. "This is really groovy." I saw a piece of tape, and all he was saying was how groovy everything was.

It was great. All these people—I mean, Otis Redding was there, and Jimi. I had known Jimi from New York, so it was like this big get-together. You looked around, and you saw people smiling and having a nice time. It was a good crowd. Paul Simon was there. We spent a lot of time talking. Al Kooper was kind of like the stage manager. And then someone stole my bass from the stage. It was a Fender Jazz Bass. That brought me back to reality.

Barry Goldberg Monterey was the first time that they showcased the band, so it was a really big deal. Albert Grossman was our manager, and major record companies were going to be there bidding on us—Clive Davis and Jerry Wexler and various other record moguls.

Jerry Wexler I went out to the Monterey Pop Festival with Otis Redding and Booker T. & the MGs, including, of course, Steve Cropper. I wasn't too knowledgeable about Michael. I just knew a little about him. I knew he was a good player—and he idolized Steve Cropper. There was complete idolatry there.

At that time, I said to Michael, "I'd love to have the Electric Flag on Atlantic." He loved the idea, because all the black artists that he grew up on and emulated were on Atlantic. He said, in that funny way of his, "Gee, I'd love to, but I'm going to have to ask Albert," meaning Albert Grossman, his manager.

The next day he came back to me. He had a way of sort of shaking his head from side to side. And he said, "Jerry, I'm sorry, we can't go on Atlantic, because Albert says that Atlantic steals from the blacks." And that was that, you know. That was the beginning of several very bad controversies that we had with Albert Grossman. Nothing of our making—just a very antagonistic and put-down attitude on his part.

Barry Goldberg There was a bidding war between Atlantic and Columbia. And Albert, you know—I guess he had a deal going with Clive. I don't know what the circumstances were, but I know that for some reason he felt more comfortable with Clive. But we all wanted to go with Atlantic. That was the natural move, because that was what we grew up on. Most of our favorite records were on Atlantic, but for whatever reason the better deal was on Columbia. And we were proclaimed as the new supergroup.

I remember hanging out with Brian Jones for hours, with Michael, and just being so dragged in the heat. They made us wait seven or eight hours before we had a chance to play. And we were just raring to come out of the gate.

By the time we actually played, everyone was so anxious and nervous and freaked out that it probably wasn't our best set. I mean, we did sets at other places—in New York at the Bitter End or at the Fillmore—that were far better. But even at that, we blew people's minds. We were still better than most of the bands there, because of Buddy, because of Michael. Even though things were faster than they should have been, because Michael had a tendency, when he was nervous, to count off things at twice the speed.

So we were off, man. But I thought we held our own, even though we were playing maybe at 50 percent. We made some of the best music in Monterey.

Buddy Miles We all were very nervous, 'cause it was our debut into the world. But people loved us. People went crazy over the band. The Electric Flag had just as much of a reaction, as far as I'm concerned, as Otis Redding, Jimi Hendrix, the Who—all of the big names. They called us back. We got three standing ovations.

Michael Bloomfield I was jacked up on adrenaline. It was the end of a long afternoon, and we were the last act to play, and we were scared shitless. Everybody we saw were old friends of ours, and it was their greatest hour. Steve Miller did a set, no one could beat it. Moby Grape came after Miller, and between guitar breaks they were giving each other fives, right when they were doing their show.

Then Butterfield came on. He had horns. He was better, he was just—we couldn't follow any of them. And then we came out, and we weren't very good. We really weren't. We were too nervous. First number, digging my pick in and getting it caught in the string—oh, it was just so terrible. But they loved us. What a lesson that was. I learned then that if you looked like you were getting it on, even if you were terrible, they'd love you. I was saying to Barry, "What's wrong? What happened to us?"

I have to disassociate myself from the hype. Monterey Pop was the perfect example of hype. It was a long blues afternoon. We were the only band with a black musician in it. The crowd had sat through endless bands, starting with Canned Heat, going through Moby Grape, the this, the that, Butter played, Steve Miller played, and they all sounded great. And this was the Electric Flag's first major gig. Probably the biggest gig we ever played. And we played rotten, man. I ain't jiving you. We really sounded lousy. And the people loved it. And I could see—oh my God, the hype, the image, the shuck, the vibes.

Peter Strazza, Marcus Doubleday, Herbie Rich,
Buddy Miles, namesake electric flag, Michael,
and Harvey Brooks.

Mark Naftalin My memory of the Flag's debut is—I saw very clearly what the elements were and how they worked together. And I thought Buddy was a super powerful drummer with a great back beat. I had always admired Nick, but I hadn't seen him presented in that way. I knew him mostly from hearing him just singing with a guitar, which is very powerful, also. But here he was shouting with the band and really getting down.

And, of course, Mike was giving it his all. But he always did. So it was interesting. I don't think that I felt that what was created there was as satisfying a vehicle for his talents as what I had known him in before, which was the Butterfield Blues Band. I thought the Flag was a very adequate vehicle for his talent. I just think a blues artist will shine more where there's more blues artistry in the setting. And if you're playing with someone like Paul Butterfield, you're not going to get any more of a concentration of blues artistry, in my opinion, unless you might happen to have Junior Wells or something like that. And so, in terms of context, that's a hard thing to replace.

Bill Graham I never got too close to the Electric Flag. We booked them a number of times. They were okay. Their music was okay—no disrespect intended. I was very upset that there was no Butterfield Blues Band, and perhaps that carried over into the Electric Flag.

There was also something in the makeup of the Electric Flag that I didn't care for musically. I'd rather not say what it was, but there were certain elements of the band that didn't fit with me. It's like I've got nothing against turnips, I just don't eat them. It's just something that's not my cup of tea.

I always thought that the Butterfield Blues Band sort of glued naturally, that the musicians just fit, as opposed to the Electric Flag. The Flag was put together for music business purposes. It wasn't a natural evolution that ended up being good because it seemed to fall that way. Listening to Butter's band, it just seemed right to me. Everything about them, from the time they walked on the stage, it was real. It wasn't a little powder, add water. It was all real. That's a group of musicians who played that kind of music, and that's what they do, that's who they are. As opposed to going shopping for a saxophone player or a drummer or keyboard player, and then trying to make things fit.

There was a difference between the two for me, even though they can say, "Hey, we're funky, and we want to get it on and lay it out." I just didn't feel the same about the band.

Michael Bloomfield The Electric Flag, which was a San Francisco band, was disliked. I don't really care, and I don't remember it that well, but I think it was like a bunch of heavyweight interlopers coming in, and saying shitty things about local bands, and not having the good old spirit. I don't think we played many free gigs. We did some benefits, but not as much as the other bands.

Peter Strazza We stuck out like a sore thumb. Plus, we had a black drummer, and we were playing soul music. We were sort of egotistical about ourselves, too. We thought what we were doing was the best. We couldn't stand anybody else, except like Otis Redding and B.B. King.

Michael Bloomfield At certain times, I'd be sitting around Winterland or one of those places, and people'd be talking about Ken Kesey. I just thought he was like some great writer who wrote *One Flew Over the Cuckoo's Nest*—that had been a favorite book of mine, even before knowing about any of this. But Kesey, Owsley—this whole structure. If you weren't related to it, you were outside of it. But they were really nice people. Something about being in that trip made them nice people, even if they played mind games.

Fine. I like to play mind games, too. I play Jewish street mind games. I'll fuck with any of their brains, anytime.

When it comes down to it, they were nice folks. But we were not part of that thing. If I was dosed with acid at a gig—and it never happened, but if it *had* happened to me—I would have tried to fight the person who did it to me. The thing is, I would have found that offensive. I would have liked to have been told—to get high only if I had wanted to.

But I did notice it was sort of a clique. And only way later, I guess after the Tom Wolfe book *The Electric Kool-Aid Acid Test*, did I realize what an experience that must have been—turning on the world to LSD. But we were a little separate from that scene, although God knows we indulged.

Susan Beuhler I'm not real sure how Michael was introduced to heroin, except the first time I ever saw it was with the Electric Flag. Because the guys that came, some of them—well, I know who they were—were junkies. And it wasn't a good thing. It wasn't. Everybody said, "Oh, it's going to be okay." You know—it's no problem. But it was. I mean, it was a problem.

Killing Floor

15

Barry Goldberg When Michael was on, there was no one I've ever played with—including Hendrix—that had that fire. No one could shake a string like Michael. No one had that tone. And no one played with such intensity and so ferociously. Not just playing, but with notes that burst like bombs.

Sometimes, after one of his solos, I had to regain my composure, my breath, and realize what had happened—a tornado or hurricane had hit. I used to scream at the top of my lungs while he was soloing sometimes, because of what he did to me. There was nothing else like it.

But there were problems.

Harvey Brooks All of a sudden there's a lot of drugs. Reefer was like cigarettes. There's a lot of heroin. The heroin seemed to be coming from the horn players. That seemed to be where it generated from, because that sort of materialized when they materialized.

Because of the drugs, the music sucked. The arrangements were good; the songs were good. When we rehearsed them they were good, and a lot of times the performances were good. But a lot of times they weren't. More often than not, it depended if the guys were able to score or not—you know, what was on their minds. To play music well, you have to have the music on your mind.

We had gotten all this equipment from Fender, guitars and amplifiers and keyboards, and it seems like somebody kept breaking into the van and stealing stuff. I always thought it was from the band. I thought it was the junkies doing it, to be honest with you. Junkies have no mercy. They have no soul. They give their soul up. They'll do anything.

Ira Kamin Michael's problem from 1967 on was junk—from '67 until he died. He told me it started in LA when he was putting together the Electric Flag. Somebody had heroin, and he took them up on it. I mean, he had always smoked pot and that was it. He didn't drink, he didn't like speed, he didn't like coke. I related to him on that level, 'cause I liked pot, too.

When he started getting into heroin, he lost himself. He really never came out of that. It's true that he was an insomniac, but it's kind of like a vicious circle: once you start having sleeping problems and then you start taking barbiturates, you run the risk of really wrecking your sleep pattern. And I think that's what he did.

Barry Goldberg Guys resented the other guys that were doing the drugs. It just ruined everything. But more than that, it was the personalities, too. You get that much talent together, and you really need something strong to bind it. Like a manager, so if there's a problem within the band, he can deal with that problem.

Albert was aware of the problems. I mean, Albert was a hip guy. He was certainly aware of what was going on and made no attempt to address it. I just didn't think that Albert was sensitive enough to the problems within the band. And I brought that to his attention at a band meeting. But his outlook was, "Hey, you guys are responsible for yourselves. And if you want to make a lot of money, just listen to what I say and get yourselves together."

But I wasn't in control in many ways. I didn't have a handle on it, and it really did a bad thing to me. Eventually, I had to get away from it—otherwise, it probably would have did me in. So I was the first one to quit.

Peter Strazza To this day, I still don't understand why Barry left, 'cause we were doing so good. So then we got Herbie Rich. Oh, man, what a monster he was. Unbelievable musician. He could play any instrument. And then we got Stemzie Hunter on alto sax. He was great, too—another great musician. They were friends of Buddy's, from Omaha.

Harvey Brooks The horn players were great players, but I think that we had serious tuning problems. Michael had a tuning problem. We didn't have electronic tuners then, and I think the tuning problems drove the horn players completely nuts.

Michael was a very physical player. He didn't change his strings every day, and we never really had a guitar-tech guy. The guys we had did everything. They were jacks-of-all-trades and masters of none. So a lot of times we'd be trying to tune up, and, depending on what was going on with the rest of the world, the tuning would be very stressful.

Michael's volume and his style of playing—I mean, the thing that made the band was Michael's guitar playing. It was really based on that. The concept of an eight-piece band, a horn band, is to play in balance and to play arrangements. But Michael used two Fender Twin amplifiers, and there is no quiet playing with two Fender Twins—only loud. Michael was very conscious of dynamics, and his arrangement concept was to have quiet moments and loud moments. But what we never were able to establish was a really good balance.

Peter Strazza Another problem with the Flag was that we signed with Columbia. This, I still don't understand. We should have been on Atlantic with Jerry Wexler producing us. The Electric Flag album is not that good. They didn't capture it on that album like they should have. They had recorded the bass and the drums on the same track, so when they went to mix it they couldn't do nothing. You've got the greatest drummer in the world, and you couldn't put him up too loud because the bass would be too loud. We definitely should have been on Atlantic with Wexler producing us, and I think that would have been a great album.

The producers were mostly for a certain type of music—not ours. That's another thing: we weren't Dylan and we weren't Peter, Paul and Mary and that type of stuff. It wasn't the right type of people producing us. And Mike's guitar didn't sound like it did when he played in person. They didn't capture the sound, the tone. The notes were there, but the sound of the guitar wasn't.

Michael Bloomfield That record was my first chance to make a studio record, to get in there and work with a studio. It was very hard at that time because Columbia had an engineering union, and there were a lot of guys who'd been recording for years and years and had no interest at all in what some of the engineers had been learning. It was now possible to play a studio like guitar players had learned to play their guitars—to get every possible sound out of it. Guys like Phil Spector, Glyn Johns, Bruce Botnick, and Dave Hassinger had learned how, but there wasn't anything like that at Columbia.

When we made the Flag record, these were guys who'd done live radio, and I would bring in stacks of records to show them where recording was going—Beatles records and such. They'd go, "What the fuck are you doing this for, man? I've been doing this for so-and-so years." So then I'd bring in records from the '50s—Sun records and stuff like that—and say, "Look, these guys have been doing it for a long time, too, and dig the sound they're getting."

I was really lucky. I got a guy named Roy Segal, an engineer for Columbia in New York, and we mixed it in a little room, called the Mixing Room. He was very open, and whatever engineering ideas I wanted to pull off on that record, he allowed me to pull 'em off.

J. Geils I had heard the Electric Flag album, and I loved the way Bloomfield played on that record. One of the great guitar performances of that era is his playing the blues on that song called "Texas." Buddy Miles sings it. I rank it right up there with some of the Clapton stuff on the Blues Breakers record. And I think it's been overlooked.

The contact we had with Mike was great. It was early on in the first Electric Flag tour. I think they had done a gig in Worcester and had run into a guy who knew us. He said, "When you get to Boston, some friends of mine that are great blues musicians live right around the corner from where you're going to play." Dick and I and Danny, the bass player from the J. Geils Blues Band, all lived together in the same apartment. So on Friday night, about ten or eleven o'clock, there's a knock on the door. It was Bloomfield and Nick Gravenites. They came in, and Bloomfield was great. He said, "This is just like being at home"—because Dick was playing Little Walter in his room, I was listening to B.B. King in my room, and Danny was playing bass to some Otis Redding cut.

We said, "Hey, come on in. Have a drink." We were, like, Wow, this is great. Because Bloomfield was a big star, a big hero. We had a piano in the front room, and we wound up jamming. Bloomfield played piano. He loved Dick's harp playing—he went completely nuts for that. I played guitar some. He liked what I was doing. And we talked about equipment. This was before they packaged different gauges of guitar strings—well, Fender was just starting to get into that—but he was telling me, "What you should do is: you buy the lightest set of strings you can buy and throw away the heavy one, move them all down one, and then buy a tenor banjo string for the top one."

We just had a great time. Finally, about two or three o'clock in the morning, there was a noise complaint. Mike was completely freaked because he had been busted not long before, in California, or he'd had some run-in with the law somewhere. At the end of this wonderful night of carrying on and talking about equipment and music and blues and harp players, Mike said, "You guys are great. Come down and sit in with the band tomorrow. I'll call you up." And we said, "Oh, okay, cool."

They were playing at a club called the Psychedelic Supermarket. It was an underground thing in Boston, right outside of Kenmore Square. It was a parking garage, really. A guy put a stage and PA in it and called it a club. It was walking distance from our apartment right down to where this place was. We went down there and, I don't know, two-thirds of the way through their set Mike had everybody get off the stage except the rhythm section. Barry Goldberg was on keyboards; Harvey Brooks, bass; and Buddy Miles, drums. We went up and did two tunes. The place loved it, he loved it, and we had a great time. We stayed, watched the rest of the show, and said good-bye to him. I never saw him again. I don't think we ever ran into him again. But it was a great 24 hours with Bloomfield.

Nick Gravenites Our record wasn't a giant hit, wasn't a million seller. We weren't at the upper echelon, with Sonny and Cher or Three Dog Night. No posh rooms or giant gigs. We were stuck at that middle rhythm & blues level, and we were doing a lot of marginal gigs. The only reason we were doing them was because we had some support from the record company. We were trying to hustle records. The gigs weren't for a lot of money; we weren't pop stars or anything like that. We were an underground band. We never made a lot of money off of it, or popularity.

Harvey Brooks We didn't have a hit record. The demand wasn't great. And it didn't look like there was going to be a lot of money there. We had a chance to do a second album, but Michael didn't have the energy for it. I think he was becoming paranoid. He wanted the music to be a certain way, and that way would be successful, but he couldn't get it.

Mike also had trouble with Nick, in the sense that Nick's a great vocalist but he's not a pop icon. And Michael was getting pressured about pop. The band has to have somebody to look at, and to this very day all that shit goes on. I always thought Nick was fabulous. I always thought Nick was a great singer and had a stylistic guitar thing.

I've always been in it for the music—the music, and to make money. I thought that Michael backing out was chicken shit. But I think ultimately what it was is that he was leaving a sinking ship. Michael felt that the band wasn't going to happen, and he couldn't figure out what to do about it. So he jumped ship.

Michael didn't want to go on the road anymore, and he didn't want to deal with Buddy. He'd had it. He thought Buddy was a clown. And it was too strenuous for him. The personnel might not have been exactly what he wanted anymore. My read on it is that it was just too much responsi-

Michael at Santa Clara Pop Festival, 1968.

bility for him. It was running wild. He couldn't control it, and his life was falling apart. Susan had left him. He was trying to get that together, and I think it just gobbled him up.

Michael Bloomfield I stone quit, man. I'll never forget the night I quit. We had been booked into three gigs in three states in one night. It was the fault of some booking agent who had obviously forgotten that these are people and we can only make so many gigs. So I flew home. That was it. I said, "I ain't gonna do it no more."

People had lost perspective on what was happening. We were getting stale; we were playing the same shit over and over; we weren't writing new songs. We were trying to live up to a mystique, trying to get this super-exciting wham-bam show, which, for me, lost the meaning of what we were about. It began to be un-good.

I thought the band was a good band. We had played fabulous in rehearsal. We had played fabulous in small gigs around San Francisco. At times it was a great, great band; at times it was a fabulous band; at times it was an atrocious band. But when it went over great, man, there was just too much of a discrepancy in reality and hype, and it got lame—very, very lame. It got very confused with quality and non-quality.

The reason I couldn't stick it out was there were just too many people, too many personal trips, that I had to be in charge of. If you're gonna lead a band, you either have to completely depersonalize it—they're your sidemen, they can just go die in their spare time, they can go to hell, you don't care what they do—or they're gonna be like a big family to you. But nothing in between. It just can't be that way.

Nick Gravenites It was conflicting goals, actually. First, of all the people in the band, Michael was the famous one. And he didn't want to be the famous one—he wanted to be just another member of the band. That was impossible. People were always pushing him to the forefront. Second, there were a lot of hard drugs in the band. There were junkies—people with real bad hard-drug problems. And that was exacerbated by the lifestyle—getting up, hitting the plane, flying here, doing this gig, flying there, doing that gig. It got to be where everybody was junked out and crazed half the time, stumbling on the plane and passing out and getting up and doing a gig. It had no real sense of identity. It was just all crazy. Third, a lot of it had to do with Buddy Miles. Buddy was a success-oriented guy. He wanted to be famous, successful. Michael didn't give a shit about that. He hated it. But Buddy didn't.

Onstage, Michael preferred to let his music do the talking. And Buddy was constantly—he would dress up, he'd put on his weird clothes, his American flag shirts and his weird pants and his wig or whatever, and he'd exhort the crowd, "Everybody get up! Everybody clap their hands!" Let's do this, let's do that—he was a rabble-rouser. And Michael hated that. It was like oil and water. All of the things that Buddy thought important, Michael thought unimportant. And vice versa.

Michael and Buddy did not get along. They just did not have the same kind of thing happening. So Michael—he cracked. He said, "Fuck this. I don't have to do this" and just left.

Actually, it wasn't Buddy's fault that the band broke up. Buddy is a good player. When the music is working well, Buddy's a good guy to work with. But there was a lot of heroin in the band, a lot of craziness. Trumpet players wouldn't blow their trumpet, cats would be late, fucked up on the gig. It just got to be too rank. I don't blame Buddy. How can you fight your way up to the top, and take one step up and two steps backwards? He couldn't do it. It was just impossible.

The band lasted only about nine months. We had a contract, but Buddy came up with an attorney. It turns out that when Buddy signed all his agreements with Albert Grossman and Columbia and everything, he was underage. He lied about his age. He told everybody he was 21 or 22, but in reality he was still a kid. So the contracts that he signed were invalid. He went to court and won and got out of those agreements. After that, the Electric Flag was essentially dead in the water.

That's what happens when you give blood. See, it was a blood band. It was full of mistakes and full of improbables and full of confusion, but it was all flesh and blood. It was just like Michael. He was a very human kind of guy, and it was a very human band.

Michael was an extremely spotty player. It depended on how he felt that day. If you give a show, then it doesn't matter how you feel. You give a show. But if you're playing from the inside, then how you're feeling is important. And that's the kind of band it was. We would give extremely mediocre performances. Sometimes, Michael couldn't hit a note—I mean, it would just be embarrassing. Other times, you'd go flying through the air with the greatest of ease. There were times when we'd be playing some heavy shuffle of some kind, and we'd just stand there looking around saying, "Are we playing this stuff or is it playing itself?" It would be that amazing. It would be so in the groove and powerful that it had a life of its own. Unbelievable.

That's the way life is, and that's the way all real things are. They have their ups and downs and middles. Everything else is show business. That's the way the band was. When we were on, we were very, very on. Nothing could touch it. But that happens when you're human—you don't sound good all the time, but sometimes you sound fabulous.

Buddy Miles I happened to love the band. Michael and I both were very, very misunderstood. But how can you be understood when a guy has got a problem with drugs? How can you do anything? Michael did not want to go any further than we went, because it scared him.

Barry Goldberg You know, it was Michael. His insomnia. His intensity, and the fact that he couldn't sleep, and his relationship with Buddy. He was really being driven crazy by not being able to sleep.

People would call him: "It's time to go to the gig" or "It's time to go to rehearsal." He couldn't relate to that. He just wanted to have that little place on Reed Street in Mill Valley, with Susie and the dog. You know what I'm saying? That's where he was most comfortable. And then, after that, his life pretty much started falling apart. I don't know what happened with Susan. They were like soulmates. We grew up together, all of us, but eventually it got to their relationship, too.

Susan Beuhler We were best friends, but the marriage couldn't continue. I came home to Chicago to get the divorce and flew back. He didn't go. I spent the day with his family, because we were all very close. I always stayed close. And his mother always kept hoping we'd get back together, because we stayed very good friends. I always felt it was because we were so young, and we were like brother and sister. We really were like family to each other, and we always stayed good friends.

The reason for our divorce was that we had no romantic connection anymore. We were just really very separate. Actually, I think the reason for the divorce was I didn't want to be a musician's wife, you know. He was always gone. We were physically separated. I remember he came back at Christmas time, in 1967, and we had a long, tearful talk about how our marriage was over.

I had my own life. He had his own life. It seemed silly to be married. And we were pretty much separate by the time we got the divorce. We just never were together anymore. So there didn't seem to be any point in actually being married. It was very amicable. His father gave me money, and it was all very friendly and nice.

I don't know if Michael was upset by the divorce. I don't really know how he felt about it, come to think of it. There was a lot of trust in our relationship. Here we were in California without too many connections, and the music business being horrible, full of people you couldn't trust. But I think Michael trusted me and felt safe, and I with him—not always, but in general. Michael remained very important to me in that sense, too, always. Not romantically, I'm not talking about that. It was just that I always felt we were connected as souls, maybe. It had nothing to do with romance.

Drugs were Michael's downfall. Back then, I never would have said what I believe now, which is that drugs change people, and drugs make people do things they wouldn't normally do. I have enough friends dead and fucked up that that's what I've come to believe—that they weren't in control, that the things that happened to them are terrible accidents due to the drugs. That, literally, they were not in control. And I think that's what happened to Michael.

Michael Bloomfield I ain't no entertainer, just a musician and a person. During the Flag, it was such a hype scene. All the stuff was getting me down, and I couldn't sleep, and my marriage was getting cruddy.

Touring is always a drag to me. Some cats love the road. They can live on the road 'til they die, and they just love it. Motel rooms are a groove for

Buddy Miles at Santa Clara Pop Festival, 1968.

them, and the groupies are a groove—y'know, plenty coke, plenty grass, plenty speed, plenty smack, plenty whatever. It's all a groove.

And you always know that you are paying for the fifth under-assistant executive's secretary's son's new bicycle or daughter's college education, or some record rack-jobber's kid's *bar mitzvah*. You're paying for it, man, through your thing. All these middlemen—they don't even listen to music. They don't have nothing to do with it. All they know is what *Billboard* says. They know that you're the buck, you're the product. And that's a drag, man.

I don't dig thinking of myself as no product. I like to produce a product, make a record and think of it as a product, and market it and whatnot. But me as a person—no sir, man. I don't dig to be marketed like at a livestock auction.

Nick Gravenites The best music Michael ever played had nothing to do with being in a band. It was always after the Electric Flag rehearsals were over and everybody had pretty much left. Buddy Miles went home. The horn players left, except for Peter Strazza. And Michael and Peter would play duets together. Peter would be playing his sax and Michael would be backing, and then Michael would do a round and Pete would be backing him.

That was the best I ever heard him play—just casually, after rehearsal. It had nothing to do with show business or selling records or being onstage or anything, and that was really where Michael was coming from. He was a pure musician. He was just concerned about the music.

That was some of the best music I ever heard in my life, by anybody. But, shit, no one else heard it. It wasn't show biz. It had to do with just being there, I guess.

Hard Cash on My Trail

16

Al Kooper Throughout the Blues Project/Butterfield phase, Michael and I were friends. Whenever we were in the same city, we would spend time together. Then I left the Blues Project, and roughly around the same time, he left the Butterfield Band. I left to put together Blood, Sweat and Tears, and he left to put together the Electric Flag, which was a pretty amazing parallel in our lives.

Then we left the bands that we started—both of us. And we came together and made the *Super Session* album because, frankly, I thought it was deemed in heaven that we come together. I got him on the phone, and it turned out he was not doing much of anything. "Why don't we just go in the studio," I proposed, "and fuck around and jam. Columbia'll put it out, and big deal."

"Okay," he says, "but let's do it in California." We picked the sidemen and set the dates. I chose bassist Harvey Brooks, my boyhood buddy late of the Flag; Bloomers chose Eddie Hoh, the Mamas and the Papas' drummer, known as Fast Eddie.

Michael Bloomfield Al Kooper said, "Listen, we're going to get together for two days, and the name alone will sell the album. Don't worry—we're just going to jam. We'll make a killing, that's all we're in it for, and it means nothing. It's nothing but a scam to make money." I said that was cool, fine.

I think those albums, *Super Session* and *The Live Adventures of Mike Bloomfield and Al Kooper*, were scams. I think Kooper had a good idea, calling something *super*. *Super* stars, *super* records—they could sell records with nothing. It was a huckster's idea that worked. The music's not invalid, and the *Live Adventures* stuff is riskier, even more valid. But I don't think the playing is so hot, even though it did sell well, and I know a lot of people, when they got into rock & roll, that was one of the records they got.

Al Kooper I think Michael was embarrassed by *Super Session*—not playing-wise but success-wise. He wanted to be in a certain niche, and anything above that niche really embarrassed him. He definitely didn't want to be a rock star. Nor did I.

I was trying to capture the way that I knew him to be—because I was very dissatisfied with his other recordings. I was very unhappy with the way he had been recorded up to then, based on what I knew of his playing. I didn't think you could go out and buy any record that really showcased what was fantastic about him. I felt my mission was to get all this great playing out of him that I knew he had in him, but that no one had been able to document on tape. So that was certainly the angle with *Super Session*. I feel really good about it. I don't hear much other stuff that got it.

Another one of the concepts of *Super Session* was to make a record based on the plethora of jazz albums that had as a concept: "Let's put so-and-so, so-and-so, and so-and-so in a room and record them." And the reason they did it was because those musicians had never played together before on a record. That was the whole concept. They were jam sessions. So I said, "Wow, let's do that with rock & roll. It's a valid art form." That was the main thrust of what that album was supposed to be. We just went in there and did what the people did on those jazz records.

Harvey Brooks That was the last time we played together. It was like an explosion. We went down there, and all that stuff just came out. Michael only did half the album, because on the second or third day he had to leave.

Al Kooper That night, we hit the studio and got right down to business. Barry Goldberg, also late of the Flag, came down and sat in on a few tracks. We recorded a slow shuffle, a Curtis Mayfield song, a Jerry Ragovoy tune, a real slow blues, a 3/4 modal jazz-type tune, and in nine hours had half an album in the can.

There was a real comfortable feeling to the proceedings, and while listening to one of the playbacks I noted that I had gotten the best recorded Bloomfield ever and, after all, that was the whole point of the album. We piled in the rent-a-car and made it back home, crashing mightily with dreams of finishing the album the next night.

The next morning, the phone starts jangling at 9:00 a.m. It's some friend of Bloomfield's, asking if he'd made the plane 'cause she was waiting at the airport to pick him up. "Huh? Michael's fast asleep in the next—hold on," I said, running into the next bedroom to find ... an envelope? And, inside, "Dear Alan. Couldn't sleep well ... went home ... sorry."

I think Michael just couldn't score in Los Angeles. Therefore, he could not sleep. And he just went nuts and said, fuck this. He made phone calls over the course of the evening until he got himself out of there. The whole heroin issue was never discussed between us the whole time that we knew each other. I think he was embarrassed by it, because I didn't do it. And he knew I didn't do it. So it was an embarrassment to him ultimately, because we never shared anything about it. We smoked pot together a lot.

The last thing on our minds was that *Super Session* was going to be a successful record—and it turned out to be the most successful record of our careers. Then I got a bad case of bandwagon fever and decided to cut a follow-up to the *Super Session* album. One of the only criticisms of that LP was that it was a studio album and, therefore, uninspired. Always one to want to shove it up a critic's ass, I decided to cut a live jam album, possibly at the Fillmore. I called Bloomfield, and he said, "Sure, I owe you one," because he snuck out of the other album.

This time he chose his friend and neighbor John Kahn on bass, and I selected Skip Prokop, who had just quit a Canadian group I was friendly with, the Paupers, on drums. I called Bill Graham and asked if he would book us in for a weekend, and could we record it? He said sure. I booked Wally Heider's remote truck to record the proceedings, got a budget okay, and things were lookin' good.

The first two nights go smoothly enough, and I've got roughly enough material for an album already. The third morning I get a call from Michael's wife, Susie, saying, "He's in the hospital being sedated to sleep. He couldn't stand it anymore." I presume she was talking about not sleeping as opposed to the gig. Well, he'd done it again. So I moseyed on down to the Fillmore office to tell Uncle Bill Graham the good news. I think I'd rather cut my dick off than tell Bill Graham half his show ain't gonna make it that night. As expected, he went nuts, screaming as if I'd murdered his best friend. "What the fuck do you want from me?" I respond, "I'm not in the fucking hospital! I'm in your office at *noon*, offering to call everyone in town. And you're chastising me. I'm here ready to play. And the other guy ain't runnin' out on your contract—it's just that he hasn't slept in a week."

All Bill knew was that it said Mike Bloomfield on the poster, and Mike Bloomfield wasn't gonna be there. He called up Michael's house and started screaming at Susie, telling her how unprofessional her old man is. She had just gotten back from taking Mike to the hospital, and she let go with a barrage that leveled him. He's screaming, and she's screaming, and—sometimes, I hate show business.

Susan Beuhler We put Michael in the hospital. It didn't bother me to do that, 'cause he was miserable. He couldn't sleep. And it was way more important that he get sleep than play for Bill Graham. Our doctor put him to sleep. It was wonderful. And Bill Graham was very upset. But at the time, it didn't seem to me that Bill Graham should be so upset. My perspective was different, I guess, because it was more important that Michael get better than play the stupid show.

Bill Graham I was very upset that Michael was a no-show. I don't think we could find him. And then somebody said that they did find him, and he was not in any condition to perform. But I was never told where he was. I was just told that he wouldn't be able to play. I don't remember too much of that, except that I felt very bad and I wasn't, as yet, aware of any problems Michael was having in his life.

Al Kooper I got on the phone and called Carlos Santana, a local hero not known outside San Francisco at the time, and Elvin Bishop, Steve Miller, Jerry Garcia, and others. Once again San Francisco responds, and every musician in town shows up and offers his/her services. It was a helluva show that night. Steve, Carlos, and Elvin all came up and did three or four songs apiece, and we ended playing way past closing time. The audience was happy. Graham was happy. Columbia Records was happy.

Carlos Santana I'll tell you how I became involved in the *Live Adventures* recording: Bill Graham called me at home, and he said that Michael was not available to play that gig. So he wanted to know if I would cover that. I said, "Well, this is great. Who's playing?" And he mentioned John Kahn and Al Kooper.

So I went down there, and, you know, I'm grateful. A lot of my friends were saying, "Hey, that's great—you get to be on an album." But I really wanted to play with Michael, even if we would have just played by ourselves. To me, that would have been better. But, as it was, I'm grateful for the opportunity.

Al Kooper The double-album set *The Live Adventures of Mike Bloomfield and Al Kooper* was the one with the Norman Rockwell portrait on the cover. The art director at CBS, Bob Cato, had told me he could get Rockwell if I ever needed him for something on a project.

I was lying in bed one Sunday watching a football game, and I was thinking: I got all this hair on my head, and I'm a hippie and wear all these funny clothes and everything, and here I am like everybody else in middle America, watching a football game on Sunday. I'm only missing the can of beer. So I said, "Man, let's get Norman Rockwell to paint us for this cover. Put these two freaks painted by Norman Rockwell on the cover of this album. This is fabulous." And Bob Cato says, "I can do it. I can put it together."

Sure enough, Norman Rockwell came and photographed us. Bloomfield came to the session—it was in the winter, and he had borrowed his brother's coat, and there were some pills in the pocket of the coat. And he took them. He didn't know what they were. I think one of them was acid or STP or something. So Bloomfield was smashed out of his mind. He had his arm around Norman Rockwell, and he was saying, "Ah, Norman, you got to come to San Francisco and paint. It's like Jerusalem. There's women nursing their babies in the street. It's incredible. You'll get some great paintings." And Norman's taking it pretty well. I was just cracking up. It was great—pure, great Bloomfield. So Norman photographed us, and then he went back and painted us from the photographs. It arrived at CBS in this really stupid frame—this

Al Kooper, Norman Rockwell, and Michael.

ornate, old frame. And he said, "Here are the Blues Singers. The most interesting people I've ever painted."

Michael was very untogether—period. Experiences that I had with him, where we played live engagements together, were horror-filled for me. Not so much the playing without a net, because that was what we did—that was the whole concept of *Super Session*. But when we're headlining at the Boston Garden—20,000 seats, sold out—and Michael's nowhere to be found, it's nerve-racking. Michael's brother, Allen, used to work for me. At the Boston Garden, Allen was there and I strapped a guitar on him. I was going to put him onstage. I figured we could buy some time that way. Allen didn't like that very much, because he couldn't play guitar. He's just about to go up there, and here comes Michael like nothing was wrong.

Later on, we played in New York at the Fillmore with Sam & Dave. In New York, Bloomfield called me—you'd think I'd get smart by now—and he says, "I'm stuck in a snow storm in Chicago. I don't know if I can get a plane out of here." And, again, I'm working for Bill Graham—so now I think I'm going to get my dick cut off or something. I didn't even call Bill Graham. I called Art D'Lugoff, who was the owner of the Village Gate. He had B.B. King in there that night. I said, "Let me borrow B.B. for the show, and we'll advertise—we'll tell everyone when they come out of the Fillmore to go down to your joint and catch B.B."

So Art D'Lugoff came down with B.B., and then Bloomfield showed up. Bloomfield came on and we played the gig, and then we brought B.B. out towards the end of the gig and gave him a plug for the Village Gate. B.B. sang "How Blue Can You Get," among other things. And in "How Blue Can You Get," at the end of the song, he'd go, "So, baby, how bluuuuuu—" and he'd start falling down. His sax player would catch him and pick him up, and he'd keep singing, "How bluuuuuu— can you get," like that. I'm behind the organ, and I'm going, God, what happens when he gets to the end and starts to fall down? What if no one picks him up? He'll fall on his ass. So I'm thinking, Well, I'll jump out from behind the organ and be very dramatic, too, and I'll go, "I'll get you, B.B." Like that. So he gets to the thing and he starts to go down, and, of course, Bloomfield's right there. He says, "Oh, let me help you up, B.B." Like that. Which is exactly what I would have done, except he was right there. So Michael was on the ball.

One time, *Hit Parader* magazine in New York—which was a magazine we all really liked at the time, that would write nice stories about everybody, and cover things that weren't covered in regular magazines, and ask the right questions and everything—wanted to do a piece on Michael and me. So Michael came into town, and I went over to his hotel to get him. We were going to take a cab down there and come in together. He answers the door, and he's completely naked. He says, "Oh, I'm not ready. Come on in." He says, "Sit down. I'll be right out." He was taking a dump. And he had the bathroom door open, so he could continue to talk to me. I went to sit down on the bed, and he says, "No, no, no. Don't sit on the right side of the bed. That's where I spit. Sit on the other side." All in complete seriousness.

I was at Michael's house on Reed Street once, and we smoked a lot of pot. It was me and Naftalin and Mike, and we were really wrecked. We were sitting in the living room just shooting the shit, and then we went in the kitchen—everyone had the munchies. And the whole time we were there, his dog was lying in the kitchen, crying. I said, "Does he want to go out?" Mike says, "Ah, don't worry about him. He's okay. He's just mad he can't participate in the conversation." And the dog's going, "Wooow, mmm, wooow, mmm," like this, all day long.

So we go in the kitchen. There's nothing, you know—it's one of those refrigerators where there's half a can of beer and some batteries. That's all. He's looking for something to eat, and nobody wanted to go anywhere. There's this box that says "Fives." So him and Naftalin are eating these "Fives," which are dog biscuits. It's true. It's a true story. And he says, "Here, you want one? It's good. Try it." And I go, "Sure, sure, give me one." I have an ulcer. I'm not going to eat a fuckin' dog biscuit. So I just took it and kind of like palmed it down to the dog, who stopped crying after he got the dog biscuit.

I was invited to a Jewish Sunday brunch at the Bloomfield's in Chicago. I can't pin the year—it must have been '69 or '70. I was in town playing an Al Kooper concert, so they invited me for breakfast. I went over there, to this incredible apartment, this rich people's place—towers, penthouse, I don't know what it was. I was impressed. I mean, it was serious. The whole Jewish family thing—except his father, who was really bizarre. He was in a riding outfit. He'd probably just come from the stables—maybe he played polo, I don't know. He didn't say much. His mother was the typical Jewish mother. She was very nice. A very sweet woman. Michael was sitting there. He'd been in the insane asylum for the past three days, voluntarily. He was explaining to his mother why he didn't stay there.

This was like the oddest thing to me—again. The guy always just completely shocked me, blew my mind. So he says, "Well, it was like *One Flew Over the Cuckoo's Nest.* How are these people going to cure me of not sleeping? I mean, I was staying up watching the fucking show in there. I didn't belong in there." So he left there, came out, and we were having a very interesting breakfast.

Michael rebelled against the money thing. His whole life was a rebellion against his roots. It made him very uncomfortable. His whole makeup, his station in life—he turned his back on it and rebelled against who and what he was.

The music was a great defense for him. It's really important, because it makes up who he is. His father had a restaurant supply business, which he sold to Beatrice Foods, one of the largest companies in the history of companies. His father was responsible for the classic salt shaker and sugar dispenser that you see in every restaurant, and the coffee makers and everything. So that's very important to his whole mission in life and who he was and how he acted and everything. I think those were what his demons were.

Michael was ahead of me in running from the notoriety thing. I got that from my association with Dylan. Up to that point, I was burning to be a famous guy. Then, after seeing Dylan, I said, "Well, this is not for me. I don't want to live my life like this." But before I got the message, Bloomfield already had the message. He didn't want to be famous.

He came from immense wealth. And I think kicking around the poor side of town and picking up the blues and everything was his rebellion against that. He was shedding that wealth. And the places he lived in were, you know, hovels. They weren't great places. And I don't think he ate dog food by accident. I mean, he certainly could have had filet mignon.

He told me a story once. They had this place in Chicago, and it was really freezing in the wintertime, and they didn't want to walk the dog. So the dog would just shit all over the place, and they'd put cardboard over it—layers and layers of cardboard. Which was fine until the summer, when they had to move.

But the ironic thing was: he became famous as a blues singer. And then the wealth was at his feet, again. The very thing he ran away from. So he had to run away from it twice. It wasn't hell hounds on my trail—it was, like, hard cash on my trail. That's what he was running from.

The drug thing has nothing really to do with what Bloomfield was. I mean, I don't think it's a key thing in a discussion of Mike Bloomfield. He was a really special guy. He was a special guy when he was high, and he was a special guy when he wasn't high—and he mostly wasn't high. He did wonderful things, and he educated a great many people.

I don't know what happened. But in any discussion of Mike Bloomfield where in the overall picture drugs are mentioned, they shouldn't be. That's not what the guy was about. That's not what his story is. His story is running away from that wealth, and it kept following him no matter where he went. That's what it was all about.

III

1968 *to* 1981

His Hands Are Rusty

17

Sam Andrew Around December 1968, Michael and Nick Gravenites helped Janis Joplin set up the Kozmic Blues Band. Janis had left Big Brother. She was very frightened about what she was going to do about putting a band together. Albert Grossman was her manager, and he was Michael's and Nick's manager, too, because of the Electric Flag and the Butterfield Blues Band.

They came in, and Michael took the time to make everyone feel good, and they whipped that band together really quick. He was kind of like an A&R man. He selected the tunes—a lot of them were Nick's—and then he went on and made sure everyone could play them. We had other music directors who were totally unessential. Michael was really the one who put it together.

Michael played on a few of the *Kozmic Blues* tracks. I still get people come up to me, if they're real sharp, young guitar players, and they'll say, "Was that you playing on 'One Good Man'?" I'll say, "No, that was Michael," and they'll go, "I knew it! I knew it!"

Michael was overseeing things for a while, but he was having problems himself. He and I and Janis were always going out to buy heroin and stuff. It was a real confused time. And we did a lot of heroin. Our connection was in a hotel maybe four or five blocks away from where we were rehearsing, and that was just too close. The three of us used to go to that hotel and buy balloons of heroin from this guy and shoot them up. That was one of the strikes against the Kozmic Blues Band. We were all doing that when we should have been focusing on the music. We did a lot of heroin together.

They kind of bailed out of the project. Really, all they were coming in for was to get it ready to perform publicly. And when it was ready, they went on to their own projects.

Bob Jones I had been the lead guitar player and instrumental arranger for We Five. We Five was a folk group, and they turned themselves into a folk-rock group and had a hit called "You Were on My Mind." I played with them for four years.

When We Five broke up, I took less money than everybody else, but I took the band van and the equipment and everything. I started a band with John Kahn, Ron Stallings, and John Chambers, called the Tits & Ass Rhythm & Blues Band. And I started playing drums about a year and a half before I started playing with Michael.

There was this band at the time called the Anonymous Artists of America, and they used to have jam sessions at their house. John Kahn was great friends with them. John and I used to practice together a lot, and we hung out. So Kahn and I went one day to that.

Michael used to go up there. We were playing, and he walked in—he had been standing in the next room and couldn't see what anyone was doing, but listening to what was coming out of the jam room. He said he heard Otis Redding singing and Al Jackson playing drums and he thought, This is really cool. Who is this? Who are these people? He thought it was two guys. He walked in the room, and it was me playing drums and singing.

So he plugged in his guitar and started playing. And that's how we met. He put together a band to do *Live at Bill Graham's Fillmore West*, and he asked me to play drums on it. Nick sang, Mark Naftalin on piano, Ira Kamin on organ, John Kahn on bass. Plus a horn section. We also did a studio album, *It's Not Killing Me*. It's basically the same band. It was around the same time.

The feeling I got from Michael was that he was unhappy with Columbia. And I think he had a contractual commitment for two more records. And the feeling I got from conversations with him was that they were trying to stick him in this mold that he had sort of gone beyond. He wanted to try other things. And he was having creative differences.

Nick Gravenites *Live at Bill Graham's Fillmore West*—well, Michael was junked out. A lot of people were junked out. It was just one of those things.

Half of my album—the *My Labors* album—is from those same sessions. I was doing this album for Columbia and had a bunch of cuts done already, but they had a lot of extra cuts from the Fillmore sessions that they didn't use on the record because they had a lot of material. And I thought the stuff they didn't use was better than the stuff they used.

We sounded pretty darned good. It captures that certain era pretty well. So I had a chance to use it, and I told them I'd split the costs with them if I could use half of it on my album. That's the way it worked out.

Bob Jones I'll tell you this story about Nick—and Michael was the same way. I'm doing the gig with Nick, and he turns around, and says, "E." And I go, "Nick, what is it? Is it a shuffle? Is it a boogaloo? Give me some idea of the time." And he turns back around, looks at me, and says, "It's in E."

The point being, you know—it was counted off, and you were expected to play. Michael's deal was: take your best shot. And often, Michael didn't care if you heard it in a slightly different way. He expected you to jump in. If you jumped in with confidence and played it with authority, he had a great time.

●   ●   ●

Christie Svane I first met Michael in early '69. I was helping Ron Butkovich in his capacity as a cook at the Fillmore West. I knew Ron because—what had happened was, my father had four wives. One of his ex-wives called one day from Chicago and said, "My godson has a jazz combo, his name is Hart McNee, he's a sax player. He wants to go to San Francisco, and he doesn't know anybody there. Can he come stay with you for a few days while he gets his footing?" My father was a great bohemian in his day, and he often wore the moniker of the first hippie. He was an older guy. He was like 50 when I was born. So my father said, "Yeah, sure."

I don't think he realized that by saying yes to Hart the entire combo and many hangers-on would suddenly be living in our house. So, one morning when I was 14, I woke up to find my father's house filled with scraggly-looking men sleeping on every surface—couch, floor, bed, rug, everywhere in the house. And Ron was one of those people.

I had a peculiar situation in that my parents had been divorced since I was about one year old. My mother moved us to Davis, California, when I was 11, in 1965. When I met Mike, I was coming to San Francisco every weekend and summer to be with my dad, which led, eventually, to being sort of a weekend hippie, as we were called in those times.

Davis is a small town. The University of California is there, and that's why we were there. My mother decided to go to college. It's only about an hour away from San Francisco, in the Central Valley, due east. So I was in San Francisco on the weekends.

One day when Ron and I were in the kitchen of the Fillmore, this incredible presence just came striding in. Michael had a unique stride. In a certain way, you could see his soul in the way he walked. The only other person I ever met who had a similar walk was Allen Ginsberg. Just a wide-open body—I'm sure if you could see auras, you would see this aura blasting out in all directions around him. Just an entirely open person.

So he strode in in that manner, behind the counter where we're selling the corn on the cob and the roast beef. He throws his arms around Ron, and he says, "I heard you were working here. How are you? I haven't seen you in so long." They hadn't seen each other since Chicago. And as soon as he went to go play, Ron turned to me and said, "*That* was Michael Bloomfield." It wasn't the fact that he was famous, but his presence was very captivating. After the gig we all went back to my father's house, which is this very wonderful, old Victorian house, with an old carriage barn in the back. It had been a farm, and the city grew up around it. There was a nice atmosphere to the place.

We came back, and Michael kept asking me if I wanted to go for a ride. It was three in the morning, and his intentions were rather transparent. I was used to being the woman of that house since I was five years old. You know, the weekend woman—my father was divorced, and I was the boss of that house. My response was to say, "No, I don't want to go for a ride. I'll make you a midnight snack. I'll make you a bed in the parlor. You can sleep there, and I'll talk to you in the morning." That's the person I was in that house at that time. I was very disappointed in the morning to find he hadn't spent the night but had driven home to Mill Valley.

●　●　●

Norman Dayron In 1969, I produced the *Fathers and Sons* album. We brought in all these great players: Muddy Waters, Otis Spann, and this great band—all in the Chess studio. I had Michael, Paul Butterfield, Buddy Miles, Duck Dunn, Sam Lay, and every blues musician in Chicago. Michael named it. He said it should be called *Fathers and Sons*, because that's how he related to Otis Spann and Muddy. He gave me that title, and he insisted that that's what it be.

Marshall Chess was instrumental in making that happen. In other words, I, alone, could not have gone to Leonard Chess and said, "I want to do *Fathers and Sons*." But Marshall championed that with his dad, and that's what got it for me.

Marshall Chess I think I met Norman through Mike. He brought him around to Chess Records. And then it leads up to the *Fathers and Sons* album, where Mike played for me. He was in terrible shape. Fear. He used to get shot up with tranquilizers and shit to come to the sessions.

Norman Dayron After the first day, Michael completely disappeared. He ran away. He was going to fly out of town. I sent my girlfriend, Jo McDermand, after him. She was photographing the session, and she was a good

B.B. King and Michael

....

friend of his and was very forceful. She caught him at the airport as he was about to get on a plane, grabbed him by the ear—physically—and dragged him back to the session. He was suitably humbled, and when he came back he just locked in the groove, got into it, and played. But he would occasionally have these episodes where he would be in doubt, or afraid of something, and he would disappear. It was a pattern on a lot of gigs.

But on the *Fathers and Sons* sessions it didn't work out, because the band was too perfect, in a way, for Michael's mental apparatus. It was too awesome for him to deal with, and he freaked out and consequently felt suppressed on the record, rather than playing his ass off. Mike's attitude was, "This is the guy that I most admire. Why do you need me?" He was intimidated by Muddy as a guitar player, even though Muddy was crystal clear that Michael was going to be the lead player, and he wanted him to be, and he tried to encourage him to be.

For me, the right piano player was Otis Spann, the right singer was Muddy Waters, the right harp player was Paul Butterfield. And I wanted the synergy that Michael and Paul had created together. Their understanding of each other was the whole idea of that record, but it just didn't work for Michael.

The live concert on the *Fathers and Sons* record was called the "Cosmic Joy Scout Jamboree." It was the success of the studio sessions, and the fact that everybody but Michael enjoyed it, that allowed for the live thing to happen. Muddy was in no way committed to doing a live concert. He didn't know how this thing was going to turn out. I think it was Marshall Chess who said, "Let's do this in front of an audience and capture it live."

It was held in a beautiful theater, the Auditorium Theater in Chicago. It was where the symphony played, and it was also used for theater productions. It was a great place. People were standing in the aisles. There were people around the block that couldn't get in. I mean, it was jam-packed.

What was magical about it was that we were going to have all these guys perform together, and it was one of those crowds of people where you could do no wrong. Michael would play one note, before he went onstage—he would be tuning up, they'd hear one note through the curtain, and the crowd would just go berserk. And they loved, equally, Muddy Waters and Otis Spann. They were very knowledgeable Chicago people. They understood what was going on. It was really quite a sensational event.

Then, around 1969 or 1970, Chess Records was sold to GRT, after Leonard Chess's death. I was living in Chicago, in Old Town. I had just produced the *Howlin' Wolf in London* sessions, and I was doing great. But when Chess closed, I had nothing else to do. Michael called me up and said, "Move to Mill Valley. It's great. We'll be partners, and we'll go into business together. We'll do independent productions of music."

● ● ●

Michael Bloomfield There was a period where I didn't play guitar at all, around 1970, 1971. I was really down and out, and I lived in this little dive. I really got into shooting junk. And I put the guitar down—didn't touch it.

See, a junkie's life is totally, chronically fucked. Shooting junk is very full-time. You either eat and move and be productive, or else you're a junkie. There's no choice. At least there wasn't for me. Shooting junk made everything else unimportant, null and void, *nolo contendre*. My playing fell apart. I just didn't want to play. And my mother went to see B.B. King playing at Mr. Kelly's—this really uptown bar in Chicago, really fancy. She told B.B., "Michael doesn't want to play anymore. His hands are getting rusty. It's terrible."

B.B. King I was in Chicago, and his mother came out and said, "My son likes you. He idolizes you." And she was feeling that he wasn't playing—something to that effect. She said, "If you would talk to him, I'm sure that would help him out." So I did. And he did start back to playing. I thought that every-

*Michael, Chris Darrow, Denny Bruce, and
John Kahn, June 1971.*

thing was really okay. I think what happens is, from time to time you can't seem to get things going exactly like you want, and you feel down about it.

I did try to tell him that it's not always going to be as you wish it to be. And whatever you do at that time won't make it be as you wish it to be, so you're going to have to take life as it comes. For some of us, it's a little harder than it is for others. And that's one of the things that we kind of got into. It had to do with music. It had to do with trying to build a foundation like he wanted. He was really into what he was trying to do. So I told him, "It's not always going to come when you want it. But it's like an old spiritual song—it may not come when you want it, but it's always right on time. So stay with it. It will work."

Michael Bloomfield B.B. King wrote me a letter, and he called me on the phone. He said, "You gotta keep those fingers in shape. You must do this. You just can't fall apart. You can't let what you've got go to hell like that. You've got to keep on keeping on. You've got to do that." And, my God, the next time I had a chance to see B.B. King, I was embarrassed to face this man who had meant so much to me and who I so much wanted to be like and play like, and he knew I didn't want to play anymore.

A lot of it is if you get rusty, man, and your chops get bad, you find it hard to wanna play. Your guitar used to feel as comfortable to you as Mickey Mantle's bat felt in his hands, and when it doesn't feel that way to you it's real hard to play.

● ● ●

Denny Bruce In June of 1971, I was working with a girl named Teda Bracci, who was in horrible movies like *C.C. & Company*, which was with Joe Namath and Ann-Margret. She was a Janis Joplin kind of blues shouter. Her manager was Allen Carr, who later put out the Village People movie, *You Can't Stop the Music*. Allen Carr and Roger Smith were managing Ann-Margret.

Teda and I got along real well, but she wasn't a great singer. She was just kind of a screamer. I got together a recording session for her with Mike, Lowell George, Mark Naftalin, and a couple of other guys, and we had fun. It was just, Let's go ahead and cut some wild slide stuff, and she'll scream.

Ann-Margret heard the tapes and said, "Dammit, I want to sound like that. I love Tina Turner. I want to sound like Tina Turner." And Ann-Margret is somebody who whispers when she sings. So I found some songs by a guy named Jim Weatherly, who later wrote "Midnight Train to Georgia." He had some really nice songs. And there was a song by the Allman Brothers, "Revival," which was so she could play a tambourine and walk around the stage, like they do in Vegas.

I got Mike, Lowell, Richie Hayward on drums, John Kahn on bass, Mark on keyboards, and a friend, Chris Darrow, to play dobro. I got everybody triple scale, which they all loved.

Michael and Ann-Margret had gone to the same high school, New Trier, outside of Chicago. They hadn't known each other, but they had mutual friends, so Mike was real excited. They had a good 20- minute chat, I'd say, before we did the session.

Ann-Margret did not want to wear headphones. She said she couldn't sing that way. So I said, "The only way we're going to get this finished is just do it live. You're going to have to sing live." She walked out into the middle of the room with a full-length mink coat on and a scarf around her neck. And she fainted—straight down. Michael was the first one to get there and try to revive her. That was great. Everyone was congratulating him. It was like a football game, when a guy makes a touchdown. And her assistant, who is this gorgeous Swedish woman, is like, "Yumpin' yiminy!" She was going crazy.

Michael then confessed to me that he had been the president of the June Wilkinson fan club. You have to go back to the '50s, where there were no

Michael's friend Roy Ruby, September 1971.

real porno movies, but you could see nudist camp volleyball. And the biggest boobs of all belonged to a girl named June Wilkinson. Bloomfield said that as a chubby teenager he used to write these letters to June Wilkinson, and he became a fan club head.

Anyway, we cut three tracks, but Ann-Margret only ended up singing on two of them. We failed at getting her a record deal. We got turned down by everybody. I really thought she'd get a deal. The thing never came off as it should have—but it was fun.

● ● ●

Dan McClosky I met Mike around 1971. My folks and Mark Naftalin's folks were best friends back in Minneapolis—my dad and Mark's dad were both professors. Then my folks moved out to California, and I moved here with them.

I used to go see Mark's younger brother, Dave Naftalin, all the time down in LA. Roy Ruby was living with Dave, so I got to know Roy. Then Roy wanted to move up north, so he moved up to Jenner, which is north of San Francisco, up by the Russian River. I would go up there to visit Roy. And because Mike was good friends with Roy, Mike went up there. So I met Mike up there when he was visiting.

I was working as a disc jockey, doing a show where I did interviews for

KPFA in Berkeley. Later on, I did interviews with Van Morrison, John Lee Hooker, Bobby Bland—people like that. But at that time, I wanted to do my first big interview with B.B. King. I didn't know a lot about him, and I was just lucky enough that Mike said if I wanted to ask him some questions, come on over to his house.

So I went over to his house. He gave me a list of questions to ask B.B. King—really good musicological questions and questions about the things he knew about B.B.'s life. I came back and played him the tape after I did the interview and he really liked it, so we became fast friends. I used to come over to Marin and sometimes stayed at his house. I had a sleeping bag, and I'd stay at his house for a couple of days, and we'd go out to dinner and stuff. He was a very interesting guy.

I did the radio-show interview with Mike in 1971. It was done at his house, in his bedroom. He had a piano in there. We recorded him playing some piano, which is on that record, *Bloomfield: A Retrospective*, that Columbia double-record set. He was in a particularly open mood when I did the interview with him. He was very, very forthcoming. And he had such a great way of telling a story and reminiscing. I mean, you just felt like you were right there with him.

Fred Glaser and Roy Ruby drove up right when we finished the interview, and Mike said, "Oh, man, you've got to talk to these guys." It wasn't planned. It happened spontaneously. It was just people sitting around BS-ing. Roy was a very interesting guy. I think Mike was one of the brightest guys I ever met, and I'd have to put Roy right up there, too. They were really smart guys.

Christie Svane I met Michael again in 1971, the night the Fillmore closed. There was a huge party. I was backstage, and Michael was there. I said, "You remember me?" And he said, "Sure I do. Come on, let's get out of here." So we jumped in his car and drove with my brother and Danny McClosky to the top of Mount Tamalpais. We saw the sunrise, and it was very romantic. He pointed down to the valley and said, "My house is right down there." And we really fell in love right there, watching the sunrise on that kind of historic moment.

We went back to his house. I was still a kid—I was 16—and he kept saying, "Stay." I said, "Oh, no, no. I've got to get back. My father will be worried about me." I'll never forget it. He kept saying, "Stay, stay."

Finally, I left. My brother Peter was driving, and I kept thinking, "Well, at the first stoplight I'll just ask him to stop, and I'll walk back up the driveway ... no, at the end of Mill Valley I'll ask him to stop, and I'll hitch-hike back to Michael's house ... no, at the toll plaza on the Golden Gate

Bridge I'll ask if I can jump out, and I'll hitchhike back across the bridge." I just kept going that way—very much in love with Michael, and very much unable to take that step into independence to hang out with this guy who was 11 years older than me. I went back to high school the next day.

The day after that, he called me at home in Davis and said, "I can't sleep, I'm in love with you, I can't stop thinking about you. I have to see you right away." And I said, "Well, I'm in high school, Michael. I'm out of school Friday at three o'clock, right after my biology class." He said, "I'll be there."

He drove up to Davis, which to me seemed like a very long drive. I guess for somebody who'd been on the road for years, it was nothing. And he picked me up. But then—right there and then—began the great painful theme in our relationship, which was about heroin. I was thrilled to be courted in this way. But right after he came in and sat down, he mentioned that he had recently gotten off heroin by going to a friend's cabin at the Russian River and just going cold turkey and sweating it out.

He told me these horror stories about how the walls were weeping, with blood running down them, and hallucinations of the radiator turning into a wolf. But he got through it. Having said all that, he then said, "You know, heroin is the best thing in the world. It's better than sex." Which didn't mean anything to me. I didn't know anything about sex from personal experience at that point. He said, "There's nothing like it. It's the most incredible feeling of total well-being." And that continued to be a real bone of contention between us. It was kind of a big obstacle and a warning sign, right from the beginning.

We drove to San Francisco, and he dropped me off at my father's house. Then Ron drove me down to Palo Alto to a gig. Right after the Fillmore closed, Bill Graham threw a giant, all-weekend party for the musicians and the employees who had been close to him. Michael came down the next day with his good friend Jonathan Cramer. Jon drove him down there to get me. They just drove down, said hi to Bill, and then I got in the car and went back up. It was, like, a seven-hour circuit for them.

I felt very pursued and happy and madly in love. And what happened shortly thereafter was really tragic for me, although it will seem silly to anyone else. Michael was recording down in LA, and he had said to me, "I'll call you Tuesday." So I sat by the phone from the moment I woke up until late into the night. As the hours went by and the phone didn't ring, it was like a weird kind of initiation. My childhood died, actually, during that day of being so horrified that I had been made a fool of in a certain way—that he didn't really care. So, at that point, I thought, "Oh, I have to wise up and play this game," which then was in full swing—free love, noncommittal relationships, and all this kind of meaninglessness.

Shortly after we got together, I went off to Europe by myself with a backpack—to go find my ancestors, to go find my roots. And then from there I went to college in Vermont. For the next 10 years, we had a passionate love affair of one-night stands or summers. I went away to college, and I'd see him in the summer or at Christmas. He'd always be keeping a candle burning for me until I got back, or saying, "Why can't you go to college out here, where we could be together?"

I didn't find out for seven years, I suppose, of this on-again/off-again relationship with Michael that he was suffering that whole time—I mean, that he really was in love with me.

Pretty Amazing Scams

Susan Beuhler I had been living in Europe. I was gone for a couple of years, and when I came back, at the end of 1971, I was in Chicago. I had a baby, Toby, independent of Michael. When my son was two months old, Michael's mother said, "Please go out to California."

She was bound and determined that Michael would be better off if I went to stay there with him. She kept thinking that he would be all right if I was there, so she gave me a plane ticket. I was happy to go because I was dying to get out of Chicago, where I felt like I was suffocating.

I kept house for Michael. I just lived there and took care of things. That was a very wonderful period of time, when we were all living in Michael's house on Reed Street. It was wonderful, happy. We were a large group—sort of an extended family. Toby Byron moved in, and that's when I met my now husband, Bonner, because he was a friend of Toby's.

Toby Byron I met Michael in early 1968. At my high school, some friends and I were promoting a concert, a benefit for Biafra. I'd found out where Michael Bloomfield lived, so I went up to his house and knocked on the door. I think I went a few times before I ever got him to come to the door.

Finally, one day, he answered the door. It was about four o'clock in the afternoon, and he was still sleeping. He was sort of pissed at me for waking him up. He came to the door in a T-shirt and nothing else. But he invited me in. And I got him to come play at our high school in the gymnasium, at this benefit for Biafra. I got him and Nick and Mark Naftalin and John Kahn and Ira to play at our benefit for 150 bucks, which I thought was a helluva lot of money. And that was really where I met him.

For quite a while thereafter I was a fan—just this kid who bugged him. Not that he treated me as though I was bugging him, but I'm sure—I look back on it, and he's 10 years older and he is what he is at that point. I'm hesitant to say "rock star," even though he certainly was by some people's measure. So I was just sort of there, hanging around and probably being a *nudge* a good amount of the time.

I'd go over and ask him all kinds of questions about music. But it was also the beginning of an awareness about a whole lot of other stuff beyond music, in culture, whether it be Lenny Bruce or Johnny Carson or loose women or drugs or whatever. And he's certainly not of my parents' generation—he's hip, whatever that is. And I'm at that age where anything he said was gospel. I was tremendously impressionable. It was real eye-opening.

Bonner Beuhler I'd gone to Europe in the spring of '72 and came back in the fall. By that time, Toby had moved into the house. I met Susie the day I came back. I was going down to Toby's room, and she was in her room. And those things—the lightning bolt hits, and you know. We struck up a relationship pretty quickly. So I spent an awful lot of time over there. Michael was gone at the time—he was in Europe with Jon Cramer, and he didn't come back 'til October.

Susan Beuhler A lot of people that were close to him always felt that Michael and I belonged together, and we should never have split up. But I don't think that was a feasible thing. Michael and I were very close, and we would have stayed very close as brother and sister, maybe—just as very good friends—but the romantic thing was gone.

Michael had a lot of problems with his family. So we built a family, he and I did—our friends around us were a family. He felt very strongly about family; he wanted family, and I think he liked having all these people around. It was very important. And when it worked, it was very, very good. There was nobody, I think, who was here, who won't remember it with pleasure. We did big dinners, we had big festivals, practically for every holiday. It was wonderful.

Everything was geared towards Michael. In those days, he'd get up around one in the afternoon. He had freshly squeezed orange juice, and he would go through different little obsessions, like when he thought vitamins were the thing. And then, for a while, Tiger's Milk was the thing. He'd mix his orange juice and his Tiger's Milk and take his vitamins, and then he'd start making phone calls, and people would start calling. People would start coming over, and it would be sort of a hang-out. Everybody would hang out all afternoon. He didn't work very much at this time, because he had some income.

Susan, Michael, and Toby, December 1972.

He had these little regimens that he had to do. For years he never brushed his teeth, and then he woke up one morning with blood all over the pillow and rushed to the dentist. And he said, "If you don't brush, you're going to lose all your teeth," so then he became a tooth-brushing fanatic. He would come out with his toothbrush and give everybody tooth-brushing lessons.

There was an enormous kitchen in this house on Reed Street—huge, with a gray slate floor. I'd painted the kitchen red and fuchsia and royal blue. It was beautiful, with a lot of windows. There was a dining area adjacent to it—a big, open room—and Mike's bedroom opened almost right into this little bit of hallway. So life would go on in the kitchen.

Let's say '72, '73—those were wonderful years. Everybody was healthy, everybody was happy and getting along. The house was the center for a number of people. And it was the time when Mary Tyler Moore and *M*A*S*H* and the Watergate hearings and *Sanford & Son* and *All in the Family* were on television, so we all gathered there on Friday and Saturday nights. We'd have a fabulous dinner, drink Lowenbrau beer, and watch TV and laugh. Things that were funny were of paramount importance in Michael's life. Finding things that would amuse Michael was important.

He was like the King. Not in a bad way, because everybody—and there were a lot of us who circulated around him—got a lot from him. But it was also very important to bring things to that circle. We were sort of intelligent, semi-intellectual young people who were interested in stuff. Things that were funny were very important, and books were very important.

Dan McClosky Michael loved music, but mostly he just loved to sit around and read. And he read great books. He was a voracious reader, and he liked the seamier side of life.

Norman Dayron He loved black humor. He liked to read Charles Bukowski. And *The Painted Bird* by Jerzy Kosinski—he loved that. He liked people like Bernard Malamud, a modern Jewish writer, who wrote *The Natural*. He would read very high-level literature.

Christie Svane When he loved a book, he would call up the author. And if he really loved a page—I saw him do this on more than one occasion—he'd rip out the page and stuff it in his mouth, just like absorbing the writing. He would call up writers in the middle of the night and say, "I love you, I love your writing, thank you so much."

Barry Melton Michael was a genius. I don't know if our relationship was so much musical as intellectual. Because I've always been a real bookish kind of person—that's probably why I ended up a lawyer and a criminal-law specialist. And Michael was very well read. We would have the most wide-ranging conversations on the most wide-ranging topics, because he was one of those people you could literally talk to about anything.

He had an almost photographic memory. He was a guy who could read a book, a complex book on logic or law, and he could tell you everything that was in there. He knew everything in the book, and he knew where it was. He would discuss it and say, "Well, if you don't believe me, look at page 38." You'd go to page 38 and there it was. I mean, he remembered the page that part of the principle was on.

He was easily one of the two or three most brilliant human beings I have ever known. I've been around some fairly smart people, and I've never met a musician as smart as Michael—ever. As intellectually well rounded, well read, and with such great analytical powers.

Susan Beuhler We liked things that were interesting. Magazines were very important. There was a big magazine store in San Rafael, so we went every week to get all the new magazines. Things that were new and things that were interesting, things that were on television—those things were very important in our household, for stimulation, for conversation.

Bonner Beuhler Sometime in 1973, I think, someone schlepped Dylan over to Michael's house. And Dylan wouldn't come over if anybody was in the house. No one could be there—everyone had to leave. This guy named Chicken Billy came over, and he wouldn't leave. Finally he left the house, but he was outside in the yard and wouldn't go away.

Anyway, being a nice guy, I left. But I climbed underneath the kitchen, which was where they were playing, so I could listen to them play. Dylan was working on all those songs from *Blood on the Tracks*. They did "Tangled Up in Blue" and all that stuff. Dylan was singing, and Michael was playing along. It was just an off-the-cuff thing.

They played the songs, but Michael didn't get the gig for whatever reason. I'm not quite sure. Michael always thought it was because his guitar wasn't right. It sounded dead. It was just after he'd had it made—it was that flame-mahogany one with the cutaway. After that he bitched about it, and we sent the guitar back. They changed the saddle on it, so it had more string tension, and it always sounded good after that.

The best thing that happened was when Roger "Jellyroll" Troy came out from Cincinnati, in 1973. That band really cooked—with Jellyroll, Mark Naftalin, and George Rains playing drums. Nick would play with them, too. Michael was into playing, so they worked quite a bit. The band was good, and Mike was proud of it.

At that point, Michael was working on the album *Try It Before You Buy It*. He had one more record under contract for Columbia, and he was working hard on it. Actually, there's some real good stuff on that. Michael really started writing good songs at that period of time. His talent for putting phrases together and writing good songs came together. It's too bad Columbia decided not to release it. They put it in the can, and that was it.

Around that time, Michael played on the *Triumvirate* album with John Hammond and Dr. John. It was Hammond's album, and then they called up Michael. It didn't gel at first in the studio, and they ended up getting rid of some of the people and bringing in some other people. I went to a couple of the practice sessions at Studio Instrument Rentals, where they were practicing. And Dr. John was over at Michael's house a couple of times. They seemed to get along pretty well. I think the problem was the producer and the material.

John Hammond Jr. I recorded with Michael again for Columbia when we made that *Triumvirate* album with Dr. John. Michael played so well. I was inspired by him.

We had an 11-piece band all set to go on the road. We had made the record, and we had done the *ABC in Concert* TV show. It was a big deal. It was like things were just about to pop. It was going to be a hit record—it was already getting pre-chart stuff. And then Columbia went through the wall. Clive Davis was fired, and the head of A&R, Kip Cohen, resigned. Every project that Columbia had was frozen. There was no more money for anything. It was a disaster. I went back to playing solo, and Michael, soon after, re-formed the Electric Flag.

Bonner Beuhler Barry Goldberg and his wife came out, and they got a house on Oakdale. They were woodshedding before they went to Florida for the Electric Flag reunion, which I liked more than most people, I guess. Going out of state was hard for Michael. It was hard for him to go anywhere. He didn't particularly like that.

Barry Goldberg Michael called me and said, "We want to get the Flag back together again." This was in 1974. So I left New York with my wife, Gail, and we tried to do it. But you can never go home again. It just didn't happen. We had a great gig at the Bottom Line, and we were signed to Atlantic, but it was just an awful experience. People had gotten really tight and weird and crazy. It didn't work out.

Norman Dayron The Flag was resurrected by Jerry Wexler, and they went down to Miami to do a record. I think Barry had a lot to do with that, trying to get that second thing, and Michael went along with it. But, see, by that point, he was a guy who had quit a band that he had been a part of—and the Flag was almost this marketable commercial entity, by that time, that had hired him back again.

Jerry Wexler When the Electric Flag was re-forming, I very foolishly thought it would be a good project for me to tackle. So I signed them up and produced them. It was Nick and Buddy and Barry Goldberg and the bass was Jellyroll—Roger Troy.

So we went to do this thing in Miami, at Criteria—and it was really a disaster. The first thing that happened was I was late coming into the studio the first day. I'd asked Tom Dowd to co-produce it with me, so Tom was there. And he got into it with Buddy Miles. Tom was miking the drums, and

Michael and Toby Beuhler.

he put an ambient mike over the set, and somehow Buddy got excited about that. He actually came over the drum set, knocking the sandbags down and coming at Tommy physically. By the time I got there, Tommy was gone.

Buddy featured himself as the man who knew everything. I found out that he was coming into the studio at night and replacing Jellyroll's bass lines with his own bass lines. It was so bad that we had to go in before the session and erase them and replace them with Jellyroll's. That was a nice little chore for a producer to have to bother with, when you're trying to make a record.

And the other thing was: I couldn't get Michael to play solos, couldn't get him to play any real lead. He was just playing rhythm. I don't know what he was waiting for. So, finally, we had to finish the record—and with everybody else gone, then he overdubbed his leads. There were some good cuts on the record, but we never got off the ground.

Bonner Beuhler To some extent, Michael didn't want to do it. Some of these projects he got drawn into—they were just things to do. They weren't really his. They'd call him up: "Do you want to do it?" "Sure." He didn't have artistic control over it. And Michael, you know, he needed the money.

Susan Beuhler I slowly started taking over Michael's finances. I didn't at first, but he wasn't doing anything about anything, so he had put me on his checking account so I could pay the bills. That was when I discovered that he hadn't paid taxes, because I said, "Hey, it's tax time—let's do the taxes." I found out that he hadn't paid taxes for quite a few years, which sort of did him in.

Allen Bloomfield When Albert Grossman was his manager, Albert took care of the taxes. Michael provided the information, and his tax returns were paid. But once he was no longer with Albert, when he was on his own, it was as if he had no responsibilities or did not have the ability to respond to certain things.

I think it was sort of a defiance—it goes back to this childhood thing of "somebody's going to bail me out, somebody's going to show me that they love me, somebody's going to be the father and take care of this business." Eventually, our father got involved in paying off those debts. Michael could jerk himself around about certain aspects of reality, but he could not completely close the door on everything Harold would say. He just couldn't.

Susan Beuhler I spent a lot of the next two years with the accountant, trying to sort out the mess. I remember many hours and many cigarettes smoked. We became very good friends with his accountant, a wonderful lady. We got along very well. She was older than we were—sort of a straight lady, but she was cool. She was another person who became, because she had to be, part of our household. That was a big thing, straightening out those damn taxes. That was horrible. That went on for ages.

Michael Bloomfield I've been involved in some pretty amazing scams. Barry Goldberg, a musician whom I have known all my life, was a genius for all sorts of scam/hustle things. One of them was the resurrection of the Electric Flag—the debacle of debacles. Another scam was a band called KGB, named after the Russian secret service.

To give you some background: During this time I was going through an intense period of musical self-awareness. I knew what I wanted to do. All of my diverse inputs were sort of coming together and solidifying. It was coming out in the way I wrote prose, painted pictures—the same aesthetic value was brought to everything, and I thought that it was valid.

Michael in airport, May 1970.

A lot of things influenced my confidence in the worth, the value, of all this. Ry Cooder is an example. I thought: Here is a man who has his eye on a certain sparrow, making record after record and constantly refining his diamond, so to speak. Not just Ry, but there were many other artists— Willie Nelson, and certain poets and novelists—and I realized that everything was coming together for me in an artistic sense. I was developing a set of Bloomfield criteria. I realized I had a way of seeing the world, and everything was filtered through this certain aesthetic mechanism. It was a pure visceral thing.

Well, right when I was going through all of this incredibly important self-realization, Barry Goldberg took me to see this manager friend of his, and the guy looked across the table and said, "Boys, let's put a super group together!" I told him he was crazy. Al Kooper had invented the term—super group, super session—and it was a pure scam. It was filthy lucre. It had nothing to do with an affinity for playing with each other. It was just a marketable name, like Fruit Loops. So I said to this manager, "Can you understand it, can you grok it, does it go through your brain what I'm saying to you, what I'm going through, what I'm going to do in terms of art and music?"

And he said, "Let's put a super group together!" This manager was not a crass guy, just a businessman. Nobody knew who the guys were in the bands that Barry and I had been playing with previously, so the manager said that we needed names. He said to me, "Look, man, we've got Rick Grech to play bass in this new band. We've got a name drummer, Carmine Appice." I told him that I wasn't interested in playing with these guys. I said, "Are you crazy?" And he said, "We'll clean up."

The band got along great—we liked each other—but artistically it was a terrible experience. I couldn't sleep. I had moved down to LA, and I took Susan's son out of school. It blew the kid's mind. We were down there living in LA. It was horrible.

The first thing we had to do was get a record company, so we went to Hollywood to showcase for record executives. It was like *Roots*. We were up on the auction block: "This is a super group, people!" All these execs who came to see us looked the same: pinkie ring, leisure suit, shirt open to the tits, fabulous complexion, and blow-dried hair. Also, some real cigar-stub guys: "Hey, Mike! I've been following your career ever since ... what was that group you were with? You were with Bloomfield, right?"

One word I heard over and over again was "bankable." We were a product, we were hula hoops, we were skateboards. We got a record deal, though. It was with MCA.

There are all sorts of executives in the record business. On the one hand you've got people like John Hammond Sr., Jerry Wexler, Lou Adler, Clive Davis, Ahmet Ertegun—these people have aesthetic values. They know what they want. They are molding specific sounds. Take Mo Ostin at Warners; he knows good music and bad music. Why do you think he keeps Ry Cooder on that label? He's not going platinum, but they know good stuff—it's hot, it's good art. They subsidize good art, and that's an attitude you don't find much in the music business.

MCA's president at the time was a corporate guy who was transferred from some other branch of this big conglomerate, and as far as he was concerned he wasn't buying music. He wasn't interested in music; he was into platinum potential. His company paid huge chunks of money for us.

It took a few weeks before I realized exactly what was happening. I began to realize the meaning of the word "band"—to band together, to congregate for some sort of common meaning, whether it be religious, or they're all gay, or they're all black, or whatever. In KGB there was no real reason to congregate at all. It finally hit me: it was product, it was beef, it was plastic. They had this big Hollywood party for us with all these guys dressed up like Cossacks. It was really bizarre.

I had quite a bit to do with the band breaking up. It took me a long time to see the scam of it, the direction of it, but finally I realized what was happening. I gave an interview to a guy from the *LA Times*, and I told all.

I told him everything that went down. And he printed it—every word. That did it. I was pissed at that guy, I was looking for his ass. I wanted to kill him. I can't explain why I blew it. It was tunnel vision, naiveté, stupidity— I was just being dumb.

Apparently, the manager had been telling these record guys that the band members had all been dreaming of playing with each other for eons. We had loved each other for so long—if only fate, destiny, would bring us together, because all our lives we had wanted to be with each other and quack, quack, quack. When it came out in the *LA Times*, the manager was furious, the guys in the band were furious, and the record company was furious.

See, every band I had ever been in got together because the people wanted to play with each other—they really did. They had known each other, and it was a serious trip. They had worked out their parts, and they were working on the same kind of musical ideology and still working and still working.

The KGB album that I played on wasn't even done with the band members playing together. They recorded it down in LA and flew the tape up to Sausalito, near San Francisco, and I overdubbed my parts—I "phoned them in," like in *Doonesbury*.

But I'll tell you something interesting. After all that I've just said, we were a good band. When we would screw around—and we screwed around a lot—we were good. We could spend all day just singing *a cappella* harmonies or doing old New Orleans horn songs, all sorts of stuff. But the KGB thing itself was undefined. Ridiculous. It was a preprogrammed mold. I exhorted them over and over to break out of that, but they wouldn't. It really upset me. When they booked us for a 50-city tour, I said this is beyond the dregs, the worst. I quit. I offered to give all the money back. I wouldn't lend my name to it.

The record came out, with my overdubbed parts on it. MCA is such an incredible merchandiser that the record sold. I swear, they could be selling pig farts, whales copulating—it wouldn't matter. They would sell it successfully. KGB sold almost half a million records—a non-band.

Shortly after KGB, I felt this overwhelming urge to do something with integrity, so I did *If You Love These Blues, Play 'Em as You Please* for *Guitar Player* magazine. I know it's my best record. It's me at my hottest. It's just great blues playing—that's all I can say. I was striving to get the sounds of various old records, and that came through. I was trying to look at not just different guitar styles, but also the whole setting, the feel, the persona, the ambiance of certain musics—sort of a musicological period movie. I mean, I wasn't just copying licks. And now I really like to hear it. The other records that I did—I hear them now, and I hear clunkers here and there. But that record I really like to hear over and over again.

Norman Dayron That record, the *Guitar Player* record, was solely Michael. It was pure, pure, pure Michael. It was totally Michael's idea. I inputted less on that than any project I ever did with him, including home recordings.

He was so overwhelmingly clear about what he wanted and what he was going to do that he really didn't need to consult anybody. He did it like an Alfred Hitchcock production. He had it all figured out in advance. For example, he has Nick singing on "Mama Lion." In normal circumstances, it would be because he was hanging out with Nick, and they would do something together. But in this case, it was because he had conceived the arrangement and wanted Nick on there.

I did have some influence on "Altar Song," in that Michael and I—believe it or not—used to talk about Greek tragedy. I had a classical education in philosophy and had read Homer and Aeschylus and Sophocles and like that. I talked to Michael quite a lot about the panegyric form of poetry, where, with religious awe, you list the names of those people whose names should be carved on the wall of eternity. I think that partly influenced "Altar Song," the way he did it in that format.

One thing that's interesting about the album is there are a lot of folk songs on there—folk blues, country blues, things like "Death Cell Rounder" or "Hey, Foreman." These are, as he says, white rural blues in the style of the Carter family or Jimmy Rodgers. Michael was into country music, too. He does give a very nice balance of country blues and city blues and acoustic ragtime playing. If you listen to "East Colorado Blues" or "Thrift Shop Rag," you can hear his origin.

This gives you the whole insight into what distinguishes him from everybody else. I could make up song lists for 10 different artists who were good blues guitar players that wouldn't have included one of these songs. That's what made Michael so unique.

On the Road to Utah and Trouble

Bob Greenspan Back in the mid '70s, I lived in southern Utah. I've always lived in remote areas in the western United States. I said, "Mike, you really should come out camping, because you need to get away from things. Maybe this is a way to get off heroin. Why don't you come out here for few weeks. This place is like another planet."

He went for the idea. He and Jon Cramer got on an airplane and flew from San Francisco to Salt Lake City, and then they took a Greyhound bus from Salt Lake City down to Moab, Utah, which is about 250 miles south of there. They were just coming off a heroin thing, and they bought new camping equipment and new hiking boots.

Michael told me, "I've never really been camping." And he certainly had never been even remotely near southern Utah, which is not like anywhere else in the world. I'm talking about the canyon lands country.

So they get on the Greyhound bus, and there's all these Indians sitting on there, coughing. Michael told me he was sitting next to somebody who puked on the bus. In a lot of ways he felt right at home with that, because he got sick and puked a lot himself. They're on the bus, coming down from their heroin bout, and they come in at about midnight to this small town. And, of course, he forgot my phone number—left it at home. He's supposed to call me so I can pick him up. They drop him off, and there's one place open, an all-night restaurant called the Westerner Grill.

He walks in there—and, of course, since it's a small town, he thinks everybody in town knows who I am. He sees this sheriff—a big, redneck-type sheriff—sitting at the counter there. He goes up to him, and he's kind of in a panic, because he doesn't want to be stranded in this town where he doesn't know anybody. He says, "Do you know Bob Greenspan?" The sheriff looks at him—God knows what he thought—and he puts his hand on Mike's shoulder and says, "It'll be okay, son. Just take it easy. Everything will be okay." The sheriff didn't know who the hell I was, and I'm sure he wondered who the hell Mike was, because Mike was such a hyper guy. I'm sure the sheriff couldn't imagine who this guy was.

And so what happened was: they walked around town 'til they found a motel and checked in. The next day I had to drive around to every motel in town and ask if these two guys came in. Finally, I found them. And they told me about this experience with the bus ride and the people puking and the sheriff. I brought them over to my place, and they just didn't know where the hell they were.

A day later, we go out on a camping trip to this remote area, which is about 50 miles from the nearest paved road. We're driving down all these dirt roads to camp in this spot—it was this huge canyon with a big alcove. During the night we had a fire going, and there was a mountain lion nearby that was screaming. I've only heard two mountain lions in my whole life, and one time was the night that I was camping with these guys. And they heard this scream. Of course, they couldn't sleep anyway, because they were used to going to sleep at five in the morning.

So they couldn't sleep, and they're in this canyon, and they hear the wailing scream of this mountain lion, which put chills down everybody's spine. A mountain lion is described as sounding like a woman, a human female, being stabbed with a knife, or being raped, or being killed. It's very much like that. These guys heard this thing and went, "What the hell was that?" They said, "We've got to get out of here. You got to get us out of here." And I said, "Hey, listen, that's a plus. It's pretty amazing that you guys heard that. I'm thrilled, because that's a mountain lion."

I told them, "It's not going to come after you." But they didn't believe me. So I sat up with those guys for a long time. Eventually, they fell asleep—around five, six in the morning. And I got up at about eight o'clock, to get these guys to go hiking. I kind of kicked Mike and said, "Hey, Mike, let's get up and go hiking." He lifts the bag up, and the sun is beating right down into his eyes, and he says, "If I had a gun, I would shoot it right off."

We hiked around for three, four, five days. And he started getting into it. Mind you, there was nothing of civilization around. I wanted to get these guys out there just to do something totally different. But Mike was sorry he had his friend Jon with him, because he was a total disaster. Jon put his backpack on upside down and everything fell out of it, and then it rolled down a cliff. But Mike and Jon were good friends. Mike used to have to help this guy out, because he was a pretty pitiful character.

After about a week, when they had to go, Mike said, "Well, it's too bad I couldn't stay longer." Even though it was so foreign and strange to him, he probably could envision that if he hung out there he could clean out, maybe.

Norman Dayron He went to the Stanford Sleep Center in the mid '70s. But I didn't think that was a big deal or anything—I mean, Michael, at that point, had a set of relationships with doctors where he would con them into giving him downers and sleep medication. Maybe "con" is too harsh a word. They loved him. They were his fans, these doctors, and they would give him sleeping pills. Michael had experimented with sleeping pills even back in Chicago, because this insomnia was an ongoing problem for him. When he went to the Stanford Sleep Center, I viewed that as just another failed attempt to get some relief.

I think that sleeping pills gave him some relief, and that's why he went back to them. This was a problem his whole life. But to tell you the truth, I saw it as part of the dynamics of his life—part of the ups and downs. Even when he went three, four, five days without sleep, he really never was that bizarre. Now, I was very close to him. He would come over to my house and spend days recovering from this or that. He had developed into this cycle of being awake and then crashing, and they were pretty long periods sometimes.

Michael had this whole part of his life that was associated with doctors. Even back in Chicago, in the very earliest days, I remember one case of him having acute insomnia and begging me to do something to help him. And I took him to the University of Chicago hospital.

Michael had this thing—when it got a little too weird, he would put himself in the hospital. It was that simple. I thought it was a fairly constructive thing. I mean, he would put himself in the hands of the physicians. He had a bizarre relationship with medicine. Michael used to read medical textbooks all the time, and he had this collection of books about medical abnormalities—things like the Elephant Man and people who had deformities and 14 fingers and a head growing out of their rib cage or something. He had this bizarre, creative relationship with the field of medicine.

But mostly it was a ritual. It was this routine, where we would put him in the hands of the doctors, and I would sit in the waiting room. They would examine him, and they would do everything they knew how to do. Ultimately, they would just not have anything all that useful for him.

Christie Svane I saw Michael sometime around 1975, when he was in the hospital for an operation on his hand. When I went to visit him, he had a stack of paperbacks that went, literally, to the ceiling. And he had read them all. I mean, it was like 25 books. He could read a book or two a day. I think he was in there that time for an operation on his thumb. He also had a terrible abscess on his arm from shooting smack.

Susan Beuhler Our life for a couple of years was not a sicky-icky thing—it was very natural and normal and nice. It didn't stay that way, unfortunately. I'm not sure why. Probably things like that can't stay as nice as they were. I always felt it was the dope—when the dope reared its head again.

We were like family. We were brother and sister. It was perfectly natural and not strange to us. Other people, sometimes, read lots of things into it, but we had made our own family. That's what we thought. And that's why the first three years—maybe it was three years—were really very wonderful, until it fell apart. I don't know why it fell apart. The dope. And it might have had a lot to do with my relationship with Bonner. Maybe that really did bother Michael, more than he ever said.

I moved out to go live with Bonner. I had to get out of the house. Michael was into the drugs and things. I had a child. I had to get out. I moved in with Bonner, and we ended up marrying. We stayed good friends with Michael, but it might have been hard on him. He never said. He was going to come to our wedding, but we stopped to pick him up and he wasn't up yet, so— that was another thing: you did things on Michael's time. Michael never did anything on your time. And that was okay.

We always considered him a part of our family, after we had our own house. He would come to eat and hang out, but that may have been hard on him. He never said—I don't know. It was a little tricky there. I really don't know, and I don't know if he told anybody.

I don't know how big a role my falling in love with Bonner played in Michael's unhappiness, or if because of it our happy household fell apart. Maybe everything was happy as long as Michael was hoping that I would stay there with him forever. Maybe some people believed that because I was falling in love with Bonner and moving away with him, maybe that had something to do with Michael's unhappiness. I really don't know.

I always thought he did what he did regardless of anybody around him. And a lot of people always said, "Oh, well, they belong together, and they'll end up together sooner or later," and they were rooting for that. But that was not the case. That wasn't how I saw it. And I don't know if it bothered him. It might have.

It wasn't the same anymore. It was very awkward. Bonner and I were together all the time, and we needed to have our own place. I think that had a lot to do with it—well, it had a lot to do with why I left.

Bonner Beuhler Most of the time when we were together the first few years, it was okay. I mean, other than the fact that it impacted his space. It was his house, and we were there all the time. Most of the time it was fun, you know, but sometimes you would—no matter how it is, you like a little space, you like not to see the people.

Susan Beuhler Michael and I were very important to each other, because we had nobody else, really. In fact, it was very scary for me to marry, because I'm not attached to my family at all. I gave up any allegiance to my family when I married Michael. I made him my family, and his family my family.

So when I married Bonner, part of me was scared that I had given up my family, which was Michael and his family. It was pretty scary there for a little bit.

I'm quite sane and stable now. I never was as crazy as he was, but I wasn't ordinary, either, in terms of the way I looked at life—none of us were. I think Michael had a chemical imbalance. He wasn't in his mind. I always felt that we were very much alike, and I know that I really understood him. I think that's why we were so close, because he trusted me and believed I understood him. But I think there were things like this chemical thing going on that I didn't understand. But I had some pretty crazy periods, too, so who knows?

I know now that drugs and alcohol change your personality. I saw it when it happened to him. I used to think that you were what you were, and what you did had to do with what you are, but I don't think that's true anymore. He was a different person when he was using heroin.

Norman Dayron After the *Guitar Player* album, Michael came to me and said, "Look, I just want to do albums with you and Bob Jones and Mark Naftalin and Roger Troy and Doug Kilmer and Ira Kamin and whoever I can feel comfortable with. I want to play around San Francisco. I want to record in my basement." Up on Reed Street, he had a little makeshift studio in his basement.

He was tired, I think, of what it took to realize his visionary ideas. He wanted to be able to express himself naturally, without the pressure of having to fulfill some high expectation of commercial success.

Nick Gravenites Norman Dayron affected Michael's life and career profoundly—for the worst. Well, I don't know if it was all him.

Let me try to put this all in context: Back in the old days when we were all young and up and coming, the record business was one of the worst businesses you could be in, if you were an artist, because it was just one big rip-off. That's all it was. And Michael was very cynical about it. Not cynical so much, but aware that behind every great fortune there's a crime. So he knew that the top people in the business pretty much got rich by screwing other people. He had no grand illusions about these people—he figured they were thieves.

Norman reinforced that idea, and he came up with these recording projects that were designed to do the exact reverse. They were designed to screw the record companies. He'd get a $25,000 advance to do a record, spend it, and then call the record company back and say, "Well, we need more." Or he'd get a large advance from a company, spend $1,500 doing an album, and pocket the rest.

Maybe Norman didn't feed on Michael's cynicism, but he reinforced it. And there's a big difference between knowing someone is a thief and doing something about it. Michael knew that the record business was stacked against the musician and the artist. He knew that. And he knew, through his experiences with the Albert Grossman office and the Electric Flag, about trying to get money out of them. Knowing the intimate histories of some of the top executives in the business, he knew it was a thiever's game.

Norman contributed that activism—actually going out and fucking the record companies. The result was, probably, that they felt good about doing it. God knows, you could applaud them for doing it. But it resulted in a lot of schlock product, a lot of stuff that didn't really represent Michael's best interests.

Michael and Norman were a pretty solid team, because, first of all, they were both junkies. I never messed with junk. It was like I was a member of another gang, another club. There's nothing that alienates relationships more than having a certain group that's junkies and another group not.

Michael was a junkie, and he hung out with junkies. They were easy to get along with. Who needed moralizing Christians on his case? That story line runs through a lot of show-business relationships. Junkies hang together. They cop together, they get high together, they do this together, they do that together. If you're not a junkie, you're an outsider. Michael and Norman, they copped and shot together. I didn't.

Al Kooper Michael had a friend named Norman Dayron who was much more of a con artist than I was. Michael always referred to me as the con artist, because I could deal with the pencil pushers, but, in fact, I'm the furthest thing from a con artist. There's nobody walking the streets of heaven, hell, or earth that can say I cheated them.

Anyway, Norman Dayron—and I don't want to put him down—he made these records with Michael that were, like, low-budget records. Norman used Michael's name to get the deals, and they made these records where they went in the studio, knocked it out in a day, and split $30,000 or something. Real "super sessions," you know. And I hope Michael was lucky enough to get that money.

That was the story on those albums. They were ill-conceived records. They were on really small labels, and they were done for a quick-cash kind of thing. I suspect that Norman Dayron made out really well on them but nobody else did. But I don't think Michael gave a fuck. Going to put out another record, great—like that. I don't think he cared very much about them.

Norman Dayron That whole period is somewhat controversial, I think, from the point of view of guys like Al Kooper. He had a very uninformed but objective standard. In other words, he was looking at Michael's output and saying, "Why isn't this better? Why isn't it more of what he's capable of?"

The thing that hurt me the most about that was their perception that I thought that stuff up just to do it for the money. Michael contracted for every one of those gigs. The record company would call me because they wouldn't know who else to talk to. All I can tell you about those recordings is that every single one of them was Michael's idea. All of those records were conceived by him, and he asked me to do the production work—to be the recording engineer, get the studio, get the contracts, handle the legal work, and so on. The stuff he didn't want to do. He was happy doing those records. I mean, that's what he wanted. There was no pressure, and we could take as long as we liked.

We would work in these little, obscure studios with people that admired us for our reputations, so they would give us cheap rates and allow us to work overtime. Michael would use whoever was around: Bob Jones, Ira Kamin, Doug Kilmer on bass. Roger Troy once in a while. David Shorey—Gashouse Dave—on guitar and bass. Nick and Mark came in for the more ambitious projects.

The total recording budget for the first Takoma record was $2,000. I think the most we ever got from them was $4,000. That was for the studio and for paying every musician.

I made some bad mistakes of integrity, and it got me a not-so-good reputation with certain musicians. I would cajole them to continue playing and promise them that someday they would be paid. Out of royalties or something, right?

For Michael, the truth is that those albums were a natural self-expression of what he wanted to do. He didn't feel there was any market for what he really wanted to do. He didn't feel there was any record company interested in letting him just play the blues and sing the songs he liked.

Maybe they are controversial, but they're incredibly valuable, because Michael really bares his whole soul on them. The conceptions of how to put the music together were all his. But they don't live up to fantasy expectations of what he might have been capable of. Some were better than others, but it was his art. Those guys who don't like me shouldn't make me the scapegoat, because Michael's art is very worthwhile listening. If you spend all your time thinking what they *might* have been or what he *should* have been, you're not in touch with reality.

There were times that everybody remembers of absolute perfection in his playing. And then you listen to what's on record, and you can always hear some crippled part of it—something that's a stutter or something that's not perfect. That's because there were so many ups and downs with him. If conditions were right, he could completely soar and enter a whole other universe that was totally creative. Up there with the greatest.

People had expectations that didn't get fulfilled. But he never had this thing like he had to make it or anything. Especially in the last 10 or 12 years of his life, he really just wanted to live his life, if you will, and let his music take whatever directions it would take. He was confident that that was going to be better for him than trying to invent a career or something.

I think he was hoping that I would bring enough of my producing talent from Chess Records to it so it would turn out okay, and I wouldn't let any really shitty stuff come out. I didn't always do that.

It was frustrating to work with him sometimes, because he would call in somebody to play piano who was a friend, who was maybe a junkie who couldn't play and couldn't get work, and he'd have this guy play. And I'd look at him and say, "How do you expect me to do anything with that?"

Mark Naftalin, Ira Kamin, and Michael,
May 1970.

One of my most frustrating moments was on one of his last albums for Takoma, which was one of the most difficult and painful, called *Cruisin' for a Bruisin'*. He had Jon Cramer play the piano, and they did this song, "Snow Blind," about cocaine. It was so painful and so crippled.

Cramer was interesting. He was another one from Chicago, from a wealthy family. A piano player, an actor, who was a very, very tortured person.

But as a producer this was a horrible experience, because here was something that was, in my view, so difficult and so lame and so painful I didn't want it on the album. And then I realized that for Michael that wasn't the point. The point was to contribute something to Jon. Only now, in retrospect, can I see the generosity and the love that was in that—that he could do that for Jon. He was doing that for Jon's well-being and prestige, so Jon could feel good about himself. He was good enough to play on a Michael Bloomfield album, and his song was good enough for Michael to want to produce.

But my point is that the whole period of recording everything from the Takoma records to the Mitchell Brothers soundtracks—those were his choices. Let it never be mistaken: those were Michael's choices in his life. He was as in control of them as he was of anything else he ever did. This is what he wanted to do.

We did pornographic-film soundtracks for the Mitchell Brothers. Again, if you want to talk about me as the bad guy, the truth is that I really wasn't. I didn't know the Mitchell Brothers—Michael did. He didn't go to those movies, particularly, but he knew them because he knew everybody. Michael came to me and said, "I've got this gig, doing soundtracks for the Mitchell Brothers. I want you to co-produce it with me. I want you to help me." And I said, "Okay. Well, what film are we going to do?" And it would be *Hot Nazis* or *Sodom and Gomorrah*. This was the kind of thing that happened.

Anybody would have to be a fool to think that I led Michael Bloomfield down any path whatsoever. It's pretty obvious. We did the soundtrack for an Andy Warhol movie called *Andy Warhol's Bad*. Did I get that gig? Do I know Andy Warhol? No. Michael's in New York, he's the darling of the New York set, and at one point he comes back and says, "Norm, Andy Warhol is sending 17 reels of 35-millimeter film out tomorrow, and I gave him your address." I said, "Michael, why did you do that?" He said, "Because I knew I wouldn't be home."

So I come home and, sure enough, there's this stack of film cans—not that we had anything to look at them on. And we had to do the soundtrack, right? So we went and did the soundtrack. We assembled a gang of stellar Mill Valley artists: Anna Rizzo, Ira Kamin, and others. We would just do these things—the Warhol film was like that, the Mitchell Brothers stuff was like that.

Anna Rizzo I met Michael through Norman. I was dating Norman, so I started hanging out with him and Michael, and I got into a lot of bad habits. I was a very screwed-up young person. And all my idols, from growing up in the music business, were either fucked up or dead. I was looking to get into trouble, so it didn't take much to talk me into anything. I was looking for the heroin and that stuff. So I got into it.

One time in the studio, during a session, before I'd ever done any heroin, I tried to talk Michael into getting me some. He looked at me and said, "You've got to be kidding me. You've never gotten high in your life." And I lied through my teeth. I said, "Yes, I have, Michael. I've done it all the time." He said, "You ain't done shit. You've never done it in your life, and I am not turning you on." He was really like a brother, and he didn't want to see me get into that shit. But I did.

Later on, we did it together all the time. I have memories of driving into the city on missions. Michael would just lay down in the back seat— he didn't even want to see the drive. And he was always trying to talk me out of it. He told me, "You don't have what it takes to be a junkie. You don't have it in you." I never understood that distinction. I didn't get it. I kind of do now, now that I've got a lot of clean and sober years behind me. I just couldn't live that life. I couldn't do it well. I didn't want to die that way.

Michael, for all his faults and everything, was a bluesman. He lived out his life as a bluesman, and in a twisted way there's a certain integrity to the way he lived his life. He made no bones about it. He made no apologies for it. He didn't try to hide anything. He just was who he was. And he was very tortured. He OD'ed lots of times—it was an ongoing thing. We'd grab some frozen peas out of the freezer and start stuffing them down his pants and putting them under his armpits, to revive him. The medics knew the way to the house on Reed Street by heart.

Michael and Norman were very karmically tied in with each other. I know a lot of people hated their relationship and felt that Norman used Michael, but they leaned on each other. They were like bookends. That's exactly what they were like. They both had incredible intellect, very sharp minds, and they were more than brothers—they were like twins. And they were both incredible storytellers. I learned a lot. Norman, basically, was my education, with the books I read and the things I took an interest in. Knowing both of them really changed my life, in bad ways and in good ways.

Everything Is Replaceable

Nick Gravenites Around 1978, Michael was getting really unreliable. I didn't know what was happening, whether he was going to show up for gigs or not. I realized I had to front my own band. I became a band leader and made my own life.

Steve Gordon I had a nightclub, the Savoy, in San Francisco. I booked Michael Bloomfield and Friends, often, and a number of times Michael didn't show up. One time he calls me up and goes, "I can't make the gig, man. Nick shot himself in the hand." And I go, "Oh, my God, is he…." Michael says, "Yeah, yeah, yeah, he's all right. Bye." And he slams the phone down.

So I call up Nick and ask, "Nick, are you all right?" He goes, "What are you talking about?" I go, "Well, Michael just told me you shot yourself in the hand, and you guys can't make the gig tonight." He goes, "You're such a fuckin' asshole," for me believing him. And he hangs up on me. Then Michael would show up the next night and be shooting the shit with me, as if nothing had happened.

Mark Naftalin During the years when we worked together as Michael Bloomfield and Friends, we would go along for a while, and then Mike would pull the plug or yank the rug. I never asked him, but I figured that those times probably coincided with the arrival of a trust fund check.

There was another factor, though, and that was the approach-avoidance thing *vis-à-vis* success. I put a lot of energy into keeping us working, often functioning as a *de facto* manager. I needed the work, and I was proud of what we did together and wanted to see it flourish. Mike was just as serious about the music as I was, but he didn't want to stay on a path. He wanted to retreat. And he did it again and again.

Sometimes he even cut out in the middle of a gig. There was one notorious incident in Vancouver where Mike took off in the middle of the night, leaving us a note on his pillow. I still have the note; it says something like, "Sorry, sorry, bye, bye." He even left his guitar in the club, and the club owner kept it. I never did find out exactly why he couldn't finish the engagement. What was the problem?

What I want to stress here is that this quality, this fear or angst or whatever it was, this need to derail—call it what you will—was a main strand in his fabric. The spotlight or the pressure or something just pushed him over the edge. There was no aesthetic of creation or ethic of friendship that could withstand it.

When Mike left the Butterfield Band, we were just starting to do one-nighters. Our star was on the rise. I felt that we had the potential of becoming the Rolling Stones of America. Certainly Grossman was hoping for this kind of result, and he was starting to work us. I don't think Mike wanted to confront that. He split.

I'm sure that putting together and incubating the Flag was a creative rush for Mike and the others. But when they started rising, he split from them, too. And, of course, there's the famous story of his splitting in the middle of recording the *Super Session* album with Kooper. When something started to get successful, he would abort it or jump ship, as the case may be. I'm not saying that he necessarily saw everything that was coming and analytically skirted it; I think it was more of an intuitive thing. He just couldn't stay with things past a certain point. He didn't want the full glare.

In our work together, we would get on a roll, with a flow of gigs and income. Then Mike would stop working for months. I, naturally, would have to find other projects, other sources of income. It was clear that he didn't want to be responsible for my cash flow. But why not? We were doing good things together. As Mike would say—"Ehh."

Bob Jones There was this cycle—I guess the check must have come once or twice a year. After a while, I figured it out and went, "Oh, shit, the trust check's come." Because you wouldn't see him. He wouldn't call, and we wouldn't work. I'd call up and go, "Come on, man, what's happening? Either I've got to take other gigs or we've got to work."

Six months would go by and then he'd start working, and then eight months would go by and he'd be, "Oh, we got to go out and work, man." It came out after a while that what had happened was that he had run out of money. He spent the trust money and had to work until the next check came. It was kind of like welfare, but on a different scale.

Basically, what would happen was that once a year he would disappear from sight. And you would have to do other things. Then you got halfway through the year, and his money would begin to get low, and he would have to start going out and working. So he would have to rebuild these bridges that he had burned, partially. That worked in varying degrees of success. And then he would get towards the last two months, I guess, before the next check was going to come in, and he would want to work a lot.

Allen Bloomfield The grandchildren, of which there were four, were provided a trust from our grandmother. My dad's mother. This trust was not an excessive trust at all. The proceeds from the interest on the shares—on the 25 percent that was Michael's share—were the income that was coming to him. He never received the principal of his fund. It had to be doled out to him. Because, based on his behavior, to give him a lump sum would have been pure madness. And he had made some serious financial omissions that had to be taken out of that money, as well.

Michael bought a house. And part of the trust money was used, because it was judicious that he have a house. The rest of that money was about $50,000 a year. And he had to pay taxes on that.

So that money was there. It was not money that would be anything more than relatively middle-class income. It wasn't opulent. It wasn't millions and millions of dollars that fell into his lap. It didn't afford him the luxury of a brand-new car every year or anything like that. He was comfortable and, yes, he certainly had access, if needed. But it was very difficult to justify the need sometimes, when the causes of putting him in debt were complete negligence and irresponsibility. And those were not the type of things you wanted to bring to your father—mopping up those messes.

Norman Dayron The real truth about that trust fund was that it was a bitch. It was not at all generous, and he had very little access to it. He really did have to earn his own living. He was due to inherit money from his grandmother, but the money wouldn't come to him until he was 37 or 39. I think he died two years before he was due for his trust fund money. I always thought that was very harsh. I thought, "My God, if you had money, why would somebody withhold it from you that long?"

The bottom line on that is, I suppose, that he had the security of knowing that at some point in his life he would come into a lot of money. But he lived the opposite of that. His house was funky, his guitars were funky, he didn't even have a working stereo. I was always fixing his stereo, and he would say, "Don't bother. I can hear it in mono; I like it that way."

Bob Jones, March 1970.

Allen Bloomfield My brother lived like a camper. He never really had any great sense of permanency. He had no attachments. Televisions, records, whatever he had, he could give a fuck about. Even his own guitar.

Dave Shorey Michael loved his fucked-up Stratocaster, even though the body had been filled in and refinished black. It had a '62 or '63 neck. That was Michael's guitar. There's a picture of it on *Count Talent*—you can see how grungy it is. The guy didn't clean it. It was filthy.

I said, "Where's the Les Paul, the flame-top one?" He said it had been dropped and the heel broken, twice, right where the neck goes onto the body. The second time it broke, he didn't even bother to have it repaired right. He just taped it up, right? He used electrician's tape and somehow put enough of it on there so the guitar was holding together.

Allen Bloomfield The material contempt that he had was just remarkable. I don't know one thing he cherished in a material way, except maybe something that B.B. King might have given him. I don't know what other things there were. They were all expendable to him. Cars, records, anything. He just wasn't attached. Those things did not mean anything to him.

Norman Dayron I grew up in a family that was sort of middle-class, and I valued material things. I didn't trash the shit. And he'd say, "Norman, loosen up, lighten up. Everything is replaceable."

Michael used to get these used cars, and he would bang them up so they looked like sculpture. He would buy them at the San Quentin auction and literally run them into the ground and then dispose of them. Just leave them by the side of the road. I once asked him about that, and he said, "Well, I have this theory of disposable cars. They're like Kleenex. You use them 'til they die, then you just abandon them and go get another one for a couple of hundred dollars."

The point I'm making is that in his consciousness everything was replaceable. He didn't value material objects, and he led a kind of blue-collar life. In his house, everything was sort of clean when Susan was there taking care of things, but it was all kinds of Goodwill furniture and beat-up, funky stuff. I think he was proud of that. He didn't want to identify with his money or his background.

Michael was proud of earning his own living. And I think it's untrue that he wouldn't do gigs when he got money from his trust fund. Michael very often wouldn't do gigs just because he didn't feel like it.

Bob Jones In retrospect, I think Mike viewed it as: now he was able to do exactly what he wanted to do, musically, and do it when he wanted to do it. I had to fight him all through the '70s. I'd call him up and go, "Michael, come on. I'm dying here, man. We have to work." And he'd go, "Okay, okay, okay." He'd call his booking agent, and we would work for a while. And then he would either get tired of it, or he would do something stupid that pissed off the booking agent, or his drug habit would get in the way. And then it would stop.

He really didn't want to go out of the house at all. He would get to the day in the week where you'd have to catch the plane to the gig, and he would be in various stages of denial. I would go to his house early. Whatever condition he was in, I would find his equipment and throw him in the van and off we'd go, either to the gig, if it was local, or to the airport to catch a plane.

In '78, it really started getting bad. And I just want to make a caveat here before I go on with this part of it: during all this time, once Michael would get onstage and you hit the downbeat, almost always it was brilliant. The actual playing was wonderful fun and almost always well done. Occasionally, he would be in such a condition that it wasn't too great. But that was, believe it or not, very rare, because he was one of those people that could play. He was gifted. He could play in almost any condition. And if we went on the road for a few days, even though he wouldn't sleep, he would basically get better as he got cleaned out.

Michael and Nick Gravenites, June 1977.

Christie Svane In 1978 I was in New York. I was an artist model for Arnie Levin, the *New Yorker* cartoonist. I was modeling for a session, and all of a sudden, in the middle of a pose, I got a psychic communiqué. I knew I had to go find a *Village Voice*, but I didn't know why.

At the break I got a *Village Voice*, and I started pawing through it frantically. It was like in *Close Encounters of the Third Kind*, when the guy was building that mountain in his living room. I don't know why I'm doing this—it was that kind of a thing. I pawed and pawed and pawed, and then I found it: Michael Bloomfield, Bottom Line, October 12th. I started shaking all over, which was kind of a common reaction we seemed to have to each other. I was just trembling and sweating.

I was living with a dancer at that time, a guy named Danny, and Michael was living with a woman named Betsy. And, really, years had passed, but knowing the trouble I might get myself into if I went alone, I begged my boyfriend to come with me. But he didn't. I went anyway, and when I walked in, there was Michael. We were just over the moon to see each other.

I remember that Johnny Winter came. He was hanging out in the dressing room, telling Michael his woes—a long list of woes. Michael was a very sympathetic ear. And it was the night of Sid Vicious and Nancy—it was the night after that had gone down. Michael opened the show saying, "I'm dedicating this to Sid and Nancy," and he started playing "Frankie and Johnny."

He did the most unforgettable version of "Frankie and Johnny." He was in top playing form, and that show was filmed.

We went to his hotel afterwards, and that night I told him that I had gotten pregnant with him when I was 17 and had an abortion. It broke his heart. He was crying and said, "I would have married you on the spot. We'd have a kid seven years old now." It was devastating and I felt terrible, but I just hadn't thought I could approach him about it at the time. Because he had said something to me right before it happened—I had spent the fall term at college and come home for Christmas and seen him, and he said, "I hope you don't want to move in with me."

I had said, "Oh, no. I wouldn't want that," which was a stone lie. But I had the habit of saying what I thought someone wanted to hear, especially him. He said, "I'm an insomniac, and it's really hard for me to live with someone. I need the whole bed to sleep, and I sleep from sunrise until noon, and I lead a really crazy schedule. I don't think you'd enjoy it. I can't adapt to another schedule. You know, I'm really idiosyncratic." So when I said I didn't want to, he said, "I'm so relieved. It's really been worrying me, because we want to be together, but I can't see us living together."

That was a crushing blow, which added more evidence on the side of: Don't ask too much from this guy. Don't think of this person as someone to marry. This is just a wild romance. So, when something so real as getting pregnant came up, I just didn't ask him. That was a very sad thing.

But what happened when we did get back together, after that show at the Bottom Line, was powerful enough to destroy the relationships we were having. That night we did that sort of classic sit-com exchange of saying, "Well, hi, how have you been? Are you living with someone?" "Yeah." "You happy?" "Oh, yeah, it's great." We both went through those lines, but by the morning it was really getting hard to hold up that front.

He went back to San Francisco, back to Betsy. And I did a stupid thing— I sent him postcards. I didn't realize that they were a very serious couple. I don't know what I was thinking. I sent him postcards saying, "What a wonderful night." Poor Betsy had to get the mail and see these postcards, and when I got through to him on the phone, he said, "That was intense." She packed up and moved back to Tennessee or wherever she was from. Apparently, that was just the straw that broke the camel's back. There were other reasons she left.

Bob Jones I stopped playing with Mike in 1979. By that time, he had pissed off and lost everyone, including his booking agency and anyone that could fulfill road-managing requirements. Basically, me and Dave Shorey were getting him to gigs. And we were doing bookings. People were calling Michael, and he was telling them to call me, so I would book him. After he didn't show up a couple of times, I wouldn't do the gig unless he would agree to me picking him up and taking him. Because I knew if I could get him in the car and get him there, then I could probably get paid. And that was unlikely if we were expected to meet there.

If I recall correctly, the last gig I played with Michael was at a college in Canada. At this point, you really couldn't get anyone to believe that you could get Michael out of the house to a gig. It was becoming obvious that there was no way to realistically play anymore. That time I got him to the gig only by dragging him out of the downstairs bathroom at the Mill Valley house and dragging him onto the plane.

Placidyl—that was the shit he was taking. When we got to Montreal, he was so full of Placidyl that it was like dragging around a retarded child. He had no idea where he was, and he was sort of a blithering idiot. But we went up there, we played, and we did good. He played well.

When I came back from that, I.... This is difficult to describe. I was convinced that he was going to kill himself some way or other. This is one of those decisions that you make based not on any one thing someone says or does, but from years and years of watching a person. You see an overall deterioration, and you've been in the scene long enough, and you've seen what happens to people that are showing these signs. You realize you're going to see the death of another one of your friends soon.

You've seen too many of your friends die. You've seen too many of the same symptoms, and you just don't want to see it anymore. At this point, it's a drag on your life. You're saying, I don't want to see this guy kill himself. It's too painful to watch. And I have long since lost my messianic tendencies. I know I can't save him. I've tried every argument. I've done everything. The plain fact is this guy doesn't want to save himself. And without that commitment, nothing I do will make any difference.

I thought, This is just too much. I can't pour any more energy down this rat hole. So I stopped. And after that I really didn't talk to him again.

Something Angelic

Ron Butkovich I started seeing Michael again around 1979. He had started drinking, which he had never done. And he stopped doing heroin and became a drunk. And, you know, it was like going from one bad thing to another.

Around that time Michael needed a back-up band. And I was in a band already. He said, "All right. You're going to be the back-up band." He'd do his solo acoustic thing and then he'd do a thing with the band.

He said, "You pay these guys and take care of everything." He didn't even care who was in the band as long as it sounded good. It was just, he'll show up and play. That's it. If he showed up. He was notorious for not showing up. Or showing up and leaving. That was a thing he used to do.

Towards the end of his life, you know, Michael still got a lot of fan mail. And he'd answer it. He'd write the people back letters. I remember one time, we come back from the gig and it's three in the morning on a Saturday night. We're sitting around, unwinding a little. He's reading his fan mail.

All the sudden he's sitting across the table and he starts this—he has this really menacing sort of laugh. And he starts laughing. I said, "What's wrong?" He says, "Ron, read this." And he hands me a letter. It's from some guy who really admires him, a guy named Dave in Alabama. And this guy Dave goes on and on in the letter. And the last line is, "Michael, please, please, feel free to call me anytime. In fact, call me as soon as you get this letter."

Michael says, "Ron, what time is it in Alabama?" I said, "Like five in the morning." He says, "Boy, this guy's in for a shock." Bloomfield calls the guy. It rings about eight times. I get on the other line and I hear a woman answer the phone. And Michael says—he had this real loud voice—he says, "Is Dave there? Let me talk to Dave." And she says, "What? Who is this?" "It's Mike Bloomfield."

This guy's sort of waking up and this woman says, "Dave, it's Mike Bloomfield." The guy picks up the phone, Michael says, "Dave? Mike Bloomfield. I just got your letter." So they go on and on. They talked for about an hour, you know.

Classic Bloomfield. And I remember once we went out to dinner, we were in an Italian, family-style restaurant, where you sit around the table with a lot of people. Strangers and everything. We were sitting around a table and people would notice Michael and everyone's really impressed, you know. He was very noticeable. People knew who he was. He was still a star. And Michael's getting sort of loaded and he gets the whole table—in this Italian restaurant—he gets this whole table to sing "When Irish Eyes Are Smiling." Everyone is singing "When Irish Eyes Are Smiling." The owners of the restaurant were getting sort of upset, but what are you going to do? This was Michael's way. He'd have unique ideas for comedy situations. You know, he could be that way. When he was on, he was nonstop entertainment.

Christie Svane In the summer of 1979, I went out to Boulder, Colorado, to teach at Naropa. I was an assistant to John Roland. He was a dear friend and a dancer, and he asked me to assist him in his dance classes. Naropa is a Buddhist college , and it has a very interesting history. Poets and avant-garde musicians and theater people collected there, and what they had in common was their interest in Tibetan Buddhism. Allen Ginsberg moved there. He helped found it and held forth there, teaching.

When I was out there, I got a telegram from Michael. I took it out of the envelope, and I was shaking like a leaf. It said, "Just call me. I may be hard to reach, but keep trying." I felt like those lines were the message of a lifetime, in a way. "I may be hard to reach, but keep trying." And I feel like I didn't know enough about how to help someone who was cross-addicted, who had a lot of problems. His main one, by now, being Placidyl.

A few months earlier I had called him, and he sounded almost unintelligible. I said, "Michael, what's wrong?" He said, "Placidyl. I'm strung out on Placidyl, and I need help." I said, "Is there anything I can do for you?" He said, "No, nothing."

Somewhere between that phone call and the telegram he checked himself into a state mental hospital. He was there at least a month. It was a substantial amount of time. He told me lots of stories about being in there. There were people in beds next to him who would put out cigarettes on their arms, just to feel something. Most people were just zombies, sitting around, no reason to live. And he would organize basketball games. Even as duck-footed as he was, and kind of awkward, whatever it was—whether it was baseball, basketball, ping-pong, whatever was at hand—he would give it 200 percent. Into it and really, really trying—but never losing his sense of humor about it.

He had gone there to get off Placidyl. And, I think, also because he didn't want to die, and he knew he was in danger. There was a very touching piece of paper I found when I came back to live with him. He had written an inventory of everything he saw in his hospital room. It was like a poem, and it was really heartbreaking. It said something like: "One green metal chest of drawers, one aluminum window, one folding chair, one gray steel bed." It was like that. It looked like some exercise of trying to affix himself to the physical world or trying to ground himself, somehow, on earth.

I responded to his telegram, and I came out to stay with him. I walked into the most surreal situation—only years later did I figure it out. There was a friend of his, a psychologist, who had moved into Reed Street with him. And as soon as I arrived, this friend summoned some old girlfriend from Los Angeles. She was a hooker, as I recall, who confided in me. She said, "You know, I had the whole thing taken out, to save the bother."

This psychologist had a plan to keep Michael off Placidyl. Now, Michael's concept was to do it the way the old black guys did it: gin. Michael had never been a drinker. He was a pothead. And the heroin was occasional and recreational. He wasn't an everyday junkie guy. But, suddenly, Michael starts drinking gin very seriously.

This psychologist had a very avant-garde strategy, which was to mirror everything Michael was doing so Michael would see a reflection of himself and react with horror at the ridiculous behavior he saw before him. And in that way, save himself. Anyway, that's the way the guy tried to explain it to me. I didn't understand it. I don't know if I believe in it, anyway. But he was so drunk and high when he was explaining it to me, I just got mad.

What this psychologist did were these three things. He saw Michael drinking himself into oblivion, continuing to use recreational drugs, and summoning an old girlfriend. So I walk into a house of someone that I love, and I find there's another guy there doing exactly the same bad things, who now has this hooker living in the house with us, to be a mirror of me. The whole thing was so sordid and lurid and horrible.

Around this time, Michael did the album of gospel music with Woody Harris. I was at all the sessions. It was very beautiful—exquisite. It was music that he profoundly loved. When I was a teenager, as soon as I set foot in his house, he said, "Wait, wait, listen." He ran and put on the Swan Silvertones. And he said, "Have you ever heard anything so beautiful?"

Woody Harris I did an album of gospel guitar duets with Michael called *Bloomfield/Harris*. I had been living in the Bay Area. Chris Strachwitz, who owned Arhoolie Records, had invited me out to California to do a record. I ended up staying there. I had a job in a recording studio and was doing backup things on sessions. During that time, I went to clubs and heard Michael play, but I had never really met him.

I had actually left California when I started playing with Michael. I had moved back to Connecticut and was living on a little farm there. Then, almost immediately after leaving San Francisco, I went back, and we recorded the album in Norman's house.

It was patently obvious to me that there were an awful lot of people in the Bay Area who were hitting on Michael all of the time. People who were, to a certain extent, dependent on him. And there were always crazy people around who were trying to get at him.

Christie Svane Things were bad, and I didn't know what to do. I was in completely over my head. I tried all the ignorant stuff of saying, "If you love me, you'll stop drinking." Meanwhile, there was a girlfriend I confided in. I told her, "I don't know what to do. I can't sort this out." And she said, "There's a program called Al-Anon. Go to it—you'll be enlightened. And if you can get him to an AA meeting, that's the only thing you can do for him." At that time, I didn't know how hip that program was. I still thought, "Oh, that's something for old winos in the gutter."

I didn't realize that the very principle of Al-Anon is to admit one's powerlessness over another person and to just give them your prayers and get out of the way. That is the only thing you can do. I was really tragically uninformed about what I was up against.

All I knew is that guys would show up at the door with the smack. I remember taking a butcher knife one night in the kitchen, just slamming it down on the butcher block and saying, "That's it. All of you guys, out of here." And everybody looked so shocked and hurt, like I was saying, "No more fun." But this was a period of nobody knowing how to help Michael get out of the addiction. He thought his way, with alcohol, was kind of earthy and tried and true.

And this doctor friend, his attitude was: "Anything but alcohol. Give him happy drugs." He wanted to give him whatever happy drugs had been invented then, just keep him away from the alcohol. I wound up hating that doctor and the whole surreal situation.

I did manage to clear out that house, which was not a good thing because I also cleared out shortly thereafter, and that left Michael alone. I went back to New York. I was fed up with the situation. I had a career as a dancer in New York. I had come out kind of on a trial basis, to see if it was worth changing my life to pick up the pieces with Michael. And the whole thing was so terrifying and bizarre to me that, after a number of months, I went back.

And then I came back out, and we tried again. This time I said, "I won't live with you. I'll live in San Francisco and maybe this way it will be saner." But it wasn't. So I went back to New York. He was lonely living alone, so he came to New York to see me. Since I kept insisting that my life and my work were in New York, he said, "Well, I'll move here. I'll sell the house and move here." It all seemed so crazy.

He came and lived with me in a little apartment I had in New York. This was a very weird period. I wasn't sure I wanted to go through with it, because it was still, for me, always this ongoing question of: Can I make a real life with this man in this condition?

He sobered up. And he lived with me for two months, sober. He said, "Okay, I'll be the house husband, and you go off to your rehearsals." I'd get back from dance rehearsals, and he'd meet me at the door and say, "How about a Dos Equis and a foot rub?"

But then one day I came home and he had just drank, like, two six-packs of beer. The drunken thing got really bad. He couldn't walk. I'd have to carry him upstairs. Finally, he looked at me and said, "I guess it's time for me to go, huh?" And I said, "Yeah." Because that was the deal: If you're going to stay with me this time, we can't do this drunken thing. So he went back to San Francisco.

Then, in December 1979, he came back. Just because on the phone he had said, "Well, how are you doing, what are you thinking?" And I'd said, "Oh, I really miss you." He got on the next plane, without us really discussing it or me saying, "Yeah, man, I'm ready for you to come back, and we're going to try this again." And then, in some terrible timing, my mother got in a drive-away car in San Francisco and drove alone cross-country in the snow, and she also descended on my doorstep. So I had these two people in my life who I didn't want right then.

I was in a dance company. We were in the middle of dance season in New York, and I felt my career was in bloom. I rented an apartment in the Village and installed them both in there. I said, "All right, the two of you, if you insist against my wishes that you're going to descend on me in New York in my tiny little apartment, I'm going to put you both in here." Actually, Michael paid the rent on the place. It was $400 a month. Bathroom in the hallway. It was on Prince Street, right around the corner from Larry

Sloman, so Larry and Michael and I hung out a lot. Sometimes, if I was mad at Michael, I'd send him over to Larry's to sleep on his couch. They liked each other a lot. Larry got Michael a gig at the Lone Star, with Kinky Friedman, the Texas Jewboy. It was great. Mike sat in and played the whole show.

Around then, a really sad thing happened. It had to do with Michael's half-brother, who was going to be *bar mitzvahed*. During this period, Michael would wake up in the morning, empty a bottle of gin into a saucepan, put in a bottle of tonic and two trays of ice. For breakfast, we would sit there and drink it in coffee cups. It was a strange period of my life. I went over to the apartment, and Michael said, "I'm not able to fly. I can't do it. I can't show up there in this condition." Michael was so worried. He loved the kid. He really wanted to be there and do the right thing, but he was a mess. It was heartbreaking for him. And it was like putting the icing on the cake of being a *meshuggener* in his father's eyes—the no-good, the loser. I did write a letter to his dad about that after Michael died, but it was too late. It was all my fault.

There was something really amazing about him, though. In New York, especially, he would often walk up to a stranger—usually an old person, a very old person who looked really alone and sad. He'd go up to a really old, crotchety woman, and he'd put his hand on her cheek or on her shoulder. He'd say, "Darling, how are you? You look beautiful today." And she would blush and twitter. She would just melt. She would look at him, as if Jesus had come and bestowed pure love on her. It was not jive. He was not doing that to prove that he had the power to do it.

No matter what condition Michael was in, that underlying thread of very pure and very real love for the whole human race was always there, and everybody felt it. And even though he would screw up as an individual, there was something angelic about him.

Valentine's Day

23

Woody Harris In 1980, I was playing classical chamber music with Maggie Edmondson, and we had an agent in New York. I mentioned to him that I had done this recording with Michael—in this completely different realm—and asked if he could try to get some gigs for us. And he got us a summer tour in Italy and Scandinavia. Four of us went on this tour together: Michael, Maggie, myself, and Christine. He had a good time. He was just really relaxed.

Flying to Italy, every time the stewardess came by with the little wagon, Mike would reach behind her and grab all the little bottles of gin that were on the trays. He would take all the little bottles and just drink them down like water, to the point where he peed in his pants in the seat.

Half of the tour was hooked into a socialist festival in Italy called D'Unita that was sort of like the Communist Party festivals. Of course, we didn't know anything about this when we were booked into it. When we played in Pisa, it was in beautiful sunlight in some old ruins, and there must have been 15,000 people there.

Christie Svane The trip to Italy was a beautiful trip. But the Italians are so attached to the mythos of the alcoholic blues guy that they would sort of taunt Michael every step of the way. They'd have drinking contests with grappa. Do you know what grappa is? It's made from grapes, but you could run a motorcycle on it. It's like kerosene. It's so strong it makes tequila look like lemonade. And Michael always had this attitude towards all games, whether it was ping-pong or a grappa-drinking contest. It was like, "Oh boy, a game. I'm in with both feet." And, you know, he was the star. The poor guy—he was just getting deeper and deeper into a hole.

Meanwhile, the manager—this 22-year-old Italian Bill Graham who had organized the tour—kept coming to me and saying, "You've got to straighten Michael out. You've got to make sure he doesn't come to the gigs drunk."

The worst part was they would scream out by the thousands, "Super Session!" And Michael would go to the mike and say, "Hey, people, I'm really glad you like that record, but that was 15 years ago, guys. Would it be okay with you if I played something that I've been playing lately? And lately I've actually been playing a lot of piano. I love to play the piano. Would you let me play the piano for you?"

And they were horrible. They'd throw bottles. "Super Session!" It was shameful, the attitude of the people. It was so hard for him. He kept saying, "I want to go home, Christie. I want to go." And I wasn't smart enough to see clearly, like, "Yeah, we should go home if you want to go home." I was thinking, "No, you've got to follow through with this. You signed a contract for this tour, so you've got to follow through."

He'd say, "You know, Christie, the only reason I agreed to this tour was because I asked Norman how to get you back, and he said, 'Work a lot. Be a performer.'" I was really saddened to hear that. But it was true—I mean, it worked. When you're trying to be in love with a guy who has lost his self-respect and isn't doing anything and just wants to watch television, it's pretty uninspiring. I was starry-eyed, thinking, "Oh boy, we get to go on a European tour." That seemed like a big thing.

He kept saying the most frightening things to me, expressions of love like, "Give me a reason to live. Give me an occasion to rise to. Let's have a kid. Nothing else matters to me now. I've been to the top." One time he said, "This will sound arrogant, Christie, but it isn't. It's the truth. I've seen it all, and I've done most of it, and I'm on my way down now. The only thing I want is to marry you and have a kid."

He'd say, "I'd out-parent you on your best day. I really know about little kids." Because he had raised Susan's son, little Toby—sort of. But the frightening thing was I just knew that there was something really wrong with that equation—to have someone put their life in your hands. I'd say, "You've got to have another reason to live. Your art, your music—there has to be something else."

And I would say some really mean things to him. One time I said, "Go ahead, be a Jimi Hendrix or a Janis Joplin, go ahead and die young." He just looked at me so hurt and crushed, like, "How could you say such a thing?" But I felt like I was speaking in self-defense, like: Look at yourself. Get off this path you're on.

Another time I said, "Okay, I'll marry you and we can have a kid, if you sign a paper and swear you won't OD until the kid's out of high school." Again, he looked horrified that I could say something so ugly. And I was baffled at his reaction, like: Doesn't he know? Can't he see that that's what he's asking of me as a mother—to have children with a father who may disappear at any moment? But he kept saying, "No, no, you don't get it. The minute I had a child, I would never do any of that again."

Once, in one of those little medieval villages, there were these two ancient woman delicately arranging a wedding dress on a mannequin in the window of a wedding shop. To prove his point, he went in the door and charged into the window and started passionately embracing the mannequin with the wedding dress. And these two frail, little old women were screaming.

All through Italy, he'd say, "Look, see that church down there? We can go get married in there right now." Or it would be Sunday morning, and he'd say, "Do you hear the bells? We can go right down—they'd marry us right now, in front of the congregation."

We parted in Italy. I went to Amsterdam and London to teach a workshop. He went on to Finland to do some more gigs.

Woody Harris He drank himself absolutely wild in Scandinavia—and it wasn't easy. We had to stand on line every morning at the state liquor store to get alcohol. It's restricted, and you have to buy everything from a state store. You're only allowed to buy so much, and it's outrageously expensive. But Michael just had to have it. So everybody would buy something and hide it under the seats in the car, and we'd ration it out to him. It was his substitute for doing drugs.

The majority of the things we did in Italy were filmed. And we made a record, *Live in Italy*. The guy who made the recording stiffed us for several thousand dollars. I never got the money for it, which was absolutely normal. I stated to Michael before we left, "If you leave this guy here with this tape, you're kissing it good-bye. You're never going to get anything from this guy." And that's exactly what happened.

When Michael came back from Copenhagen, he landed in New York and left everything there—he left his guitars, he left everything. He just got out of the plane and came out to visit a friend that we had in Connecticut. He paid $300 for a taxi to take him from JFK up into Connecticut. And he was so drunk that he threw up all over the inside of the cab. It certainly couldn't have been worth the 300 bucks to drive him out there.

Christie Svane, Paris 1986.

We played at the Bitter End in New York for several nights. Michael was playing piano and acoustic guitar. And we did a live thing for French television at the Bottom Line, also in New York. They paid for the whole gig for one or two evenings, which wasn't cheap. It has some really funny and really good stuff in it with Michael. He started the first thing, and I'm sure the guys at French TV didn't know quite how to respond. He sat at the piano with his sunglasses on. All these people were cheering, and he sang, "I got drunk. I pissed on the floor. I wiped it up with my toothbrush. I don't brush my teeth much anymore." Michael didn't play a note. He sang that into the microphone, *a cappella*, and then he started playing. The cameramen must have dropped their cameras when he sang that.

It was a really, really good show, and it was well received. Michael was really hot that night because Danny Kalb came. He hadn't seen him in years, and Michael got a little bit nervous. I'd never seen him like that. He wanted to show Danny that he could really do something.

We played in Boston several times. Also in Washington, D.C. And there was a club in Pennsylvania—the Main Point. We played there two or three times. We had some really good performances. And then we played in McCabe's in Santa Monica, and that was pretty much it.

Norman Dayron In November 1980, Bob Dylan came to San Francisco to play a series of concerts at the Warfield Theater. During that time, he went over to Michael's house in Mill Valley, on Reed Street. Maria Muldaur took him there.

Maria Muldaur I'd known Dylan since 1962, and I was friendly with his band, especially his back-up singers. So on their day off, Dylan and the whole band came over to my house. We made this huge meal, and while everyone was enjoying themselves, Dylan was very nervously sitting aside from everybody. He kept looking around, and finally he said, "Bloomfield, Michael Bloomfield, lives around here in Mill Valley, doesn't he? Can we call him up? I'd love to go see him." So I kept calling, and I honestly don't remember whether the line was busy or nobody answered.

We were all going to go see Etta James later that night. She was playing in the city. And Bob said, "Gee, I just hate to feel like I came all this way up to Mill Valley and didn't see Michael." So I said, "Well, I know where he lives, and I can take you there. We can at least see if he's there."

I knew that Michael was having problems. I knew, through the grapevine, that Michael had taken to drinking a lot and wasn't exactly a smooth drunk. I mean, he was a way sloppy drunk, in a kind of jolly way. I never saw him be belligerent, but there are some people that know how to navigate drunk and Bloomie wasn't one of them.

And I knew there were other things going on, because I knew Susie and everybody around him, and I'd see him from time to time. I knew there was some bad stuff going on. Part of me was very hesitant to bring Bob over. I thought, "Bob obviously cares about Bloomers, because he's spent the whole evening preoccupied with how he could get ahold of him. But what if I bring him up there and there's some weird, debauched thing going on?" But then I thought, "Okay, whatever's supposed to happen will happen."

So we all piled into a couple of limos, and I got in with Bob and directed the driver to Bloomers' house. Thinking that I really didn't want to intrude—I didn't want it to be a scene—I said, "Why don't you all wait here? Bob and I will walk up." We saw lights on, so we walked up the driveway. I heard a TV, and I told Bob to wait further back. I thought, Let me peek in here. And if it's really something not for public consumption, I'll tell Bob there's nobody home.

So I stood on tippy-toe and looked in, and there's Bloomfield in his bathrobe looking quite disheveled, as he always did, with that Wolfman hairdo of his. He was watching some old movie on television. I tapped on the window and said, "Michael, it's Maria." "Oh, hey, hi, what are you doing here?" I said, "I've got somebody here who wants to see you." So I motioned for Bob to come up and said, "Look who's here. Look who I've got here."

Bloomfield did a double take. He was so happy to see Bob that he just threw his arms open and gave him a big hug and said, "Come in, come in, sit down. Wow, what a surprise, what a treat. My God, the last person I would have thought would be standing in my doorway." The place was not terribly well kept but not too awful, either. I was relieved. And no one seemed to be there with him.

They had a great time. They turned down the TV, and they had a great visit for about half an hour. I sat off to the side. I was there, but I just let them visit. Bob said, "You've got to come down and sit in with us, man. Maria came down, and Jerry Garcia came down." Mike said, "Oh, I don't know, I'm not playing much these days." And Bob said, "Oh, man, you've got to come—I want you to come." He really urged him to come.

And then Bob said, "You want to go with us? We're going to go see Etta James." And Mike said, "Oh, no, I'm just in for the night. I'm going to finish watching this movie." But Mike promised he'd go down and play, and he thanked me for bringing Bob over.

As we were leaving, Mike said, "Wait a minute, Bob, there's something I want you to have." He went and got this Bible. He said, "This has been in my family at least for a couple of generations. It was my grandmother's and probably her grandmother's before that." It was a very thick, little, square Bible. I'd never seen a book like it. The cover of it was raised, filigreed silver. It looked very old, very well worn, and the names of the various Bloomfield ancestors were written in the front of it.

Dylan was a little taken aback. For Mike, it was like he was acknowledging that he knew Dylan was seriously into God and spiritual things at that time. And it was something he wanted to pass on to him. Bob took it, and they embraced. And Bob said, "Okay, now, I want you to come down and play." And we went back down the driveway and got in the car.

On the way into the city, Bob was looking at the book and going, "Wow, man, look at this book." He was really touched that Michael would just, out of the blue, give him his family Bible. He seemed to really appreciate it.

Norman Dayron Michael calls me up and says, "Bob Dylan was here." I said, "Oh, yeah, bullshit." He said, "Bob Dylan was here. He wants me to sit in with him, but I'm not going to." I said, "Well, God, I'd really like to see that." He goes, "Nahh." And I said, "You're going." And he said, "Well, why am I going?" And I said, "Because I want to see it. I want to go." It had been years since I had seen Bob Dylan. And I thought, well, this would be cool, you know—"Like a Rolling Stone," "Highway 61 Revisited," whatever.

The day of the show we go to the Warfield Theater, and there's this huge line. Michael was wearing tattered blue jeans. You could see his knees through them. You could see his ass through them. And he's wearing house slippers, these old brown slippers that you just slip on, and maybe he had his old motorcycle jacket on, or not—I don't know. And a Brooks Brothers plaid shirt or something.

We go to the box office, but we can't get in because they don't know who we are. And we don't know where the backstage is. Michael is not feeling very well. He looks at me with those beagle eyes—very forlorn.

He used to call me "Profundo"—that was his nickname. So he said, "Profundo, this is a misconceived idea." This was his way of putting me in my place, because I was this University of Chicago professor, you see, who knew everything. And he always wanted me to know that I didn't. Calling me Profundo was a sarcastic way of keeping me in my place, which was very funny. In fact, I'm grateful for it, because now in my old age I know I didn't know shit.

So I go back to the box office and say, "Look, there's this guy out here called Michael Bloomfield. He's, like, a really good guitar player who used to play with Bob Dylan, who's actually on his records. Bob invited us to this show, and we want backstage passes." They looked at me like they were going to call the police. But someone believed something, so they got security and went down to Dylan, and he said, "Oh, let the guy in."

We went down to the dressing room, and it really was nice. Dylan hugged Michael, and Michael introduced me to him. They gave us backstage passes, and then Bob brought out Michael during the concert. And he gave him a 10-minute introduction. He took 10 minutes to tell this young audience of his, this new generation audience, that here in their midst in San Francisco was this legendary guitar player, who he thought was, perhaps, the greatest guitar player alive. And who had added so much to his music. And now he was going to bring him onstage. So Michael shuffles onstage in his bedroom slippers, looking somewhat embarrassed, plugs in and plays the most pure, the most perfect accompaniments, the most intelligent, most brilliant playing that I'd heard in God knows how long, putting in all the right stings and the overtones and the slide.

It was like he knew about it and figured it all out in advance and rehearsed all of the songs. Of course, he hadn't done any of that. The crowd went berserk. *Berserk*. I think most of them didn't even know who Michael was. Some of them did, the ones who were true San Francisco old-timers, who knew Dylan, knew Michael, and they were just blown away that here they were, together.

Photo by Norman Dayron

Norman Dayron and Michael, Fall 1980.

When Michael started playing, the music came alive like nothing you've ever heard. I mean, it was just like that killer slide guitar on the *Highway 61* album—only it was louder and cleaner and more mature and more thoughtful, faster and cleverer. It was really quite a job he did, and it surprised the hell out of me, because he was not in great shape that night.

After the concert, Michael tried to run out of there. But the way the theater was, we couldn't get out of there without going through the dressing room area and going by Dylan again. Bob came up to Michael, and I won't say there were tears in his eyes, but I would say it was as close as it could be. And he said, "God, I had forgotten what a difference your playing made in my music, and how important it was to it, and how much I had missed it." Michael, I think, was very moved. I think he appreciated what was said. I was much more moved, because at that time Michael was in his downward spiral, and I wanted him to hear that. I wanted him to perk up, like: "Michael, look—look what this guy thinks."

I'm not sure, but I think Michael was okay with it. He played well and enjoyed himself. He had a good time. And I believe that Michael said to me, when I dropped him off, "God, you know, that was fun. I really had a good time. We should do that again." He spoke of it as if it were not this one-time thing with Bob Dylan that would never occur again, but rather like, Gee, that was pretty good. We ought to do that again—like going to the movies, you know. We ought to do more Bob Dylan concerts.

Christie Svane I was back in New York when Michael played with Dylan. He called me and said, "I played with Dylan tonight." I wasn't sure if it was true or not, because one of the most frustrating things about Michael was you never really knew if he was making it up. As a lover, one of the absolute worst things for me was I never knew when he was making it up. But it would boomerang—it would really hurt him that I didn't believe him.

He said, "No, no, no. Bob asked me and I went. I went in my bedroom slippers. I played the Warfield in my bedroom slippers, and I played fantastic. It was great to see him, and he didn't have his character armor anymore. He's a much sweeter guy."

At that time, I was in New York preparing for this chance of a lifetime, a European tour, a three-month performing and teaching tour, starting in February. Michael kept saying, "I'll pay you double not to go." And I said, "But this is what I've been building towards my whole life. This is my chance to really get out there." He couldn't convince me not to go.

Betsy heard about the situation, and she called me. She said, "You know, I've never met you, but I want to ask you: Don't go. Maybe you don't know how fragile Michael is. Somebody has to be there with him." And I said, "Betsy, I think he's stronger now. And I have to do this."

I said to Michael that I really, really was lovesick and heartsick. And all we could do was speak on the phone. We spoke every day, for hours, on the phone. I said, "When I come back from this trip, all I want to do is be with you, and we'll take it from there." He said, "Great, that's all I need to hear. But call me every single day. If I can hear your voice once a day, I can make it through." I said, "Okay." And I left.

But when you fly from New York to Europe, it's a six-hour time difference. We landed in Brussels, and then there was a long train ride to Amsterdam. There were several legs before we got to Paris. By the time I got to Paris, a day and a half had already gone by, and I had lost track of what the time would be in California.

When we finally got to Paris, the Moscow circus happened to be in town, for the last night. Our hosts said, "Come see the circus, and then we'll take you back to the apartment and get you all settled in." I'll never forget it. At the circus they had trained bears. Do you know how they train a bear to dance? They make it stand on a red-hot metal plate and they play music, and the bear lifts up one foot at a time to get it off that metal plate. And that's why it looks like they're dancing. From then on, when they hear that music they remember that experience, so they're reliving that torture when they hear that music.

I didn't know that then. But at the Moscow circus I watched the bears, and I started weeping. For the first time in my life, I understood somehow what Michael had felt like. Why when we were in Italy Michael was saying, "I want to go home, I don't want to finish this tour, I don't want to be this person for these people."

When we got back to the place where we were staying, the phone rang. It was my mother, saying Michael's body had been found in a car. And it was Valentine's Day.

Crying Time

Allen Bloomfield It's still so clear to me: the phone call from Susan, Michael's ex-wife, telling me that he was found dead in the car with no identification, with the doors locked and the key suspended in the ignition. He was sent to the county morgue as a John Doe. Susan had identified him. In shock, I went into the living room and sat down and started to cry. All I could think about was that he died alone, with no one to hold him, no one to say good-bye.

I notified my father, who was remarried. He, in turn, called my mother, also remarried, and arrangements were made to meet in San Francisco at the coroner's office. The building was a cold, formal, institutional structure, much like a large post office. A woman sat at the desk in the center and, without a trace of compassion, had us sign in. We walked down a dark hallway and were told to stop in front of a large glass window.

At this point, my father suggested to my mother that this may be very disturbing and suggested that she not view the corpse. She said, "No way. I want to know if this is my son." They pulled back the cheap hospital curtains, and laying there on a stainless-steel table was Michael, with his arms outstretched, eyes half open, and face contorted in a grimace. Dead, dead, really dead. Cold as ice. Irretrievable.

My mother proceeded to pass out. Her new husband was shocked by all this and understandably confused. My father did not falter and navigated the situation in a detached manner.

We then proceeded to Michael's house in Mill Valley. It was a small contemporary house that had been neglected, as all material things were by my brother. His solution to any home problem was to call the Roto-Rooter man.

The door was not locked. I wandered around Michael's house. It was so reflective of his nature. There were pictures on the wall: B.B. King, Ray

Charles, George Jones, Tammy Wynette, William Burroughs, and Charles Bukowski. As I moved into his bedroom, I was not surprised to see the stacks of books everywhere. Since he was a kid, an avid nighttime reader, he would tear off a little corner of a page he was reading and munch on the paper. True to form, most, if not all, of the books looked as if they were food for rodents.

The best way to describe his lifestyle would be: a visitor without roots, surrounded by articles of music. A sense of impermanence with no concern for any material thing, really—just the function that it served. A broken piano with a metal dog leash over the strings to add some tonal resonance. Guitars—scratched, cracked, with glued-on pickups, all there to serve his inspiration. Stacks of records without covers, tapes without titles. A stereo, crude and primitive—speakers with the cloth covering long gone; a turntable that was taken out of some console and set on a board-and-brick shelf, using pennies to weigh down the tone arm. How like Michael to shun the state-of-the-art technology!

In order to file the final tax return, we gathered all the paperwork that we could find. We then proceeded to select a coffin, which was in some way tied into a synagogue that officiated the service in San Francisco, and based on what you paid, they would receive a kickback. Obviously, this is a time when feelings of guilt and remorse fill the family, and when you walk into the showroom there are very few words that adequately express the shock of shopping for the final resting place of the body. There were 50 caskets, each with benefits: excellent lining, hermetically sealed, lead-lined.

I must digress here to explain that on many road trips the family took to the West, Michael and I would constantly badger our father to pull over at the Giant Indian Teepee, the House of the Great Green Mamba Snake, the Tombstone Museum. More often than not, they were passed by like so many Burma Shave signs. But once in a while we were granted a request. The one that comes to mind is the House of the Snakes and Other Oddities. From the outside it looked like a weather-beaten farmhouse—paint peeling, dirt yard, porch, swinging screen door. Inside, there was a pine-walled interior and a large counter with a postcard carousel and a small caged chimpanzee exploring his armpit. On the other side of the counter were all the snakes—coiled, uncoiled, watching us watching them. The floor was alive, undulating in color. The owner comes out from somewhere and greets us and asks if we would like a tour. Who could resist?

The chimp's name is "Zippy," and he loves to have the top of his head scratched. Standing next to us, the owner takes a pole with a loop of rope hanging in a noose and reaches over the counter and collars a rattlesnake and pulls him up on the counter. "Boys, this here is a one-way ticket to hell." He then proceeds to pin his head down on the wood so we can get a closer look at his body. Diamondback, incredible markings, five rattlers in a skin sheath like dried rawhide with stones inside. The body is cool but not moist. His underside is tan, and it contracts and expands for mobility.

The old guy then slides his hand up the length of the snake's body and grabs him right behind the head. He takes a shot glass and while the snake is thrashing, mouth open, he extracts the venom from the fang into the glass. I saw these clear drops of poison slide down the side of the glass. In a single motion, he slides the snake over the top. We hear a plop and look at each other. Before continuing the tour, the snake man takes out a hip flask of booze, throws some into the shot glass, and downs it.

"I've been bit so many times by them sons o' bitches, I've grown a taste for it. Hey, you folks want to see something real unusual? I don't believe the collection exists anywhere else in the world." Michael and I had been weaned on *Science Fiction Theater* hosted by Truman Bradley, and nothing could totally capture our imaginations like an overture like that. Hell, yes, we'd love to see whatever collection you got. The snake handler pulled back a red-velvet curtain and invited us inside a large living room that was filled with pictures and statues, assorted diagrammatic drawings, and utensils used for the sole purpose of inflicting pain and death on the recipient.

This was the ultimate house of horrors. The collection showcased a variety of homicides that had never been solved, and each murder had a uniqueness: the act, the method of action, the implement, the conditions of the event were all there. One that stands out in my memory was of a guy who used to kill his victims by driving a dagger through their skulls. They had a bronze casting of a head with a knife driven up to the hilt embedded in the head. Then there was the sweet old lady that killed off her family by mixing ground glass into the food. This was by far the oddest museum we had ever encountered.

The reason this comes to mind is that I had the same strange, spooky feeling looking at all those caskets and urns in the showroom. I had to bolt. I started to freak out, remembering the Evelyn Waugh novel *The Loved One*, which was made into a film. Liberace plays a casket salesman, selling all this shit, and the family wants to know if the eternal light over the crypt should be natural gas or propane. He responds with a smile, "Propane burns bluer."

The funeral services were held in San Francisco, as well as Los Angeles, where Michael was finally interred in the family crypt. The turnout in San Francisco consisted of every type of human form you can imagine: musicians, fans, friends, promoters, pushers, hookers, deli countermen, the down and out. They all came to say good-bye.

Susan was so impassioned. She said to the rabbi, "You fucker, you tell the truth about how wonderful he was." It was from that level: it wasn't going to be a show; it wasn't going to be some vacant speech that never touched on the being of a person. The temple was packed, and the rabbi was looking out at a congregation that sat in such profound stillness that only speaking the truth could bring comfort to these sincere and deeply grieving mourners. The eulogy was all right, but somehow I got the sense that the only thing that could express what we were all feeling had to be the sound that only Michael could have played at that very moment. You know, like the slow riff of "Easy Rider." Hell, yes, it was crying time.

The coffin was closed for the service, but when it was concluded, many wanted to see Michael for the last time. And they brought gifts for the journey to come. So we opened the casket, and there was Michael, fixed up wearing a black suit, white shirt, and black tie. Standard uniform of the dead. My mother said, "Who is that man? That's not Michael." My father looked on in cold silence.

Susan and her husband were heartbroken—emotions were tearing up their hearts. Then the gifts were placed with him. There were amulets and poems, fragrances, reefer, guitar picks, pressed flowers, ripped clothing, and pictures of the past. In some strange way, this new and narrow house started to take on the qualities of his old house. When the time came to close the lid, I was surprised that only I kissed him good-bye. I remember thinking that Michael would have thought that might not be an act that he could have done. "Little cold, Allie." Well, fuck it—you do what you feel sometimes.

The next stop was Los Angeles, a place he hated and where he would remain. This service was for the family, primarily, and friends from there. Barry Goldberg gave a beautiful eulogy, which was directed more to Michael than anyone else. "Boris, we're really going to miss you. Life will never be the same. You brought me so much love, introduced me to my wife, took me farther musically, and made me see the humor of the world." The service was concluded with the playing of Michael's interpretation of "Mood Indigo." And then he was entombed in my mother's family's crypt. And that was that.

I have a dark and ugly suspicion that Michael was rearing to clock, get loaded, float along and kick back, never doubting the situation. He tied off with a hangman's noose. Then he overdosed on a drug he never used, detested due to his bipolar illness, and punched out.

Norman Dayron The report in the newspapers was that he died from an overdose of cocaine. When everybody read that, they thought that was bizarre and absurd. He never used cocaine. He didn't like it. And he would never use it even if there was nothing else around. He would drink—if he was reduced to obliterating himself, he wouldn't do it with cocaine, he would do it with alcohol. If he didn't have heroin and he was feeling like he wanted to put out the fire, he would drink.

Leading up to his death, Michael was on a self-destructive path unlike anything I had ever seen in the 20 years that I had known him. I'd never seen him do anything like that, where he'd be drinking gin and passing out. I would see where he pissed in the bed.

Michael seemed to be suffering a lot of pain. I had seen him quite often during that period, and it got to the point where it was very uncomfortable to even be with him. I couldn't stand it, and I felt very guilty about it, because I felt that as his friend I should take care of him. But he wouldn't let anybody take care of him. He was doing things like chug-a-lugging Tanqueray gin. He used to keep a quart of gin in the freezer, and he would drink it. He was never an alcoholic, but he would do it to obliterate himself. He used to describe the pain he felt as a red-hot wire between his ears, like a toaster wire. So leading up to his death there was a lot of pain.

After Michael died, I was interested in finding out more about what really happened. I was also interested in finding out who was responsible. In a nutshell, he died in what was probably a pretty swanky apartment in Diamond Heights, of a combination of drugs—some kind of unknown designer drug, designed to be synthetic heroin, and cocaine. There were two other people there. I don't want to mention their names.

Three or four months before Michael died, he took me into the city to score some heroin. He wanted my company. He was very excited about it, because this guy was somebody that he liked having as a friend. He was a white guy, an ex-convict, a very dangerous guy. Michael was proud of his relationship with him. It was like: I know this really dangerous guy. Michael like hanging out with people like that from time to time. It was like playing with fire, because the guy was an armed robber and a dope dealer. I believe he was a dope dealer who didn't use dope, which was kind of dangerous because he never knew what he was selling.

I remember driving down Divisidero to this guy's house—it was a basement apartment on Divisidero. It was about halfway up Divisidero, before you get to Castro. I remember meeting this guy and being in his apartment. I believe it was through him that Michael met the connection that he had the night he was killed. I believe it was in that guy's circle. The connection was a lowlife who lived in a funky manner, was a certain kind of person— a certain kind of hard guy.

Michael listens to playback of his last album, Cruisin' for a Bruisin', *Wally Heider's Studio, 1980.*

On the night he died, I think Michael probably asked them to give him a large amount of powder, whatever it was. I don't believe that it was heroin. It was some kind of designer drug that asphyxiated him. And they probably gave him a shot of cocaine to try to wake him up, because that was what was found in his system. Then they probably panicked, like: What are we going to do with this guy? I mean, they damn well knew who he was.

They didn't want to call attention to their operation. And they tried their best, I think, in all good faith, to try to help him. Their idea of helping him was to shoot cocaine into him. At some point he died. And then they just took the body outside. A couple of guys grabbed him like he was a drunk and moved him to his car and sat him behind the wheel.

What those guys who dumped his body did worked, because there wasn't enough connection to them—there was no systematic search of the buildings in the neighborhood. Probably within a day, those guys had moved out or had flushed everything.

The connection later left town. He was a lowlife character and wasn't somebody I had known before. I sort of tracked him down and promised him that I just needed to know, because I was Michael's friend—I just wanted to know what happened. And that was as close as I could get to it. That's my memory of the facts that I put together, and I really don't know how accurate they are.

The bottom line about Michael's death, for me, is that in the period leading up to his death, maybe the three or four months prior, he was hell-bent for destruction. He was suffering a lot emotionally. I'm not sure what all the reasons were. I also think he had fantasies that would get him out of wherever he was that he wasn't happy with. He always loved having a family around him, and at that point he really didn't. And he was doing those unusual things, like drinking a quart of gin and passing out in his own piss. That was not usual for him, even on the worst Placidyl days. That was not a pattern.

In all of our relations, we always had projects, and we always had things that we were planning on for the future—what we were going to do next. And we didn't have anything going at all. On those times when I accompanied him into San Francisco on his various errands and runs, as he used to call them, I could feel he was sort of heading for something, and it was like an endless maelstrom of some kind. There was no project at the end of it. There was no music around. I don't know what it was. Sometimes it seemed to be very positive; sometimes it seemed that he was getting his head above water. I'd see him, and he'd be sitting in the sun completely coherent and happy.

I think it was an accident. Yes, he was suffering—but I also think it was an accident. I don't think I should characterize it that he was hell-bent for destruction because he had reached the end of his rope. Because that was not true. I think the truest characterization is that he was leading a somewhat dangerous life and what happened was accidental. It was one of those spins of the wheel.

Eventually, statistics have to go against you. Something bad has to happen. You just can't keep getting away with it. The fact that none of us got AIDS or anything from dirty needles—none of us got sick from that—that was a piece of luck. So I think the odds were, mathematically, that you couldn't keep doing shit like that and not have something happen.

The official police inquiry hit a dead end very quickly. Essentially, a blues musician was found in his car. I think the police concluded that here was a guy, a musician, who had overdosed. They wanted to tidy it up as quickly as they could. Claim the body and the car, and that was it.

Michael's mom wanted him to be near her, in LA. He's buried in Los Angeles Hillside Memorial Park. It's a well-known Jewish cemetery.

Final Words

Nick Gravenites The totality of Michael's character is the thing that impressed me most. Not only his musical ability but also his intellect, his sense of humor, his compassion, his generosity—all those things that make up a human being. Those are my fondest memories.

He had a certain charisma. People wanted to be around him—to touch the hem of his garment. And the effect he had on me and the people around him who knew him and loved his music was life changing.

When people write stories and books about Michael as the young guy who was successful but had a lot of problems, had drug problems and died of an overdose—on the surface, all of that is true. But it doesn't really come close to the real effect Michael had on me. It was a lot more profound than some trite Hollywood story. This was a major league guy. I'm not talking about making it in show business; I'm talking about his human qualities. Michael's friends, the ones who were closest to him, really loved the guy. He helped them live their lives. He helped them make something out of their lives, in many ways, very profoundly.

He was quite a forceful personality. He was quite a wit. And he also had a very deep character. He was very generous, very soulful. I can still think in those major terms, those big terms, when I think about Michael. He was a huge giant of a person.

Interviewees

Sam Andrew Guitarist with Big Brother & the Holding Company and the Kozmic Blues Band with Janis Joplin.

Applejack Friend of Michael's from Chicago; played harmonica in the Elvin Bishop Band.

Bonner Beuhler Michael's friend. Married to Susan, Michael's ex-wife.

Susan Beuhler Michael's ex-wife. Stayed with Michael and helped him to maintain the practical aspects of his life for some years after their marriage had ended.

Elvin Bishop Guitarist for the Paul Butterfield Blues Band both before and after Michael's involvement. Continues to enjoy success as a solo artist.

Allen Bloomfield Michael's younger brother.

Harvey Brooks Bass player on many records; worked with Michael on Bob Dylan's *Highway 61 Revisited* and *Super Session*. Member of the Electric Flag.

Denny Bruce A&R man with Takoma Records who produced an Ann-Margret demo recording session that featured Michael and Little Feat guitarist Lowell George.

Ron Butkovich Friend of Michael's from Chicago.

Toby Byron Originally a fan of Michael's who approached him while in high school to play at a benefit for Bangladesh. Now produces documentary and music-related films.

Jack Casady Bassist with the Jefferson Airplane and Hot Tuna.

Marshall Chess Son of Leonard Chess, the owner of Chess Records.

Billy Davenport Drummer in the second incarnation of the Butterfield Blues Band, which recorded *East-West*.

Norman Dayron One of Michael's closest friends and the producer for most of his later solo efforts.

J. Geils Guitarist with the J. Geils Band

Fred Glaser Friend of Michael's since junior high school in Glencoe, Illinois.

Barry Goldberg High school friend of Michael's who became a professional musician and played with Michael, Harvey Mandel, Steve Miller, Bob Dylan, Duane Allman, Charlie Musselwhite, and others. Now resides in Los Angeles, where he scores motion picture soundtracks.

Steve Gordon Ran the Savoy, a nightclub in the North Beach area of San Francisco where Michael performed.

Bill Graham The foremost concert promoter of his time. His interview was generously provided by Bob Sarles of Ravin' Films.

Nick Gravenites Chicago native; one of Michael's friends and collaborators. Founding member of the Electric Flag. As a singer, songwriter, and producer contributed to the efforts of Big Brother & the Holding Company, Quicksilver Messenger Service, and blues luminaries such as Muddy Waters, Otis Rush, James Cotton, Sam Lay, and many others.

Bob Greenspan Lifelong friend of Michael's. As a teenager, played in some of Michael's early bands.

John Hammond Jr. Blues songwriter and guitarist; son of the late John Hammond Sr. Played with Michael on three albums over a period of several years.

Woody Harris Guitarist who recorded an album with Mike and performed with him in Europe and the U.S. in 1980.

Chet Helms San Francisco rock promoter and manager of the famed Avalon Ballroom.

Bob Jones Drummer and singer on some of Michael's best solo recordings; formerly played guitar with We Five, who had a hit in the '60s with "You Were on My Mind."

Ira Kamin Friend of Michael's and keyboard player from Chicago. Moved to San Francisco to join Tracy Nelson's Mother Earth and later played on *It's Not Killing Me,* Michael's first solo album for Columbia Records. Performed in many of Michael's musical configurations throughout the '70s.

Jorma Kaukonen Guitarist with the Jefferson Airplane and Hot Tuna.

B.B. King Big city blues progenitor and the King of the Blues Guitar. He thought of Michael as being "like my own son."

Bob Koester Owner of the Jazz Record Mart in Chicago and producer of many jazz and blues recordings on his Delmark Records label. He employed several young blues enthusiasts, including Michael, who went on to achieve fame in the recording industry.

Al Kooper Session player on Dylan's *Highway 61 Revisited* with Michael. Produced and played with Michael and Stephen Stills on *Super Session,* which won a gold record award. Founding member of the Blues Project and Blood, Sweat and Tears.

Sam Lay Original drummer with the Paul Butterfield Blues Band.

Norman Mayell Drummer in Michael's band at Big John's for a year; recorded with Michael on demo tracks for John Hammond Sr. and was later a member of Sopwith Camel.

Dan McClosky Recorded interviews with Michael, Roy Ruby, and Fred Glaser for a San Francisco radio station, in which they recounted their experiences in the clubs of Chicago's South Side.

Country Joe McDonald Founding member of Country Joe & the Fish; political activist and pioneer of the "psychedelic sound."

Barry Melton Guitarist with Country Joe & the Fish.

Buddy Miles Drummer who was approached by Michael to play and sing with the Electric Flag. Later formed the Buddy Miles Express and played with Jimi Hendrix in Band of Gypsies.

George Mitchell One-time employee of the Jazz Record Mart who co-managed the Fickle Pickle with Michael and accompanied him on a trip to St. Louis with Big Joe Williams.

Maria Muldaur Member of the Even Dozen Jug Band and the Jim Kweskin Jug Band before embarking on a solo career and recording the hit single "Midnight at the Oasis." She continues to record and perform blues, gospel, and country.

Charlie Musselwhite One of the premier harmonica artists of his generation; met Michael while working at Bob Koester's Jazz Record Mart.

Mark Naftalin Keyboardist of the Paul Butterfield Blues Band and Mother Earth. Mark performed and recorded with Michael throughout the '70s. Mark hosts a blues radio show in the San Francisco Bay Area, produces The Marin County Blues Festival and heads Winner Records.

Fritz Richmond Member of the Jim Kweskin Jug Band, performer at the Newport Folk Festival in 1965.

Anna Rizzo San Francisco musician and friend of Michael's who appeared on a number of his recordings.

Paul Rothchild Producer of the Paul Butterfield Blues Band, the Doors, and others.

Roy Ruby Boyhood friend of Michael's who died of a heroin overdose in 1974. The interview with him was provided by Dan McClosky.

Carlos Santana Acclaimed guitarist and leader of Santana; member of the Rock & Roll Hall of Fame.

Eric Von Schmidt Acclaimed folk performer who ran the Blues Workshop at the Newport Folk Festival in 1965.

Dorothy Shinderman Michael's fan and longtime supporter, his loving and devoted mother.

Dave Shorey Member of Michael's band in the late '70s.

Peter Strazza Saxophonist with the Electric Flag.

Christie Svane Michael's very close friend.

Bob Weir Guitarist with the Grateful Dead.

Jerry Wexler Legendary producer at Atlantic Records.

Afterword
....

I first became aware of Michael's recordings as a high school student in Portland, Oregon. I got the strong impression that his notes and phrasing came more from his heart than his hands. Michael once said that the "music you listen to takes on more import than the notes being played. It becomes the soundtrack for your life." His music became just that for me and countless others, because it was expressive beyond technique. His playing conveyed raw emotion and a "cry" that spans eras and transcends ethnicity.

I was living on the island of Oahu in 1981 when I received news of Michael's passing some weeks after the tragic fact. My hope had always been that I might meet Michael some day and tell him how much his music meant to me. I knew if I couldn't meet him I would at least have to learn more about Michael from his friends and associates. Not knowing his story left a void within me that had to be filled.

Michael Bloomfield, The Rise and Fall of an American Guitar Hero, was written by Ed Ward in 1983. This book helped to fill the widespread vacuum of knowledge about Michael and gave fans a glimpse of Michael's life and music career. But there was so much more to be said. And so my quest began.

My first calls were to Norman Dayron, who I knew had been a friend and associate of Michael's for many years. Once Norman had determined to his satisfaction that I was operating out of a sincere motive, he consented to speak with me, and ultimately became one of this book's major contributors. When I told Norman that I was writing a book on Michael, I didn't know at that moment whether or not a book would become the ultimate result of my efforts, but it was my sincere desire.

What I didn't know at the time I started the project was that Jan Wolkin had begun interviewing Michael's friends and band mates in 1994, a year before I started my gathering process. It was Ellen Naftalin who first said to me, "Have you ever heard of Jan Wolkin, the guy who does the *Bloomfield notes?*" I had not. Jan, with the assistance of Neal McGarity, was gathering information, editing interviews on his computer and sending the resulting newsletters out to several hundred of Michael's friends and fans. I called Jan, introduced myself, and told him of my efforts to compile information on Michael.

Jan seemed wary at first, listening patiently to several excited phone calls during which I recounted my interviews with music figures that were not only great subjects, but also central to Michael's story. I told him of my conversation with B.B. King on the back of his tour bus, of spending a weekend with Mark Naftalin at his home north of San Francisco, of Carlos Santana calling me one night and talking for over an hour, and of finding Fred Glaser after searching for over a year. Jan took this all in without saying a lot, and regularly side-stepped my suggestion that we pool our efforts and tackle the book as a team.

I learned early on in our talks that Jan was a collector of details, names, dates, and places—a veritable database of Bloomfield information. It was at the end of one of these long conversations, just when I was about to sign off and hang up, that Jan finally agreed to co-author the book. I was encouraged at the prospect and immediately e-mailed him all my interviews. He later described being a bit overwhelmed by the sheer volume of material. It was his first real indication that between us we had a good start on developing a comprehensive document.

The third member of our team was my sister Paula Hankins who transcribed all the interviews, aided by her court reporting skills and enormous patience for wading through countless hours of taped interviews in her "spare" time. She had no idea in the beginning who Michael Bloomfield was, but she became quite knowledgeable on the subject in the process. She deserves a great deal of credit for making this book a reality.

For the most part, people opened up gladly the minute Jan and I approached them for their stories about Michael. There was something about Michael's character and charisma that caused people to want to impart their impressions of the man and his presence. Many times we'd just ask the first question and be treated to hours of recollections.

Michael Bloomfield was so much more than a great guitarist. Raconteur, musicologist, renaissance man, mensch, painter, ultimate appreciator are some of the words used to describe him. I've heard it said often that if you knew Michael, you were changed by him, and that when he walked into a room, his charisma and energy made it difficult to focus on much else.

We present this book in order to underscore Michael's contribution to music and give the reader a sense of the man behind the guitar. We hope it continues to spark the fascination we found in him.

—Bill Keenom

Acknowledgments

We interviewed more than eighty of Michael's family members, friends, and colleagues while researching and compiling this book. We want to thank them all for sharing their memories with us. Without their cooperation, this book would not have been possible.

Thanks to Allen Bloomfield for his help in developing this manuscript. Thanks also to Allen for his encouragement over the past several years, and his faithful representation of The Michael Bloomfield Estate.

Michael Bloomfield's mother, the lovely Dorothy Shinderman, has always been Michael's biggest fan. Thank you, Dorothy, for your hospitality and the great interviews that gave us a sense of the history of your family.

Thanks to Norman Dayron for his hospitality, detailed recollections, historic photographs, and his expertise as the producer of the fine recordings found in this book.

Thanks to Susan Beuhler, Michael's ex-wife and lifelong friend, and her husband Bonner for their memories.

Thanks to Mark Naftalin for his help and encouragement and for his historic photographs.

Thanks to Ellen Naftalin for her help and encouragement, and for her role in bringing the authors together.

Thanks to Bob Sarles of Ravin' Films for generously supplying interviews taken from an upcoming documentary project on Michael Bloomfield.

Thanks to Dan McClosky for the use of his KSAN interview with Michael Bloomfield, Roy Ruby, and Fred Glaser from 1971.

Thanks to Bonnie Simmons for her help in researching interview material aired on KSAN.

Thanks to Bob Simmons for the use of his interview with Michael Bloomfield and Nick Gravenites.

Thanks to Christie Svane, for sharing her home with us, and for freely offering her memories. Thanks also to Billy and the girls, and of course, Annie.

Thanks to Scott Summerville, a true friend and mentor, for guiding Bill around San Francisco and Mill Valley. Thanks also to Scott and Vale Vale for permission to use a portion of *Me And Big Joe,* recently republished by RE/SEARCH Productions.

Bill thanks his wife Bonnie and notes that, "Bonnie is my heart, and truly deserves my debt of gratitude for her patience and partnership in this project." Bill also thanks Florence Keenom for teaching him to read, and Jennifer, Jacob, and Kevi for their love and support.

Jan thanks Sidney, Sylvia, and Stephanie Wolkin for their love, support, and encouragement. He thanks his dad for not smashing his guitars, his mom for her faith, and his sister for being a good friend. He also thanks his uncles Irv and Joe Strobing for being good guys.

Special thanks and appreciation to Paula Hankins for accomplishing the finger-numbing task of transcribing every interview, word by word, line by line. Thanks also to Paula's assistants Heather Ferguson and Patrice Devore.

Thanks to Toby Byron, Fred Glaser, Barry Goldberg, Nick Gravenites, Bob Greenspan, Mike Henderson, Bob Jones, Al Kooper, Charlie Musselwhite, Dave Shorey, Bob Welland, and Ed Ward. These gentlemen all played an important role in the researching of this book.

We would like to thank all those who contributed photos to this book: Susan Beuhler, Allen Bloomfield, Norman Dayron, Raeburn Flerlage, David Gahr, Grant Jacobs, Charlie Musselwhite, Mark Naftalin, Don Paulsen, Christie Svane, and Leonard Trupin. Thanks also to Vince Carroll, our man in the digital imaging realm.

Thanks to Ward Gaines for his research and for the encouragement to continue when the going got tough; Tom Ellis III, the writer and Texas harmonica-microphone man, for sharing from his list of contacts; to Mark Armstrong of The Monarch Company in Atlanta, long distance assistance.

Thanks to all those at Miller Freeman Books for their efforts, especially Matt Kelsey, Dorothy Cox, Jay Kahn, Nancy Tabor, and Nina Lesowitz.

Thanks to Jim Roberts, our copy editor. We feel fortunate to have an editor who brought knowledge and skill to our project, and understood what we were trying to accomplish.

Thanks also to R. Stewart and Alicia Douglas, Russ Dugoni, Skye Emanuel, Dave Fimbres, Mike Gottlieb, Ferda Guzey, Kohel Haver, George Jones in England, and Sue Windsor.

CD Notes

W e want to express our sincere thanks to Norman Dayron and Allen Bloomfield for allowing us to include the CD that accompanies this book. Following are their comments about the CD.

Allen Bloomfield Michael's speed and versatility on these recordings is truly awesome. Because the structure is loose and intimate, one gets a rare insight into the emerging talent that flowed almost effortlessly from his hands and voice. It is also really raw and at times repetitive. This comes with the nature of these recordings: they were never intended to be released as a polished product but rather as a work in progress.

Norman Dayron These recordings were made in Chicago, at one of two locations. The acoustic cuts were made on January 28, 1964, in the living room of my student apartment at the University of Chicago, which was located in Hyde Park at 5319 South Kimbark Avenue. Very often Michael would come over to my house, and we would just play and sing and mess around. I had a little mono tape recorder; actually, it wasn't so little—it was a half-track Tandberg (made in Norway). I also had a full track Ampex mono machine. These recordings were made on the smaller one, at least the acoustic ones were.

"Bullet Rag" was the type of thing you might have heard if you walked into the Fret Shop when Michael was hanging out there. Michael would play a fast, finger-picked song like that, and people would be amazed. I had two guitars; one was a very old Martin with a slotted headstock, a wide triangular neck, and a shorter-scale fretboard. The top of that guitar had caved in, and it had been rebuilt. But I think on "Bullet Rag" he was playing my other guitar, which was an early 1950s Martin 000-28. "J.P. Morgan" was a song Michael could not perform without an enormous smile on his face. You can hear his exuberance in that recording. I don't know if there was some kind of subtle acknowledgment there, of his status as an inheritor who hadn't yet inherited anything.

Michael was always wanting to play more than one part. He'd want to play the bass part, the rhythm part, the melody, the harmony. We had heard some of the multiple part recordings that people like Les Paul had done. I understood that the basic principal was that you disabled the erase head so that everything you put on the tape would build up in layers and never erase. He loved that idea, and he persuaded me to cut the wires on the erase head so we could do that. The recording of "Kingpin" was done that way. Michael played two parts, a rhythm/bass part and a lead part. That was the first time Michael had ever over-dubbed anything, or tried to do a multiple part recording.

The electric recordings were made on October 15, 1964, at Big John's, on the near North Side on Wells Street. I don't think Big John's had ever had live electric music in it before Michael Bloomfield played there. After the first night, the place was completely sold out every night. The word went out like wildfire. Michael was only 21 years old, but the energy he had and the power of his playing was such that really within one set, the word went out on Wells street and the place jammed up, just got full of people. Big John's holds a special place in everybody's memory as being this really unique place. It was all word of mouth. It was never advertised. The people who hung out there were poets, writers, photographers, and the actors from the first Second City.

Michael would say, "Hey man, look, you just gotta record everything because that'll give me a chance to hear what I'm doing." I told Michael we were never going to make a good recording of an electric band without some kind of set up before hand. You have to remember this was the kind of place that barely had a PA for the vocal. How do you record a screaming electric band with loud lead guitar and electric instruments? I didn't really have the equipment to do that. But I knew if I could get in there and set up earlier before people came in that we would have a chance.

I used only two microphones, one for the band and one for the vocal. And it was recorded into an Ampex monaural full-track tape recorder, which we hid off in a corner by the bathroom. I would come in in the afternoon around three or four and set up the mikes. And I would usually tape the vocal mike, which would be a little lavalier-type mike, usually it was an Altec salt-and-pepper-shaker type mike, and I would tape that to the PA mike and then put a Neumann U67 condenser way back, and try to find a sweet spot in the room where all the sounds would blend, where if you stuck your head in that spot you could hear just the right amount of bass and just the right amount of lead. I would have figured that out from previous performances when the room was full of people.

I would just hang that one condenser microphone in that one place where the room reflections gelled and where it sounded as much like a record as it could, and I would just use the vocal mike as a spot mike to emphasize and bring out the vocal, because that would usually be drowned out by the band. I'd have to tape down the cables because there'd be all kinds of drunks and people hectically serving beers, so I'd tape down the cables so nobody tripped and hurt themselves or disconnected the mike feed.

"Gotta Call Susie," "Blues for Roy," and "Country Boy" were all that raw energy of Big John's. The recordings, to my mind, are particularly wonderful and useful because they show Michael with all the hormones and testosterone and energy of a 21-year-old saying, "Don't hold me back, man," just straining at the bit, yearning to express himself, and he's got all this room to do it. That's why some of the cuts are like 10, 12 minutes long. And, also, he would play seven sets a night. They would start around nine o'clock, and he wasn't off stage until two-thirty or three in the morning. It was grueling. So playing long songs also helped to fill out all of those sets.

"Intermission Blues" was the type of thing Michael would play between sets. He loved to play the piano so much he would sit down at this huge, old, upright piano they had in Big John's and keep playing while the rest of the band took a break. It was all very loose. You can hear the bell on the cash register going off in the background.

1964, this was really pretty much at the peak of the blues scene that had been building up since after the Second World War. The great players were playing; Chess Records was at its peak. It was a very rich and vibrant time in Chicago's music history. There was every kind of blues playing all over the city. And Michael was right in the middle of it all.

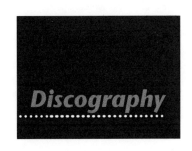

Discography

7" Single

Michael Bloomfield
"Analine"/"Peepin' and Moanin'
Blues"
Takoma B-5059, 1977, promo single

**Michael Bloomfield/
John Paul Hammond/Dr. John**
"The Trip" (non-LP version)
Playback (CBS Custom label) AS51
ZSM 158374

The Paul Butterfield Blues Band
"Come on In" (non-LP version)/
"I Got a Mind to Give Up Living"
Elektra 45609

The Chicago Loop
"(When She Needs Good Lovin')
She Comes To Me"
Dyno-Voice 226, 1966
"Richard Corey"
Dyno-Voice 230, 1967

Nick Gravenites
"My Baby's Got a Whole Lot of
Soul"/"Drunken Boat"
Out of Sight Records

12" LP

Beaver and Krause
Gandharva
Warner Bros. WS-1909, 1971,
one song

Chuck Berry
Fresh Berries
Chess 4506, Bloomfield guitar
uncredited

Michael Bloomfield
American Hero
Thunderbolt THBL-100, 1984

Analine
Takoma B-1059, 1977

Between the Hard Place and the Ground
Takoma 7070, 1979

Bloomfield—A Retrospective
Columbia C2-37578, 1983, two-
record set

Count Talent and the Originals
Clouds 8005, 1978

Cruisin' for a Bruisin'
Takoma 7091, 1981

*If You Love These Blues, Play 'Em as
You Please*
Guitar Player 3002, 1976

I'm with You Always
Demon Fiend-92, 1987, recorded live
1977 at McCabes, LA

Initial Shock
Cobra 10, 1989, Italian reissue of
Red Hot & Blue

It's Not Killing Me
Columbia KH-30395, 1970

Live Adventures
Masters 20784, Dutch release of
   American Hero

Live in Italy
Mama Barley 001, 1980, Italian

Livin' in the Fast Lane
Waterhouse 11, 1980

Michael Bloomfield
Takoma 7063, 1978

Red Hot & Blue
United Distributors Lyrics, Ltd. UDL
   2328 UDL2322, 1981

Live at Bill Graham's Fillmore West
Columbia CS-9893, 1969, more on
   My Labors

**Michael Bloomfield/Nick
   Gravenites/Paul Butter-
   field/Maria Muldaur**
Steelyard Blues
Warner Bros. BS-2662, 1972, movie
   soundtrack

**Michael Bloomfield/John Paul
   Hammond/Dr. John**
Triumvirate
Columbia RC-32172, 1973

Michael Bloomfield/Woody Harris
Bloomfield/Harris
Kicking Mule 164, 1979

Mike Bloomfield/Al Kooper
More Live Adventures
Better Days 002, 1974, bootleg re-
   corded at the Bottom Line, NYC

Super Session
Columbia CS-9701, 1968

Super Session
MFSL 1-178, half-speed master

*The Live Adventures of Mike Bloomfield
   and Al Kooper*
Columbia KGP-6, 1969

Brewer and Shipley
Weeds
Kama Sutra 2016, 1969

The Paul Butterfield Blues Band
East-West
Elektra EKS-7315, 1967

The Paul Butterfield Blues Band
Elektra K-294, 1965

Dick Campbell
Sings Where It's At
Mercury SR61060, 1965

James Cotton
Cotton in Your Ears
Verve FTS-3060, 1969

Pure Cotton
Verve FTS-3038, 1968, "advice and
   enthusiasm"

The James Cotton Blues Band
Verve FTS-3023, 1967, Bloomfield
   co-produced

Taking Care of Business
Capital SM814, three songs

Michael d'Abo
Broken Rainbows
A&M 3634, 1974, one song

Tim Davis
Take Me as I Am
Metromedia BML1-175, 1972, two
   songs

Bob Dylan
Highway 61 Revisited
Columbia CS-9189, 1965

Highway 61 Revisited
Columbia CS-9189, 1965 with alternate "From a Buick 6"

Stealin'
Berkeley 2010, bootleg, *Highway 61*
   outtakes

Electric Flag
A Long Time Comin'
Columbia CS-9597, 1967

The Band Played On
Atlantic SD-18112, 1974

The Trip
Sidewalk/Tower ST 5908, 1967; re-
  issued on Edsel ED211

Sleepy John Estes
Broke and Hungry
Delmark DS-608, 1964

Millie Foster
Feels the Spirit
MGM SE4897, 1972

Barry Goldberg
Barry Goldberg and Friends
Record Man CR-5105, 1969

Barry Goldberg and Friends Live
Buddah BDS-5684, 1976

Blasts from My Past
Buddah BDS-5081, 1971

Two Jews Blues
Buddah BDS-5029, 1969, listed as
  "The Great"

Nick Gravenites
My Labors
Columbia CS-9899, 1969

John Hammond Jr.
Mirrors
Vanguard VSD-7924, 1968, two songs

So Many Roads
Vanguard VSD-7917, 1965

Woody Herman
Brand New
Fantasy 8414, 1971, four songs

Janis Joplin
*I Got Dem Ol' Kozmic Blues Again
  Mama!*
Columbia KCS-9913, 1969

KGB
KGB
MCA 2166, 1976

Kingfish
Kingfish
Relix RRLP2005, 1973, one song
  with John Lee Hooker

Sam Lay
Sam Lay in Bluesland
Blue Thumb BTS-14, 1970

Melton, Levy, and the Dey Bros.
Melton, Levy and the Dey Bros.
Columbia KC31279, 1972

Mill Valley Bunch
Casting Pearls
Verve V68825, 1973, a/k/a *Mill Valley
  Session* on Polydor

Moby Grape
Grape Jam
Columbia MGS-1, 1969, with Wow,
  one song

Mother Earth
Livin' with the Animals
Mercury SR-61194, 1969, as "Makel
  Blumfeld," one song

Charlie Musselwhite
Leave the Blues to Us
Capital 11450, 1975

Peter, Paul and Mary
Album
Warner Bros. WS-16481965,
  one song

Yank Rachell
Mandolin Blues
Delmark DL-606, 1963

Otis Rush
Mourning in the Morning
Cotillion SD-9006, 1969, Bloomfield
  co-produced

Mitch Ryder
What Now My Love
Dyno-Voice DY-31901, 1967

Southern Comfort
Southern Comfort
Columbia 1011, 1971

The Usual Suspects
The Usual Suspects
Tomistoma, 1981, one song

Various Artists
Chicago Breakdown
Takoma 7071, 1980, one song with
     Little Brother Montgomery

Fathers and Sons
Chess LPS-127, 1969

Folk Song '65
Elektra S-78, Butterfield Blues Band,
     "Born in Chicago"

Newport Folk Festival 1965
Vanguard VRS-9225, 1965, Butter-
     field Blues Band, "Mellow Down
     Easy"

Rare Blues
Takoma 7081,1980, one song with
     Little Brother Montgomery

San Francisco Blues Festival
Jefferson BL 602, one song live, 1976

What's Shakin'
Elektra KL-4002, 1966, Butterfield
     Blues Band; reissued on Edsel
     ED249

You Are What You Eat
Columbia OS-3240, 1969, one song

Eddie "Cleanhead" Vinson
Cherry Red
Bluesway/ABC BL-6007, 1967

The Zeet Band
Moogie Woogie
Chess 1545, 1969

CD

Beaver And Krause
In a Wild Sanctuary/Gandharva
Warner Brothers Archives 9362-
     45663-2

Michael Bloomfield
A True Soul Brother
Skyranch SRM 652328, French

American Hero
Thunderbolt CDTB-1009, British

Best of Mike Bloomfield
Takoma 7115, out of print

Best of Mike Bloomfield
Takoma 8905-2

Between a Hard Place and the Ground
Thunderbolt, reissue of *Red Hot &
     Blue*

*Blues, Gospel and Ragtime Guitar
     Instrumentals*
Shanachie 99007

Cruisin' for a Bruisin'
Takoma 7091, mastered at the wrong
     speed, out of print

*Don't Say That I Ain't Your Man!—
     Essential Blues 1964–1969*
Columbia CK57631

I'm with You Always
Demon-Fiend CD92, British,
     recorded live at McCabes, LA

Initial Shock
Cobra 10, Italian (not the U.S. Cobra
     label); reissue of *Red Hot & Blue*

Live at the Old Waldorf
Columbia CK65688

Living in the Fast Lane
ERA 5006-2

Red Hot & Blue
Universe, UV 006

Rx for the Blues
Eclipse 64736-2, same as American
   Hero

Rx for the Blues
Success 22540cd

The Gospel of Blues
Laserlight 12 356

The Root of Blues
Laserlight 12 357

Try It Before You Buy It
CBS Special Products A21265, out of
   print

Uncle Bob's Barrelhouse Blues
Pulsar PULS 013

**Michael Bloomfield/John Paul
Hammond/Dr. John**
Triumvirate
Columbia RC-32172

Mike Bloomfield/Al Kooper
*More Live Adventures of Mike Bloom-
field and Al Kooper*
Four Aces Records FAR 009, Italian
   bootleg, recorded at the Bottom
   Line, NYC, March 31, 1974

Super Session
Columbia CS-9701

Super Session
Columbia CK-64611 0, gold "Master-
   Sound" disc, includes bonus track

*The Live Adventures of Mike Bloomfield
and Al Kooper*
Columbia C2K 64670

The Paul Butterfield Blues Band
East-West
Elektra 7315-2

Strawberry Jam
Winner 446, live

East-West Live
Winner 447

The Original Lost Elektra Sessions
Elektra/Rhino R2 73505

The Paul Butterfield Blues Band
Elektra 7294-2

An Anthology: The Elektra Years
Elektra 62124-2

Droppin' In
Colosseum 97-C-021, bootleg

Unicorn Coffee House '66
Colosseum UCH 1966, bootleg

James Cotton
Best of the Verve Years
Verve 314 527 371-2

Bob Dylan
*Bob Dylan Live with Al Kooper and
Mike Bloomfield*
Document DR 015 CD, bootleg

Farewell Bloomfield
Cuttlefish Records CR004/CR005,
   bootleg recorded live November
   15, 1980, at the Warfield, San
   Francisco, Mike on two songs

Highway 61 Revisited
Columbia CK9189

Highway 61 Revisited
DCC GZS-1021, gold CD

Highway 61 Revisited Again
92-BD-09-04, bootleg

Live in Newport 1965
Document DR 004 CD, bootleg,
   Mike on three songs

The Bootleg Series
Columbia C3K 47382

Thin Wild Mercury Music
Spank Records SP 105, bootleg

Electric Flag
A Long Time Comin'/Electric Flag
Columbia CK9597, with unreleased
   tracks

Old Glory: The Best of the Electric Flag
Columbia/Legacy CK57629, with
    unreleased tracks

The Electric Flag—Live
Thunderbolt CDTB 1006, British

The Trip
Curb Records D2-77863, 1996

Sleepy John Estes
Broke and Hungry
Delmark DD-608

Barry Goldberg
Barry Goldberg and Friends
Sequel nex cd 160

Barry Goldberg and Friends Live
Unidisc BDK 5684

Nothin' But the Best of the Blues
Laserlight 17 058

Nothin' But the Blues
Laserlight 17 057, reissue of *Barry
    Goldberg and Friends Live*

Two Jews Blues
One Way Records OW 27672

John Hammond Jr.
Best Of John Hammond
Vanguard VCD 11/12

Woody Herman
Brand New
Fantasy, OJCCD-1044-2

Janis Joplin
*I Got Dem Ol' Kozmic Blues Again
    Mama!*
Columbia CK 9913

Matt Kelly
A Wing and a Prayer
Relix RRCD2010, one song

Kingfish
Double Dose
Relix RRCD2035, from *Kingfish* LP,
    one song with John Lee Hooker

Percy Mayfield
Blues Summit
Pilz 449300-2, two songs by Joe
    Turner with Mike Bloomfield and
    Mark Naftalin

Tracy Nelson
The Best of Tracy Nelson/Mother Earth
Reprise 9 46232-2

Yank Rachell
Mandolin Blues
Delmark DE-606

Merl Saunders & Friends
Merl Saunders & Friends
Fantasy 7712-2, two songs with Mike

Joe Turner
Shake, Rattle and Roll
Pilz 449319-2, live, with Mike
    Bloomfield and Mark Naftalin

Joe Turner/Live
P-Vine PCD-908, with Mike Bloom-
    field and Mark Naftalin

Various Artists
Blues with a Feeling
Vanguard VCD2-77005, three songs
    live from Newport '65

Chicago Blues Masters, Vol. 3
Capitol 7243 8 36288 2 7, James
    Cotton tracks from *Taking Care of
    Business* LP

Fathers and Sons
MCA CHD 92522

*I Blueskvarter, Chicago 1964,
    Volume One*
Jefferson SBACD 12653/4, Swedish

*Love Power—Hard to Find Hits of the
    60's* [sic]
Sequel Records NEM CD 669, with
    "(When She Needs Good Lovin')
    She Comes To Me" by the
    Chicago Loop

Monterey International Pop Festival
Rhino R270596, Electric Flag,
two songs

Takoma Blues
Takoma CDP 72822, two songs with
Little Brother Montgomery

What's Shakin'
Elektra 9 61343-2, five songs by the
Butterfield Blues Band

You Are What You Eat
Columbia CK3240, one song by the
Electric Flag

Eddie "Cleanhead" Vinson
Cherry Red
One Way Records MCAD 22169

Muddy Waters
Muddy Waters—The Chess Box
MCA CHD 3-80002

Samples

**Diamond D and the Psychotic
    Neurotics**
Stunts, Blunts, & Hip Hop
Mercury 314-513934-2, "Check One,
Two" has sample of "Stop" from
Super Session

Movie Soundtracks

Andy Warhol's Bad

Medium Cool

Steelyard Blues

The Trip
Background music for various
Mitchell Brothers films

Movie and TV Appearances

BBC, Butterfield Blues Band, 1966

Bongo Wolf's Revenge

Blues Summit in Chicago, PBS
1974, with Muddy Waters,
Nick Gravenites, et al.

Festival, a documentary of the Newport Folk Festival

Speakeasy, TV show hosted by
Chip Monk; Mike appeared with
Al Kooper

ABC in Concert, with Dr. John and
John Hammond Jr.

Various performances at the Bottom
Line, NYC, 1978 and 1980, filmed
by French TV

By Neal McGarity

Music Critic for
The Hartford Courant

A Selected Critical Discography

Super Session

Or, "The Guitar That Shook the World." Could it be possible you bought this book and don't own this album? Not very likely. As the original liner notes suggested, you should be ashamed not to say you love it.

For anyone raised on the Beatles, Elvis, and the Beach Boys, *Super Session* came as a life-changing event. Bloomfield's astonishing display of technique—and his cool, self-assured delivery of sledgehammer emotional power—opened a brave new world to rock fans accustomed to getting their music in neat little three-minute packages.

Mike plays guitar as if he came down from a higher plane to play on earth. But some long-overdue major kudos belong to Al Kooper, whose motivation for organizing this project was to capture and display Bloomfield's awesome talent better than previous records had done. Needless to say, Al succeeded mightily. (And he "baits" Bloomfield perfectly on organ.)

Super Session indeed made Bloomfield a bona fide Guitar God—and, perversely, he spent the rest of his life trying to shake off the glory this record created for him.

The Live Adventures of Mike Bloomfield and Al Kooper

A largely successful attempt to capture the spirit of *Super Session* in a live setting, this second excursion with Al Kooper kept alive the possibility of continuing greatness for Bloomfield in 1968. In hindsight, it was one of the last glorious outings before the fame-hating Bloomfield began a slow downward spiral.

The breathtakingly precise guitar attack Mike unleashed on *Super Session* is still largely on display here on long jams and cover tunes. Oddly, fans are once again cheated out of a full dose of inspired Bloomfield playing by that damned insomnia thing. (This time, Carlos Santana and Elvin Bishop step in when Mike crashes from lack of sleep.)

Bloomfield's sweaty workout on Albert King's "Don't Throw Your Love on Me So Strong" has to be considered a career highlight. Mike conducts a blues clinic on this 11-minute thrill ride, masterfully harnessing the musical power of tension and release. A devoted disciple of Albert King, Bloomfield's focus on this track is total—he seems to have an out-of-body experience as he drives agony through every guitar note. And his pain-drenched vocals were never better.

Thoroughly spent after this emotionally wringing trip, Bloomfield somehow (amazingly) finds more gas in his tank and machine-guns his way through a great instrumental closer, "Refugee," an all-too-brief hard rock treat. Then, just like a gunslinger who's killed everything in his path, Bloomfield drops his weapon on the floor and walks offstage.

Don't Say I Ain't Your Man

This sturdy overview of Mike's early and mid-career work offers rewards to both the novice and serious fan. Hard-core devotees will want the disc for the first four songs, rare and unreleased demos recorded with John Hammond, Sr. prior to Mike's various Columbia record outings. Mike hasn't found his groove yet on these early tracks, but the talent, though unfocused, is clearly there. Novices will find an impressive smattering of gems from Bloomfield's prime—including work with the Butterfield Blues Band and well-chosen samples from *Super Session*, *Live Adventures*, and *Live at Fillmore West*. Essential.

The Best of Michael Bloomfield

"Best," of course, is a very relative term in the music business. While not really Bloomfield's best, this Takoma disc is a reasonably satisfying sampling of Mike's non-Columbia work, including early-'60s outings with Little Brother Montgomery (when Mike was a mere guitar "babe") and a smattering of his work with Takoma in the latter third of his career. Mike lets loose some great finger-picked acoustic blues on "Effinonna Rag" from his Takoma days. But the real reason to own this CD compilation is "Hitch Hike on the Possum Trot Line," the only track currently available on CD from Bloomfield's dazzling 1971 work with Woody Herman on *Brand New*.

Live at the Old Waldorf

What can you say about a CD in which the only great track is not even recorded at the venue advertised on the CD cover?

Probably the most widely promoted and distributed Michael Bloomfield release of the '90s. Columbia jumped on the fact that these were never-released performances. Sounds good for a PR pitch, but newcomers will not understand Bloomfield's "Guitar God" status after listening to *Old Waldorf*. His chops are merely mortal as opposed to divine. The highlight is the opener—a blistering "Sweet Little Angel" recorded at the Record Plant that finds Mike nicely targeting some stinging licks and Roger Troy growling the vocals like a man deeply in lust. It's bumpy sledding thereafter, with Mike lazily shucking through on slide guitar. Gravenites sounds sluggish on his vocal contributions.

I'm With You Always

Recorded live at the tiny McCabe's guitar shop, this is Bloomfield loose, relaxed, and clearly having fun. Featuring sharp and very sturdy performances, this mostly acoustic disc is well worth seeking out. "Darktown Strutter's Ball" has to be considered one of Mike's best acoustic blues performances. He also reels out some nice electric chops on "Don't You Lie to Me."

Try It Before You Buy It

A respectable collection of tracks rejected for release by Columbia in the '70s, but miraculously rescued from the dusty vaults by One Way Records. Lots of fun surprises here, especially Mike's enthralling Spanish-style acoustic guitar on "When it All Comes Down." His trademark sweet tone may be missing from "Your Friends," but this grungy electric Chicago-style blues is satisfying nonetheless. Roger Troy's heartfelt vocals and Mike's focused guitar create a delicious gospel atmosphere on the ballad "Let Them Talk," with great "church-style" organ from Barry Goldberg.

Blues, Gospel and Ragtime Instrumentals

This collection of late-period Bloomfield instrumentals is so laid back it comes awfully close to being an "easy listening" dinner-party record. The CD begins with a groan-inducing remake of Leo Sayer's sappy "When I Need You," with Mike serving up some syrupy-sweet slide guitar. Some tracks are renamed— "Memphis Radio Blues" is really "WDIA" from *If You Love these Blues, Play 'Em as You Please*. Bloomfield's late-period work is profiled to much stronger effect on *Best of Michael Bloomfield*.

Living in the Fast Lane

Sure, there are some throw-aways on this late-period Bloomfield release, but there are also ample rewards for the faithful. "Andy's Bad" has aged surprisingly well with its quasi-trip-hop beat and electronically enhanced jivey vocals—it damn near fits in with today's music scene. "When I Get Home" is yet another good argument that Roger Troy's real calling should have been gospel, and "Watkins Rag" and "Dizz Rag" are exceptional '20s-style country blues.

Cruisin' for a Bruisin'

In a rather cruel twist of fate, Bloomfield's final album was remastered on CD at an incorrect, faster speed. When singing, Mike sounds like an agitated street pimp on Methedrine. It's probably a good thing this 1987 CD is long out of print. You need to seek out the vinyl LP to fully appreciate this enthusiastic performance from Bloomfield.

The Root of Blues (Laserlight)
True Soul Brother (Sky Ranch)

Here's something to get riled about: two different labels—one American, one French—threw themselves a "cut and paste" party with Bloomfield's lovingly rendered work.

Both of these CDs present material from Mike's *If You Love These Blues, Play 'Em As You Please* LP, recorded for *Guitar Player* magazine in 1977. On the vinyl original, Mike presented a wide variety of historical blues covers and fondly discussed the musical contributions of the original artists. Both of these CDs omit Mike's wonderful insights.

Though either of these CDs is deserving of a place in any Bloomfield collection, the impact of his original recording is considerably lessened without Mike's chatter. Be especially wary of Laserlight's edition, which is minus three tracks from the original (two of which unexplainably show up on another Laserlight Bloomfield release). The Sky Ranch CD includes those tracks as well as tracks from the 1979 *Bloomfield/Harris* LP.

Count Talent and the Originals (vinyl only)

A throw-away project from a Bloomfield in sad decline. However, Mike gives a three-minute flash of his earlier brilliance on "You Were Wrong," laying down a furious guitar attack alongside Roger Troy's gravelly and convincing vocals. Forget the rest.

Live at Bill Graham's Fillmore Various Artists (vinyl only)
My Labors Nick Gravenites (vinyl only)

If you need an excuse for keeping your turntable in this digital era, these two vinyl gems offer plenty of justification. Maybe someday the gods will smile on Bloomfield fans and these two stellar LPs will appear on CD. The albums belong intertwined because a fiery 1969 Fillmore West performance by Bloomfield, Gravenites, and friends was split in half and spread across the two releases.

Fillmore West weaves in live tracks from Fillmore shows by Taj Mahal and others with the Bloomfield performances. *My Labors* features another section of the Bloomfield/Gravenites Fillmore show on side one, and Gravenites and Bloomfield cutting some nifty studio tracks on side two. Both albums are indispensible for the serious fan.

Two excellent tracks from *Fillmore West* are available on the CD anthology *Don't Say I Ain't Your Man*. But the performances on *My Labors* are even stronger—especially the live "Killing My Love," with Bloomfield angrily rampaging on guitar. "Gypsy Good Time," also live, is a criminally underrated song by Graven-ites and may be the best performance ever by Bloomfield and Gravenites to-gether.

Triumvirate Bloomfield/John Paul Hammond/Dr. John

More a statement on the clueless-ness of Columbia Records than an enter-tainment experience. The label, in an ill-conceived plan to build an audience for Bloomfield, attempted to clone the super-session concept by teaming him with free agents Dr. John and John Hammond Jr. on this outing. What's sur-prising is how little chemistry exists between these kindred blues spirits.

The Paul Butterfield Blues Band

A tough, uncompromising Chicago blues package that quickly triggered a blues-rock movement among young white bands in the U.S. that continued for decades. For 1965, Bloomfield's soul-jarring guitar work was without compar-ison and loudly announced his arrival to the music world.

East-West The Paul Butterfield Blues Band

By the time of this 1966 sequel, Bloomfield had developed a large following, and *East-West* was truly much anticipated. Fans were amply rewarded, as Bloom-field raised the performance bar for himself. The more emotionally complex and inventive guitar styles displayed on *East-West* offered strong reassurance that Bloomfield was deep with talent and not just a skilled but one-dimensional bluesman. Mike delivers jaw-dropping guitar acrobatics on "Work Song," while "I Got a Mind to Give Up Living" finds Bloomfield and Butterfield taking a won-derfully slow and soulful cruise deep into broken-dreams territory. The much-heralded title track was a major turning point for Bloomfield, as he smashed through traditional blues and rock structures in search of new free-form styles of music. Perhaps more influential than the band's debut, *East-West* positioned Bloomfield even closer to the edge of greatness.

What's Shakin' Various Artists

The title and kitschy cover art may be very dated, but the music on this "var-ious artists" disc from the '60s is a real treasure trove. Besides the five sturdy Butterfield Blues Band tracks, there are a couple of good early Eric Clapton rar-ities. Butterfield's vocals and Bloomfield's guitar sound absolutely sinister to-gether on "Lovin' Cup," and Mike's axe wails righteously on "One More Mile," which would reappear later with even more ferocity on *Barry Goldberg and Friends Live*. Another bonus is a winning early solo track from Al Kooper, who sounds like little Stevie Winwood in his Spencer Davis days on "I Can't Keep from Crying Sometimes."

The Original Lost Elektra Sessions The Paul Butterfield Blues Band

More historically interesting than musically striking, these tracks from the band's first recording sessions for Elektra are nice, compact blues packages, but offer little breathing room for Bloomfield's guitar. Mike is more a solid blues anchor on these songs than the fire-breathing guitar monster who would appear just around the corner. Sonny Boy Williamson's "Help Me" and Willie Dixon's "Spoonful" are the strongest performances by the band.

Droppin' in with the Paul Butterfield Blues Band

This lovingly prepared bootleg—complete with rare and superb photos—offers a number of exciting live Butterfield/Bloomfield performances, mostly from the Fillmore West in 1966. *Super Session* may have exalted Mike to Guitar God status, but this two-disc set presents him as a Guitar Godzilla. Bloomfield is simply a ferocious beast on this must-have bootleg, wielding a guitar tone that is truly menacing.

Bloomfield's fury comes gushing out with a frightening intensity on "The Sky Is Crying." On other tracks, such as "Our Love Is Drifting," he eases up the fireworks but skillfully delivers an equally intense emotional wallop. The obscure "Willow Tree," from a September 1966 Fillmore West performance, is the real gem of this set, as Bloomfield and Butterfield drive each other to a hallowed blues ground that's well out of the reach of mere mortals.

Strawberry Jam The Paul Butterfield Blues Band
East-West Live The Paul Butterfield Blues Band

Both of these albums are taken from audience recordings made in 1966 and 1967. *Strawberry Jam* includes four cuts with Mike; the rest of the album features the Butterfield Band after Mike's departure. "Just to Be with You" is the standout Bloomfield track. The title track, recorded post-Bloomfield, features a beautiful Butterfield performance of a previously unreleased composition written by Mark Naftalin.

East-West Live is a definite oddity, with appeal mainly for hard-core Bloom-O-Philes. This disc has only three live tracks—each a lengthy, different take of the instrumental "East-West," recorded at three different venues. These three versions trace the development of this ground-breaking instrumental.

The sound quality on these disks is acceptable, considering that these historic performances were recorded on less than studio-quality equipment.

The Paul Butterfield Blues Band: An Anthology—The Elektra Years

This two-disc compilation offers an excellent overview of Butterfield's Elektra career, including much of the great work with Bloomfield from the Butterfield

Band's first two albums, some neat rarities with Bloomfield, and the best moments from the uneven records released after Bloomfield's departure.

The rarities include an early alternate version of "Born in Chicago" and "Come On In," a long-unavailable single that leans more towards rock than blues. Butterfield's vocals and Bloomfield's guitar sound absolutely sinister together on "Lovin' Cup," (which first appeared on *What's Shakin'* in 1966), and Mike's axe wails righteously on "One More Mile." Some tracks from *Lost Sessions* are also included. Even if you already own the mandatory first two Butterfield Band albums, this collection is a superb supplement.

Highway 61 Revisited Bob Dylan

Mike Bloomfield's musical legacy is so often sadly overlooked, but his work on this historic Dylan session assures him some measure of immortality. Certainly one of the most important—and daring—rock records ever made. Dylan made the switch from traditional folkster to surreal hipster on this record, and Bloomfield's inventive guitar work is the glue that holds much of the experiment together. For Bloomfield, a radical departure from his recent Butterfield blues repertoire, and, in retrospect, probably the most challenging guitar assignment he ever tackled.

The Trip The Electric Flag

This first, mostly instrumental, excursion for the Flag holds up surprisingly well, given that the music was used for the purpose of supporting a "Grade Z" hippie dope film. Most of the tracks are adventurous and very impressionistic jams—you won't find a lot of R&B or blues here. The music may be loosely structured, but the band's interplay is remarkably tight. Bloomfield digs in heartily on the anthemic "Fine Jung Thing," and the rest of the band marches along admirably with his limber and freewheeling guitar. The 1996 CD edition unfortunately trims some music from the original release.

A Long Time Comin' The Electric Flag

One of the few "super group" records that actually lived up to all of its hype, although the group imploded shortly after its release. Touted by Bloomfield as "An American Music Band" that would weave blues, jazz, soul, and other roots music into one exciting package, Mike and crew delivered the goods on this ambitious and bold experiment for 1968. *A Long Time Comin'* smoothly toggles back and forth between a variety of blues and horn-driven soul styles, even making effective satire out of a President Johnson "sample" that kicks off Howlin' Wolf's "Killing Floor."

Bloomfield's guitar work covers an equally impressive scope. "Texas" offers fierce, hard blues without any wasted notes, "Wine" finds Mike adeptly handling a '40s boogie-woogie style, while on "Easy Rider" Mike wrings an otherworldly cool blue tone from his Gibson, as notes seem to sensuously drip from his guitar. No serious Bloomfield collector should be without it.

Live Groovin' Is Easy **The Electric Flag**

This CD, also available as *Small Town Blues,* goes in two directions. Five of the nine tracks are marginal outtakes from the recording sessions for the ill-fated 1974 Flag reunion, while the remaining four tracks are live—though it's hard to tell whether it's the '60s lineup performing or the re-heated '70s version of the Flag. High Point: Bloomfield appears to be feeling genuine blues pain on the live "My Baby Wants to Test Me" and dishes out some crisp, penetrating notes. Honorable Mention: Buddy Miles's respectable live rendering of the soulful "You Don't Realize."

Two Jews Blues **Barry Goldberg and Mike Bloomfield**

Bloomfield's limited work with Barry Goldberg is very underrated. *Two Jews Blues* offers two very impressive pieces of the Bloomfield-as-Guitar-God canon: "Blues for Barry and" and "Jimi the Fox." The latter, a Hendrix tribute, crackles with crisp, exciting licks from Mike, while the longer jam "Blues for Barry and" finds Mike in the *Super Session* mode, i.e., allowing plenty of elbow room to search for—and find—righteous riffs. Nice, understated organ work by Goldberg.

Barry Goldberg and Friends Live

In the category of the most heavenly Bloomfield performances that the fewest people have heard, the obscure *Barry Goldberg and Friends Live* is the clear winner. No "best of" compilation is really complete without some representation from Mike's three performances on this disc. Bloomfield was "on" and smokin' the night these tracks were recorded. "One More Mile" is stretched out to often-thrilling effect by an on-fire Mike. Goldberg turns in some great blues organ work, and the tracks featuring guitarist Harvey "The Snake" Mandel are top notch too. Consumer note: The Canadian CD of this disc adds extra applause between the tracks, for some odd reason.

Fathers and Sons **Various Artists**

Is *Fathers and Sons* a good blues record? You bet. Is it a showcase of Bloomfield's talents? No way. Mike plays the role of dedicated blues journeyman on this part-live, part-studio effort, allowing Muddy Waters to be front and center. Muddy's performance is top rate, and Butterfield never sounded more fiery than he does on the live "Mojo."

Chicago Blues Masters, Vol 3. Various Artists

There's absolutely no mention of Bloomfield in this package, but his hard-to-find work with James Cotton on the vinyl *Taking Care of Business* can be found on the second disc of this two-CD harmonica blues anthology. Bloomfield gives particularly strong backing to Cotton on "Nose Open."

Brand New Woody Herman

Supposedly, Miles Davis recommended Mike Bloomfield to Woody Herman, who was looking to make a "hip" big band record as a way to jump start his career in the early '70s. However Mike got involved in this session, it was an inspired idea and a credit to Mike's sense of daring to accept such an offbeat assignment. Bloomfield hinted that he could go jazzy on *East-West*, but who knew he could cook this hot in a big band setting? Mike and Woody's crew swing here like nobody's business.

Gandharva Beaver & Krause

Historically, this 1971 album plowed early ground for "New Age" music and electronica. That aside, it also sold about a dozen copies at the time of its release. Always up for a new adventure, Mike is curiously found jamming away in the middle of dueling Moogs on "Saga of the Blue Beaver." For completists only.

The Best of Tracy Nelson/Mother Earth

This CD anthology is a nice snapshot of a young Tracy Nelson using her lusty blues voice to knock over buildings. Mike is on board for one track, "Mother Earth" (from the 1968 LP *Living with the Animals*), and he delivers appropriately slow and smoky blues guitar behind a pained and passionate Tracy. Good piano work from Naftalin, too. Mike was credited as "Makal Blumfeld" on the vinyl original, to avoid contractual issues.

Casting Pearls The Mill Valley Bunch

A communal musical gathering of sorts, with Mike's Bay Area musician friends noodling around in a variety of musical styles. This record is really hurt by consistently bad vocals, except for the few turns that Nick Gravenites takes behind the mike. Bloomfield fanatics will want the disc anyway, if only for Mike's hard-charging wah-wah guitar attack on the instrumental "Jimmy's Blues." Also, the slow, smoldering "Bedroom Blues" is solid teamwork between Bloomfield and Gravenites.

Sources

Additional material from the following sources:

Dan McClosky—from his interview with Michael Bloomfield and Roy Ruby, 1971.

Bob Simmons—from his KSAN interview with Michael Bloomfield, aired January 31, 1978.

Bob Sarles/Ravin' Films—material excerpted from Bob Sarles' video interviews with Bill Graham, Mark Naftalin, Al Kooper, B.B. King, Carlos Santana, Jack Casady, Jorma Kaukonen, and Bob Weir

Bloomfield notes—Neal McGarity's interviews with Nick Gravenites, Barry Goldberg, and Al Kooper are excerpted.

Paul Rothchild—from *Baby Let Me Follow You Down: The Illustrated Story of the Cambridge Folk Years.* Eric Von Schmidt and Jim Rooney, 2nd edition, Amherst: University Of Massachusetts Press, 1994, copyright © 1979 by Eric Von Schmidt and Jim Rooney.

Me And Big Joe. Michael Bloomfield with Scott Summerville, RE/SEARCH Publications, 1999, copyright © 1980 by S. E. Summerville and Michael Bloomfield.

Backstage Passes and Backstabbing Bastards. Al Kooper, Billboard Books, 1998, copyright © 1998 by Al Kooper.

Guitar Player Magazine, July 1979—Tom Wheeler's interview with Michael Bloomfield.

Bob Dylan's comments are taken from his introduction of Michael Bloomfield at the Warfield Theater, San Francisco, November 15, 1980.

About the Authors

Jan Mark Wolkin was born in Brooklyn, New York. He grew up in Rahway, New Jersey, and is a graduate of the American University. From 1994 to 1996 he published the *Bloomfield notes* newsletter. His work has also appeared in the *All Music Guide to the Blues, Blues Access* magazine, and *Vintage Guitar* magazine. He has assisted in the release of several posthumous Bloomfield CDs.

Bill Keenom, a Portland, Oregon native, lived in Hawaii from 1978 to 1988. A long-time Bloomfield fan, Bill has written a number of biographic articles on West Coast sports figures, and won an award for Excellence in Scholastic Journalism from the University of Oregon. He currently plays bass guitar in the Donna Jose Band and markets promotional items and art reproductions online at OceanZero.com and MotherArt.com respectively.

Index

S. Beuhler on, 52–53
Bloomfield, Michael
  bar mitzvah, 9–10, 11
  on blues clubs, 19–29
  childhood, 3–9
  death, 229, 230–236
  discography, 253–259
  drinking problem, 214–224
  drug problems. *See* drug problems
  early musical influences, 10–12, 18
  father, 6, 8, 17, 18
  fire-breathing act, 131
  first guitar, 9, 16–17
  grandfather, 8–9
  Hyde Park, 30–43
  insomnia, 150, 157, 163–164, 197
  marriage, 41–42, 43, 46–53
  relationship with Susan Beuhler,
      183–187, 190, 198, 199
  relationship with Christie Svane,
      180–182, 211–212, 216, 218, 219
  state mental hospital stay, 215–216
  teenage years, 9–18
  trust fund and, 206–208
Bloomfield, Sam (grandfather), 8–9
Bloomfield, Susan. *See* Beuhler, Susan
Bloomfield/Harris, 217
Blue Flame Lounge, 39, 77, 78
bluegrass music, 30, 60
"Blues for Roy," 251
Blues, Gospel and Ragtime Instruments, 263
Blues Project, 132–134, 161
Blumenfield, Roy, 133
Booker T. & The MGs, 145
"Born in Chicago," 97–98, 112, 121, 129
Botnick, Bruce, 152
Bottom Line, 211, 212, 223
Bowie, Lester, 142
Bracci, Teda, 178
Brand New, 269
Brooks, Harvey
  on Bloomfield, 109, 154–155
  on effect of drugs on band, 150
  on Monterey Pop Festival, 144–145
  on *Super Session,* 161, 162
Broonzy, Big Bill, 99
Bruce, Denny, 177, 178–179
"Bullet Rag," 249
Burnett, Johnny, 54
Butkovich, Ron, 60, 79, 173, 214–215
Butterfield Blues Band, 93–98, 111–138
  Bloomfield and, 111–138
  Bloomfield joining, 94–98
  Bloomfield leaving, 136–138
  Blues Project and, 132–134
  first West Coast appearance, 120–121
  Monterey Pop Festival, 146

Newport Folk Festival, 102–109
  Santana on, 112, 128–129
Butterfield, Paul
  Bishop and, 94–96, 136
  Bloomfield and, 36, 40, 85, 93–98, 114,
      135–137
  Blue Flame Lounge, 78
  Fathers and Sons, 174, 175
  Musselwhite on, 85, 86, 94–95
  Out of Sight Records, 79
  Sam Lay on, 114
Byron, Toby, 183–184

C
Cabale Creamery, 93
Cafe Au Go Go, 98, 132, 133
Canned Heat, 146
Carmen, Tony, 9, 18
Carpenter, John, 120, 121
Carr, Allen, 178
Carter family, 194
Casady, Jack, 130
Casting Pearls, 269
Cato, Bob, 165
CD notes, 249–251
Cellar Boheme, 37
Central Day YMCA High School, 38, 39
Chambers, John, 172
Charles, Ray, 30, 139
Charles River Valley Boys, 93
Charters, Sam, 29
Chess brothers, 75, 113
Chess, Leonard, 174
Chess, Marshall, 174, 176
Chess Records, 75, 176, 203, 251
Chicago blues, 19–29, 35
Chicago Blues Masters, 268–269
Chicago, Illinois, 3–18, 24, 28, 55
Clapton, Eric, 123, 128
Club 47, 93, 98, 106, 132
Cohen, Kip, 188
Collins, Judy, 45, 97
Columbia Records
  Bob Jones on, 172
  Electric Flag and, 152
  Live Adventures, 164
  Triumvirate, 187–188
  Try It Before You Buy It, 187
Cooder, Ry, 191, 192
Cooke, John, 94
Cornwall Academy, 15
Coryell, Larry, 141
"Cosmic Scout Jamboree," 175–176
Cotton, James, 78, 133
Count Talent, 209, 264
country blues, 30
"Country Boy," 251